Make Our Hearts Like Yours

MAKE OUR HEARTS LIKE YOURS

Daily Meditations on the Sacred Heart of Jesus

Thomas J. Kronholz

Our Sunday Visitor
Huntington, Indiana

Nihil Obstat
Msgr. Michael Heintz, Ph.D.
Censor Librorum

Imprimatur
✠ Kevin C. Rhoades
Bishop of Fort Wayne-South Bend
April 2, 2024

The *Nihil Obstat* and *Imprimatur* are official declarations that a book is free from doctrinal or moral error. It is not implied that those who have granted the *Nihil Obstat* and *Imprimatur* agree with the contents, opinions, or statements expressed.

30 29 28 27 26 25   1 2 3 4 5 6 7 8 9

Our Sunday Visitor Publishing Division
Our Sunday Visitor, Inc.
200 Noll Plaza
Huntington, IN 46750(260) 356-8400

ISBN: 978-1-63966-178-7 (Inventory No. T2881)
1. RELIGION—Holidays—Easter & Lent.
2. RELIGION—Christian Living—Family & Relationships.
3. RELIGION—Christianity—Catholic—General.

eISBN: 978-1-63966-179-4
LCCN: 2024950086

Cover and interior design: Amanda Falk
Cover art: AdobeStock

Printed in the United States of America

This book is dedicated to the Most Merciful Heart of Jesus.

In memoriam

Rev. William R. Krizner

In paradisum deducant te angeli

Contents

Preface

I saw water flowing from the right
side of the temple, alleluia.
And all to whom that water came were saved,
and they shall say: Alleluia, alleluia!

— Antiphon for the Sprinkling Rite on Easter Sunday

The Sacred Heart of Jesus is the revelation of God's love for man, incarnate of the Virgin Mary and born at Bethlehem. It is an inexhaustible fountain of mercy, opened upon the cross of Calvary. Resurrected on the third day, it is the ever-living source of the sacraments whereby man may drink unto eternal life. The Sacred Heart is thus a summary of the entire Christian message — for it is divine love made flesh, ever offered to the Father in atonement for sin.

Devotion to the Sacred Heart of Jesus has its roots in the Apostolic Faith, though its full flowering has only been realized in the modern age. Contemplating the rich symbolism present in the Old Testament, the Fathers of the Church identified the Sacred Heart in a host of images and figures, including Noah's ark (see Gn 7-9), the Ark of the Covenant (Ex 26:34), and the rocky cleft of the beloved (Sg 2:14). Meditating upon the New Testament, the saints never tired of considering Christ's self-description as "meek, and humble of heart" (Mt 11:29), Saint John's mystical repose upon the breast of Jesus (Jn 13:23), and the fearful piercing of Christ's side (Jn 19:34).

With ardent longing, He who emptied His Heart upon the cross revealed it anew to St. Margaret Mary Alacoque, seeking a return for such love. Gathered together, the following meditations allow Christ's special love for each soul to be more fully known. In this collection, one will find stirring hymns of praise, solemn prayers of consecration, and poignant meditations from every age of the Church. Together, these texts give witness to the historic nature of devotion to the Sacred Heart.

Like my previous work in *Mystery of the Altar: Daily Meditations on the Eucharist,* coauthored with Kenneth J. Howell, I have arranged the texts according to the liturgical calendar so that the Sacred Heart may be contemplated in harmony with the feasts, seasons, and saints recognized each day. I have examined newly translated passages with an eye toward the literal, yet with the poetic sensitivity due the subject. Texts native to the English language have been preserved, as far as is reasonable, in their original form. Each reading is prefaced with introductory remarks that illuminate its spiritual theme and concluded with a summative prayer that applies its message.

The Church Fathers, medieval mystics, and modern saints well understood that theology is not simply the acquisition of knowledge, but the loving contemplation of Christ that leads unto union. Following the path of Christian meditation, they found that the love of God is no chimera, but something manifest before all, incarnate in the Heart of Jesus. It is my prayer that the collective witness of these saints may draw readers ever deeper into Christ's side, that all might freely drink of this fountain of mercy.

January

January 1 | *Solemnity of Mary, Mother of God*

On this day, the Church honors that most blessed of women in whom the Sacred Heart of Jesus first began to beat. In Mary, the Word was made Flesh, manifesting God's great love for man. Bl. Columba Marmion (1858–1923) here summarizes the devotion to the Sacred Heart and teaches that its roots are found in the Deposit of Faith.

> What is the Incarnation? It is the manifestation of God to the world. God reveals himself to us through the humanity of Jesus. *Nova mentis nostrae oculis lux tuae claritatis infulsit.* ["The light of your glory has newly shone upon the eyes of our mind."] This is the revelation of divine love: "For God so loved the world that he gave his only-begotten son" [Jn 3:16] and this Son has loved man unto handing himself over for their sake: "Greater love has no man than this, that a man lay down his life for his friends" [Jn 15:13]. *Majorera hac dilectionem nemo habet.* The entire seed of devotion to the Sacred Heart is contained in these words of Jesus. And to show that this love had attained the highest degree, Christ Jesus desired that immediately following His last breath on the Cross, His heart would be pierced open by the soldier's lance.[1]

Sacred Heart of Jesus, Incarnate Love and Unfading Light, make known the depths of Your mercy that all might turn to You. Mary, Mother of God, lead all souls to your Son, pressing them to His Sacred Heart.

January 2 | *Sts. Basil the Great and Gregory of Nazianzus*

In the following letter to Maximus, a man of great nobility, St. Basil (330–379) describes the path of Christian virtue as a continual conformation to Christ. He proposes the Heart of Jesus as the pattern of sanctity and a safeguard against pride, extolling the treasure of virtue.

> Indeed, it is no small gain that a man of illustrious lineage and a member of a great household should adopt the life of the Gospel, bridling the inclinations of youth by reflection, and subjecting the affections of the flesh to reason. … In a word, it renders one a disciple of Our Lord who said, "Learn from me; for I am gentle and lowly in heart" [Mt 11:29].
>
> And in truth, dearest son. … Youth fades more quickly than spring flowers, and beauty wastes with sickness or age. Riches are uncertain and glory is capricious. The pursuit of arts and sciences is tethered to the present life, and the charm of eloquence, which all covet, reaches only the ear. The practice of virtue, however, is a precious possession for him who has it and an edifying display for all who observe it. Make this your study — so you will be worthy of those good things promised by the Lord.[2]

Sacred Heart of Jesus, fountainhead of all virtues, inspire in me a sincere desire for Christian perfection. Increase in me those holy habits, which You crown with an eternal reward. St. Basil the Great, pray for us!

January 3 | *The Holy Name of Jesus*

On the tenth day of the Christmas season, the Church honors that Name above every other name as it joyfully calls upon Christ Jesus. *Summi Parentis Filio*, an anonymous eighteenth-century text, exultantly sings Jesus' name.

O Son of the Father Most
    High,
Father of the world to come,
blessed Prince of Peace:
to You we raise hymns of
    praise.

He whose breast was wound-
    ed,
pierced by love's price,
inflames with love's fire,
those who draw nigh.

Jesus, sorrowful victim!
Who compelled You, the
    innocent,
to endure that searching blade
that broke open Your side?

O blessed fount of love!
O fair flow of water!
O flame to consume all sin!
O Heart of burning charity!

Within Your Heart, O Jesus,
enclose and nourish us.
Grant us the joy of Your grace,
and at last, the reward of
    heaven.

To the Father and Son,
be praise, honor, and glory,
together with the Holy Para-
    clete,
unto the ages, without end.[3]

Sacred Heart of Jesus, infinitely exalted above the earth, raise me up to You. Make me participate in that heavenly conversation in which all extol Your glory. Saint Longinus, you who pierced heaven's heart, pray for us!

January 4 | *St. Elizabeth Ann Seton*

St. Elizabeth Ann Seton (1774–1821), a convert from Anglicanism, founded the first women's religious order in the United States, the Sisters of Charity. Her sincere love of God is evident in her many letters documenting her journey from motherhood to widowhood, and ultimately to consecrated religious life. In this letter, Elizabeth recounts the momentous occasion of her entrance into the Church and begs that her heart be buried within the Heart of Jesus.

> A day of days for me, Amabilia. I have been — where? To the Church of Saint Peter, which has a cross on top instead of a weathercock — to what is called here, among so many churches, the *Catholic Church.* When I turned the corner of the street it is in, "Here, my God, I go," I said, "my heart all to You." Entering it, how that heart died away, as it were, in silence before that little tabernacle and the great *crucifixion* above it.
>
> "Ah, my God! Here let me rest," I said, as I went down on my knees and my head sunk on my bosom.
>
> I was called to the little room next to the sanctuary, and made my profession of faith ... but not without begging Our Lord to bury deep my heart in that wounded side.[4]

Sacred Heart of Jesus, opened upon the cross, give entrance to my soul that I may take refuge within. Let flow those streams of blood and water, granting us the drink of eternal life. Saint Elizabeth, pray for us!

January 5 | *St. John Neumann*

St. John Neumann (1811–1860), a Redemptorist bishop, emigrated from Bohemia to the United States to serve immigrant communities. His personal writings reveal a tender heart of piety and deep concern for the moral life. In the following passage, Saint John contemplates the Infant Jesus, spiritually laying the twin gifts of love and purity upon the Child's breast. Placing his own heart at the disposal of Jesus' Heart, he unreservedly expresses the desire to fulfill His holy will.

> You, O my most amiable Jesus, sleep in the poor crib of my heart. Are You, by chance, weary of my incessant weeping over my sin? Forgive me, O Divine Babe! While Your eyes are closed in slumber, I will adorn Your crib with the most lovely flowers. When You awaken, Your little eyes will be delighted; You will be better pleased with Your new home. Dearest Mother Mary, teach me how to adorn the dwelling of Your Divine Child!
>
> On Your breast, O Divine Infant, I will lay the white lily of purity and innocence, for You are the All-Holy. I will become like unto You. To it, I will add the rose of love as a proof that I sigh for Your love alone. … Deign to purify me from my sins, cleanse me in Your own Precious Blood![5]

Sacred Heart of Jesus, impeccable and undefiled, purify my soul. By Your holy and blessed infancy, grant me a new life of grace. St. John Neumann, devoted son of the Church, pray for us!

January 6 | *Epiphany of the Lord*

Today marks not only the traditional date of Epiphany, but also the death and entrance into heaven of St. Charles of Sezze (1613–1670), a Franciscan whose life was marked by radical poverty and self-divestment. In his treatise, *Interior Path of the Soul,* he contemplates the Incarnation as it relates to the cross, teaching that the cross was embedded within the Sacred Heart of Jesus at birth and fully manifested at Calvary.

> From His Nativity until His death, His immaculate life was a continual cross in which He suffered hunger, heat, cold, ignominy, flagellation, beatings, and nails. As a true lover of the cross, He carried it in the depths of His Heart throughout life and willed it to be revealed before all upon Mount Calvary, spread upon His shoulders. …
>
> Completing the work of our salvation upon this cross, redeeming and fulfilling all that the eternal council had determined concerning His death, His passion bringing victory and triumph over His enemies, shutting closed hell and opening wide heaven, the rubied cross thereafter remained sprinkled with His vermillion blood. O wondrous stronghold of Our Savior! At the time He was stretched out, dismissing His distress, and with fading voice, He sweetly spoke: "O beloved cross, my sweet hope, for thirty-three years I have carried you in my heart and with ardent desire have I longed for you."[6]

Sacred Heart of Jesus, uniting humanity and divinity, wed my heart to Yours. Teach me to love as You loved. Saint Charles, pray for us!

January 7 | *St. Angela of Foligno*

St. Angela of Foligno (c. 1248–1309) was an Italian penitent and mystic whose contemplative writings plumbed the depths of the mysteries of the Faith. In the following meditation on the passion, St. Angela offers insight into a most astonishing paradox of God's omnipotence: He who holds all things in existence upheld the very instruments of His passion. For love of man, the Sacred Heart endured insults, buffets, and transfixion.

> Not only did sinful man rise up against Him, but even the elements and insensible beings received power from their Creator to cause Him suffering and affliction, as if He had no power to resist. ... He empowered the lofty cross that it should bear Him on high, His Body scourged, bleeding, and pierced as He hung there, showing Him naked unto all. He caused — O marvelous to hear! — the lance to enter and pierce through His Divine side and Heart so that the blood and water issued out from His Heart and Body, falling upon the earth. If He had not in truth granted them the power, and not shown himself as helpless and weak, there is no doubt that a single creature would have been able to hurt its Creator; in truth, it would have abhorred such a deed.[7]

Sacred Heart of Jesus, incomprehensible mystery of love and abode of justice, I place my trust in You. Help me to endure all things for Your sake, abandoning myself to Your will. St. Angela of Foligno, pray for us!

January 8 | *St. Lawrence Justinian*

St. Lawrence Justinian (1381–1456) was an Italian prelate whose outstanding life of holiness and care for the poor led to his appointment as the first patriarch of Venice. His mystical writings express a passionate love for the Lord and contemplate the spousal love between Christ and the soul. In this passage from *On the Fire of Divine Love,* Saint Lawrence describes the Sacred Heart as a place of repose and everlasting peace.

> O most amiable wounds of my Jesus! O most happy lance! O fortunate nails that have pierced the Sacred Body of my God! O that I had been this lance, I would have never withdrawn from the side of Jesus! For, it is here that my eternal repose is found. And I would cry out that this is my home, the refuge of my choosing.
>
> O folly! O callousness of the sons of men! It is in these open wounds that you may taste the Passion of the Savior, the sovereign good, the brilliance of the eternal light and the splendor of the divine majesty. Why then do you hesitate to enter? O soul, made in the image of God, how can you still resist? Here is your Spouse, who comes full of tenderness, wounded and glorified for you.[8]

Sacred Heart of Jesus, furnace of divine charity, inflame my heart with Your love. Help me to spread that holy fire which You came to cast upon the earth. St. Lawrence Justinian, zealous disciple of Christ, pray for us!

January 9 | *Bl. Pauline Jaricot*

Bl. Pauline Jaricot (1799–1862) was a consecrated virgin who established an association of like-minded women to make reparation to the Sacred Heart of Jesus. In this letter, Pauline illustrates how the heavens and earth proclaim the glory of God.

> Do you not know that the sun which heats the earth and shines to produce a thousand excellent fruits — however wonderful this may be — is but a weak and obscure image of the Son of Justice. … And that the ocean is only a slight figure of the immense goodness of the Heart of Jesus Christ, the victim of His own love on our altars, plunged in an ocean of mercy and love, burning day and night in a sea of flames without being consumed? And that the planets which receive the light of the sun, represent the teaching Church, which receives from the Son of Justice … all His power, all His beauty, all His light, and all the brilliance of His teachings in the midst of the darkness of the fallen world so as to guide its pilgrims toward the heavenly city? … If you know how to love, the magnificent spectacle of nature would remind you at every step, and every instant, of the immense love that Jesus Christ manifests to you in His adorable Sacrament.[9]

Sacred Heart of Jesus, boundless in mercy, surround us on every side. Let all creation proclaim Your praise and every tongue confess Your glory. Bl. Pauline Jaricot, help of missionaries, pray for us!

January 10 | *St. Gregory of Nyssa*

St. Gregory of Nyssa (335–c. 395) was a Cappadocian bishop who defended the unity of the Trinity against the heretical views of the Arians. In the following tract, he describes the profound unity of wills that Christians ought to have with Christ, including virtues of mercy, compassion, and meekness of heart.

> Our Lord is called merciful and compassionate by the prophet [see Ps 103:8], and He wills us to be so. … If, then, anyone has modeled himself according to the divine will through attentiveness and diligence, and has become kind, merciful, and compassionate, or meek and lowly of heart [Mt 11:29] — such as many of the saints are attested to have become in the pursuit of such excellences — does it follow that they are therefore one with God, or united to Him by virtue of any one of them? Not so. That which is not in every respect the same cannot be one with Him whose nature thus varies from it. Accordingly, a man becomes one with another when in will, as Our Lord says, they are perfectly one [Jn 17:23]; this union of wills being added to the connection of nature. So also, the Father and the Son are one, the communion of will and the communion of nature running, in Them, into one.[10]

Sacred Heart of Jesus, temple of the Triune God, unite all souls in Your love. Make our wills one with Yours, cleansing us of every imperfection. St. Gregory of Nyssa, bishop and mystic, pray for us!

January 11 | *St. Paulinus of Aquileia*

St. Paulinus of Aquileia (c. 726–c. 802) was a highly educated priest, appointed by Charlemagne to rebuild the foundations of academic learning. Here Saint Paulinus draws upon the words of Saint Paul to describe the unity of heart found between Christ and Christians, emphasizing the unbreakable nature of this communion.

> If we diligently seek to enter that great council of our salvation so as to not lose the heavenly inheritance that the Lord has prepared from the beginning of the world; if we serve Him in justice, holiness, purity of heart, and sincere charity, we may cry out with the apostle: "Who shall separate us from the love of Christ? Shall tribulation, or distress, or persecution, or famine, or nakedness, or peril, or sword" [Rom 8:35] or the other things that follow? "Neither death, nor life, nor angels, nor principalities, nor things present, nor things to come, nor powers, nor height, nor depth, nor anything else in all creation, will be able to separate us from the love of God in Christ Jesus our Lord" [Rom 8:39]. This saying truly describes the early Church, which was "of one heart and soul" in the Lord [see Acts 4:32]. They were of one will, for they had been united in the love of Christ.[11]

Sacred Heart of Jesus, glory of the angels and delight of the saints, let my heart ever exult in You. Graciously grant me perseverance unto the end. St. Paulinus of Aquileia, defender of the Faith, pray for us!

January 12 | *St. Aelred of Rievaulx*

St. Aelred of Rievaulx (1110–1167) spent his youth serving on the court of the Scottish king, for which service he was offered an episcopal position. Aelred instead chose to enter the Cistercian Abbey of Rievaulx, where he was eventually named abbot. In this sermon, he movingly represents a dialogue between the merciful God and a repentant sinner.

> Thanks be to You, good Jesus, truly merciful in all Your works. If there, within the soul wherein God sees, the heart of man is converted unto God in humility, then the Heart of God turns unto it. God's Heart thus expresses His pity and compassion, "My heart cries out for Moab" [Is 15:5]. Moab cries out in penitence: Christ calls for mercy. Moab cries in fear: Christ cries in mercy. Moab sobs in acknowledgment: Christ calls for remittance. Moab, seeing the winds rise up, grows fearful and cries out: Christ, stretching out His hands to the faltering and trembling turmoil, says, "O you of little faith, why did you doubt?" [Mt 14:31].
>
> In this way does He respond to the frantic cries and distress. [Truly, Lord,] You grant marvelous tenderness and sweetness; when the heat of passions rise up, You pour out the cooling dew of deliverance; when the mind is beset with wrath, hatred, and so forth, You likewise act within, bringing tranquility.[12]

Sacred Heart of Jesus, solace of sinners and merciful savior, increase our trust in You. St. Aelred of Rievaulx, pray for us!

January 13 | *St. Hilary of Poitiers*

St. Hilary of Poitiers (c. 310–367) was a Western bishop whose robust defense of the orthodox Faith was marked by a prudence and diplomacy that carefully distinguished doctrinal errors from mere variations in language. In his *Commentary on the Psalms,* Hilary observes that King David, the "man after [God's] own heart" (1 Sm 13:14), foreshadowed the meekness and humility of the King of Kings.

> The doctrines of the Gospel were well known to holy and blessed David in his capacity as prophet. … He did not take vengeance on his enemies through war. Though he did not oppose force of arms to those who laid in wait for him, he acted after the pattern of the Lord whose name and meekness he foreshadowed. When betrayed, he entreated; when endangered, he sang psalms; when he incurred hatred, he rejoiced; and thus he was found to be a man after God's own heart. …
>
> David, whose actual sufferings prophetically foretold the sufferings of the Lord, did not oppose his enemies by word or deed; rather, in obedience to the command of the Gospel, he would not render evil for evil in imitation of his Master's meekness. In his affliction, betrayal, and flight, he called upon the Lord and was content to use his weapons only in his struggles with the ungodly.[13]

Sacred Heart of Jesus, abandoned by friends, help me to forgive those who betray me. Teach me to surrender myself to Your holy will. St. Hilary of Poitiers, pray for us!

January 14

St. Methodius of Olympus (c. 260–c. 311) expresses his love of allegorical interpretations of Scripture in this passage from *Banquet of the Ten Virgins*, which describes consecrated virginity as the great jewel that captures Jesus' Heart.

> Consider now, O virgins, that in saying to the bride, "You have ravished my heart, my sister, my bride" [Sg 4:9], He refers to the clear eye of understanding, cleansed by the inner man to look more clearly upon the truth. For, it is certain that there is a twofold power of sight — one of the soul and the other of the body. … Those who live chastely adorn themselves with ornaments truly composed of precious stones — namely, of freedom, of magnanimity, of wisdom, and of love; caring little for those material decorations. For, those temporal decorations are like leaves that blossom for an hour and dry up with the changes of the body. Thus is seen a twofold beauty in man, of which the Lord accepts that which is within and immortal, saying: "You have ravished my heart … with one jewel of your necklace" [Sg 4:9], showing that He has been drawn to love by the splendor of the inner man, shining forth in its glory, even as the psalmist testifies: "The King's daughter is all glorious within."[14]

Sacred Heart of Jesus, containing the elixir of eternal life, adorn me with virtue, and fill me with Your wisdom. St. Methodius of Olympus, pray for us!

January 15 | *St. Macarius of Egypt*

St. Macarius of Egypt (c. 300–c. 390) sought a life of prayer and penance in the desert. In the following saying, Saint Macarius speaks on the preeminent value of Christian humility. By establishing the Sacred Heart as the great exemplar and pattern of our lives, we may make our hearts thrones upon which Christ may reign.

> Let him force himself to humility of mind in the sight of all men, considering himself less and worse than others, seeking not the honor, praise, nor glory of men, as it is written in the Gospel. Let him ever keep the Lord and His commandments before his eyes, desiring to please Him alone in meekness of heart; for the Lord says, "Learn from me, because I am meek and lowly in heart, and you will find rest for your souls" [Mt 11:29].
>
> Let him persevere in prayers, always beseeching and believing, so that the Lord may come and dwell in him, and may perfect and strengthen him in all His Commandments. Thus the Lord himself may make of his soul His dwelling place so that one day, what he does now by force with a reluctant heart, he may do willingly.[15]

Sacred Heart of Jesus, throne of mercy and model of compassion, destroy all my illusions of pride. Conform my heart to Yours that I might ever manifest Your charity. St. Macarius of Egypt, model of asceticism, pray for us!

January 16

At the monastery of Helfta, a Benedictine saint, Mechtilde of Hackeborn (c. 1240–1298) developed an intense devotion to the Sacred Heart of Jesus. In this text from her revelations, Jesus provides instructions for honoring His Sacred Heart upon retiring for the night.

> Before sleep, draw from My Heart a sigh in union with that praise it dispensed in favor of all the saints and as a supplement of what was owed by all creatures. … The soul ought then sigh for its own sins, and those of others, in union with that compassion which drove Me to bear the sins of all. Sigh also for the love and desire it has to obtain all that is necessary for the glory of God and their own needs. It will thus unite itself to the divine desires I had on earth for man's salvation. Lastly, sigh in union with all the prayers that poured forth from My Heart, and from those of my saints, for the salvation of all, living or dead. It ought to desire that each breath during the sleep of this night might be accepted by me as an incessant sigh. As it is impossible for Me to refuse anything to a loving soul, I will fill them according to the plenitude of My divine Truth.[16]

Sacred Heart of Jesus, perfect sacrifice, make me one with Your self-offering. Let my living and breathing become a perpetual prayer, offered for Your glory. St. Mechtilde of Hackeborn, espoused of Christ, pray for us!

January 17 | *St. Anthony the Great*

St. Anthony the Great (251–356) was among the first Christians to seek a life of wholehearted conversion in the deserts of Egypt. Following his example was Abba Rabba, who here speaks on the essential virtue of humility, reproving some prideful older monks for refusing to heed the spiritual council of a younger monk, Theodore.

> Have you never heard that it is written, "Every one who is arrogant is an abomination to the Lord"? [Prv 16:5] For, whoever exalts himself shall be humbled, but he who humbles himself shall be exalted [see Mt 23:12]. Therefore, deliver yourselves from your false superiority, for do you not know that the mother of the beginning of wickedness is pride? You did not only leave Theodore and depart from him, but you fled and departed from the word of God and fell away from the Holy Spirit. O you truly wretched men who deserve sorrow of every kind: How is it that you cannot understand that it was Satan who was working in you, and that, because of this, you made yourselves remote from God. O what a great and wonderful thing it is that God humbled himself, and took upon himself the form of a servant, taking on his body, dwelling in him, and becoming obedient even unto death for our sakes![17] And yet, we who are low by nature, puff ourselves up with pride![18]

Sacred Heart of Jesus, guide us on the path of humility and through its narrow gate. St. Anthony the Great, pray for us!

January 18

Born in 1647, St. Margaret Mary Alacoque had visions of the Sacred Heart that helped inspire its modern devotion. While attending a local carnival celebration, Margaret — a pious youth — unexpectedly beheld a vision of Christ, scourged and bloodied. Spiritually reproved, she became a Visitandine nun, serving Christ with prayerful, undivided zeal. Here Margaret recounts a vision in which Christ showed His Heart to her as a purifying fire, a means of illumination, and the path to divine union.

> On the first day, Our Lord presented His Sacred Heart to me as a furnace of love, into which I seemed to be immersed and so penetrated with its flames that I thought I should have been reduced to ashes. I heard these words: "This is the divine purgatory of My love where you must purify yourself during this life. Later you shall find in it an abode of light and finally one of union and transformation." He allowed me to feel this so effectually during my retreat that sometimes I hardly knew whether I was on earth or in heaven, so entirely was I filled with God and lost in Him. … I made my confession with so many tears and such contrition that I thought my heart would break with sorrow at having offended such infinite goodness, whom all the time I felt sensibly present within me.[19]

Sacred Heart of Jesus, purify my heart! Efface my sins by that fire of mercy poured out in sacramental confession. St. Margaret Mary, pray for us!

January 19

St. Bernard of Clairvaux (1090–1153) was a Cistercian abbot and leading spiritual figure of his age. This excerpt from his *Homilies on the Song of Songs* styles the pierced Heart of Jesus after the rocky cleft in the Exodus desert (see Dt 32:13). Bernard gazes beyond the violence and injustice of Jesus' death, perceiving the peace and reconciliation secretly wrought by His sacrifice.

> As for me, whatever is wanting in myself I claim with unwavering confidence in the Heart of the Lord, from which all mercy flows. Nor is it without cleft through which that mercy flows; for, [the soldiers] pierced His hands and feet, and His side they pierced with a lance. And by these openings, I may draw honey from the rock and oil from the hardest crag; which is to say, to taste and see how sweet the Lord is. He was meditating thoughts of peace, and I knew it not. For, who has known the mind of the Lord or been His counselor?
>
> Yet, the nails that pierced Him have become for me, as it were, master keys to open the treasury of the Lord's will. . . . And how has it ever shone forth more wondrously, O Lord, sweet and gentle, and of great mercy, than in the cruel wounds that You endured for our sake?[20]

Sacred Heart of Jesus, show forth the power of Your redemptive love. Triumph over every evil for Your greater glory. St. Bernard of Clairvaux, pray for us!

January 20

In his *Catena Aurea,* St. Thomas Aquinas quotes a lengthy passage from Origen (c. 184–c. 253), who speaks of Christ's agony in the Garden and the radical depths of his humility.

> He took with Him the self-confident Peter and the others that they might see Him falling on His face in prayer and learn not to think great things, but little things of themselves, and not to be hasty in promising, but careful in prayer. And therefore, He went "a little farther" [Mt 26:39], not to go far from them, but that He might be near them in His prayer. Also, He who had said, "Learn from me; for I am gentle and lowly in heart" [Mt 11:29], now commendably humbling himself, falls on His face. He shows His devotion in prayer, and as the beloved and well-pleasing of His Father, adds, "Not as I will, but as you will" [Mt 26:39]. …
>
> And as He began to have fear and sorrow, He prays accordingly that the cup of His passion may pass from Him, yet not as He wills, but as His Father wills. … Indeed, the believer must in the first instance be disinclined to incur pain, seeing that it leads to death and that he is a man of flesh; nevertheless, if it be God's will, he acquiesces because he is a believer.[21]

Sacred Heart of Jesus, crushed in the winepress of Gethsemane, grant me perfect submission to God's will. Have mercy on us, and bless us with Your peace.

January 21

Like St. Mechtilde of Hackeborn, St. Gertrude the Great was placed as a child into the Benedictine monastery at Helfta, where she inherited that saint's love for the Sacred Heart and greatly advanced its devotion. Here, she breaks forth in praise of this most loving of hearts. Perceiving her own weakness, she offers the Sacred Heart as an atoning sacrifice, supplying for all that is lacking in her.

> O Love, Your self-oblation, worthy of a God, has opened unto me the door of the most tender heart of my Jesus. O Heart full of sweetness! O Heart overflowing with compassion! O Heart superabounding with love! O Heart whose gentle mercy falls as the dew! O Heart, dearest object of my love, deign to absorb my heart in You. You who are more precious to me than most precious pearls, call me to the banquet of life. Pour out for me the wine of Your consolations, all unworthy as I am. In Your divine charity, raise up the crumbling ruins of my soul and enrich my utter misery with Your boundless wealth.
>
> O Love, take this Divine Heart — this censer wherein burns such fragrant incense, this victim so august — offer it for me upon the golden altar. . . . Offer it to supply all that has been lacking in me.[22]

Sacred Heart of Jesus, sacrificial gift poured out for mankind, join us to Your self-offering, and lavish us with its riches! St. Gertrude the Great, heroic in love, pray for us!

January 22

St. Ildefonsus of Toledo (607–667; memorial, January 23) was a Spanish bishop and defender of the orthodox Faith. In this passage he recounts the prayer intoned over the newly baptized, highlighting the intrinsic connection between Christ and the sacraments, which flow from his heavenly Heart. Additionally, Saint Ildefonsus ardently prays for the gift of charity.

> The Lord Jesus Christ, who has washed you with water from His side and redeemed you with the effusion of His blood, will himself confirm in you the grace of Redemption you have received. He, through whom you were reborn of water and the Holy Spirit, will make you to share in His heavenly kingdom; He who has given you the beginnings of your holy faith, will grant both the completion of the work and the fullness of charity.
>
> ...
>
> Give me that fire, O Lord, which Thou didst send when coming on earth; and "would that it were already kindled" (Lk 12:49). Grant me to burn with the fire of charity, to shine with the splendor of obedience, to grow ardent with love, to be saved from destruction amidst dangers, to escape happily from perils, to hasten to Thy sweetness, to come tranquilly to Thy presence, to be satiated forever by the manifestation of Thy presence, and to praise Thee without end forever in eternity.[23]

Sacred Heart of Jesus, You regenerate all those souls reborn of water and Spirit. Complete the work You have begun in us, leading us to eternal life. Saint Ildefonsus, pray for us!

January 23 | *Bl. Henry Suso*

A Dominican priest and student of Meister Eckhart, Bl. Henry Suso (1295–1366) zealously pursued union with God through devout contemplation, rather than scholastic studies. In this mystical exchange, Our Lord directs Blessed Henry to pursue an integrated life of virtue, drawing strength from His Heart. Within this fount of blessing, all may be renewed by the Precious Blood of Christ.

> A sharp spear was thrust into My right side and forthwith a stream of Precious Blood gushed out, and with it a fountain of living water.
>
> You ought to thirst after the salvation of men. You should direct your good works toward a perfect life and persevere to the end. Your will must be subject and your obedience prompt to your superiors. Your soul, and all that belongs to it, must be surrendered into your heavenly Father's hands; and your spirit must ever be dying out of time into eternity in prefiguration of your last journey. Behold, thus will your cross be shaped after My miserable cross and worthily accomplished in it. You should wholly lock yourself up in My love-wounded Heart in My open side, and dwell there, and seek there your resting place. Then will I wash You with the waters of life and robe you with My Precious Blood in purple. I will associate myself to you and unite you with myself eternally.[24]

Sacred Heart of Jesus, crucified for love of me, transform me in Your self-giving love. Bl. Henry Suso, pray for us!

January 24 | *St. Francis de Sales*

In this excerpt from *Introduction to the Devout Life*, St. Francis de Sales (1567–1622) writes that Christ, who possessed all the perfections of the Godhead, beheld all souls from the cross and held each in the love of His Heart.

> It is certain that the Heart of our dear Jesus beheld your heart from the tree of the cross and loved it, and by this love obtained for it all the good things you will ever have; and among them your resolutions. Yes, Philothea, we may all say with the prophet Jeremiah: "O Lord, before I had a being, You beheld me, and called me by name," since the divine goodness actually did prepare for us all the general and particular means of our salvation, and consequently our good resolutions.
>
> As a pregnant woman prepares the cradle, the linen, and swathing clothes, and even a nurse … so Our Savior, designing to bring you forth to salvation and make you His child, prepared all that was necessary for you upon the tree of the cross: your spiritual cradle, your linen … all that was needed for your happiness. …
>
> O how sweet to think that the tender Heart of God thought upon Philothea, loved her, and procured her a thousand means of salvation, as if there had been no other soul in the world to think on.[25]

Sacred Heart of Jesus, help me to surrender to Your providence over all things. St. Francis de Sales, pray for us!

January 25 | *Feast of the Conversion of Saint Paul*

Today, the Church celebrates that miraculous working of grace which transformed a persecutor of Christ into an apostle. The stirring Latin hymn *Tinctam ergo Christi sanguine* (c. sixteenth–eighteenth century) voices the sentiments of one who longs to be conformed to Christ and crucified to the world (see Gal 2:20). Here, the instruments of Christ's passion become the means of man's own moral reformation, holding him fast in fidelity and restraining him from every evil.

Turn then upon me, O spear
all stained with the Blood of
  Christ,
that did exact the price of sin,
and pierce my heart, my feet,
  and my hands.

I beseech You who are afflicted,
on account of transgression:
anoint my wounded soul,
healing it by Your Blood
  divine.

Then, powerless to approach
  sin my feet shall be;
hands shall cease their injury;
and from my heart cast open
shall fevered passions flee.

To You, O Jesus, transpierced
by nails and lance, be glory!
With the Father and the consoling Spirit,
now and for ages without end.
  Amen.[26]

Sacred Heart of Jesus, pierced victim and opened gate, conform me to Your image. Make of my hands and feet true instruments of praise, and turn my heart to You. Saint Paul, you who were miraculously converted to Christ, pray for us!

January 26

Best known for *The Imitation of Christ*, Thomas à Kempis (1380–1471) also wrote the equally praiseworthy *Meditations on the Life of Christ*. Drawing upon images from the Old and New Testaments, Thomas here describes Jesus' open and wounded side as the birthplace of the Church.

> In former times, Moses, the servant of the Lord, struck the rock in the wilderness so that waters gushed forth in abundance, quelling the murmuring of the people who now drank from this stream with joy. But Longinus, a rugged soldier with spear in hand, struck with great force the rock when he opened the right side of Jesus, whereupon blood and water flowed forth. And it was from there that our chaste mother, the Church, has drawn the sacraments of salvation. For, as Eve is called the mother of all living, drawn from the side of Adam, her husband, so also the holy Church is called the Mother of all the faithful and is formed anew out of the side of Christ, her Spouse. …
>
> Whoever drinks from the sacred and divine fount of this wound, or once takes a draught of love from therein, shall forget all his evils. He shall no longer be inflamed by the heat of worldly and bodily desires, but shall ardently burn with the unspeakable love of eternal things.[27]

Sacred Heart of Jesus, living fountain, let me drink of Your waters which heal every wound of sin. Mary, Mother of the Church, pray for us!

January 27 | *St. Angela Merici*

St. Angela Merici (1474–1574), foundress of the Ursuline Order, delivered these final instructions to superiors. She exhorts them to imitate the tenderness of the Shepherd, who guides his flock with compassion, correcting when necessary.

> In every circumstance, be gentle and courteous to them. Listen to the Master saying: "Learn from me; for I am gentle and lowly in heart" (Mt 11:29). Of the Almighty Creator and Ruler, it is also said that He "orders all things well" (Ws 8:1), and the Master says of himself, "My yoke is easy, and my burden is light" (Mt 11:30). Therefore, it is fitting that you employ the utmost gentleness. Above all, take care never to use compulsion. God has made us all to have free will, and to no one's will does He do violence. He leads them to obey by use of reason, through inviting motives and by gentle persuasion. Thus He says in the Apocalypse: "I counsel you to buy from me gold refined by fire, that you may be rich (Rv 3:18). "I counsel you," He says; not, "I compel you."
>
> However ... correction may be required in certain circumstances and may prove useful at times to certain persons. Only, in order to make them useful and reasonable, one should be moved by charity and zeal for the spiritual welfare of souls.[28]

Sacred Heart of Jesus, Good Shepherd, lead me on the path of meekness and humility, reproving me with love. St. Angela Merici, pray for us!

January 28 | *St. Thomas Aquinas*

In his *Commentary on the Gospel of John*, St. Thomas Aquinas (c. 1225–1274), the greatest of scholastic theologians, addresses the dual movements of the soul proper to Christian conversion: it must turn *from* the world even as it turns *toward* Christ.

> Regarding the first, it is noted that we ought to forsake four things if we wish to follow Christ: (1) In forsaking earthly things by despising them, "Whoever of you does not renounce all that he has cannot be my disciple" [Lk 14:33]. (2) In leaving relatives and parents for the sake of God, "He who loves father or mother more than me is not worthy of me" [Mt 10:37]. (3) In abandoning his own body by mortifying it, and (4) in denying his own will. Of these latter two: "If any man would come after me, let him deny himself and take up his cross daily and follow me" [Lk 9:23].
>
> Regarding the second, we ought to imitate Christ in four ways: (1) In humility: "Learn from me; for I am gentle and lowly in heart" [Mt 11:29]. (2) In piety, "Be merciful, even as your Father is merciful" [Lk 6:36]. (3) In charity, "This I command you, to love one another" [Jn 15:17]. (4) In the bitterness of tribulations, "Christ also suffered for you, leaving you an example, that you should follow in his steps" [1 Pt 2:21].[29]

Sacred Heart of Jesus, model of charity, free me from vanity that I may seek Your favor. Saint Thomas, pray for us!

January 29

Bl. Mary of the Divine Heart (1863–1899) was a German noblewoman who renounced worldly comforts to serve Christ in the Congregation of Our Lady of Charity of the Good Shepherd. Devoted to the Sacred Heart from her youth, her ultimate achievement was to persuade Pope Leo XIII to consecrate the world to the Sacred Heart of Jesus, an act he carried out in 1899. Here, Blessed Mary ponders the depths of Christ's charity, proclaiming that Christ loved humanity even unto the opening of His Heart.

> We should, first of all, study to recognize more and more this adorable Heart as a furnace of ardent love, an ocean of mercy. When we draw near to this burning fire, we shall feel our hearts also inflamed with burning love, for who could remain cold and insensible at the sight of so much goodness, so much love. He loved us in immolating himself for us. He gave everything for us. His whole life was consecrated to our salvation, and even after His death, He allowed His Heart to be opened, that we might find in it a place of salvation and repose. And how can we speak of the institution of the Blessed Sacrament? No human language can express the depth of this ineffable mystery of love.[30]

Sacred Heart of Jesus, Bread of Life, You gave yourself for the life of the world. By this holy and inestimable gift, consecrate us to Your service. Blessed Mary, pray for us!

January 30

The *Ancrene Riwle* is an anonymous rule of life, written for anchoresses seeking union with God in solitary enclosure. Here, the author extols the wounds of Jesus as refuge, shield, and resting place.

> Name Jesus often and invoke the aid of His passion, and implore Him by His sufferings, by His Precious Blood, and by His death on the cross. Fly into His wounds; creep into them with thy thought. They are all open. He loved us much who permitted such cavities to be made in Him that we might hide ourselves in them. And with His Precious Blood, ensanguine thine heart. *"Ingredere in petram, et abscondere in fossa humo."* "Enter into the rock," says the prophet, "and hide in the dust"; that is, in the wounds of Our Lord's flesh [see Is 2:10]. …
>
> He himself calls thee toward those wounds, *"Veni columba in foraminibus petrae, in cavernas maceriae"* [Sg 2:14]. "My dove," says Our Lord, "come and hide thyself in the cavities of my limbs, and in the holes of my side." Great was His affection for the dove for which He made such hiding places. See now that thou, whom He calls dove, have the nature of a dove, which is without gall, and come to Him boldly, and make His sufferings thy shield [against the enemy] … "which is thy laborious sufferings" [Lam 3:65].[31]

Sacred Heart of Jesus, strengthen us by Your passion, and fill us with Your Spirit. Sacred Heart of Jesus, have mercy on us!

January 31 | *St. John Bosco*

Seeking to minister to youths marginalized by the Industrial Revolution, St. John Bosco (1815–1888) founded the Society of St. Francis de Sales. To regularly reach the laity, he published the *Salesian Bulletin*, from which this passage beautifully portrays the intimate life of the Holy Family. The tender hearts of Mary and Joseph are here matched only by the sweetest Heart of Jesus.

> Who, however, would deny that Jesus and Mary, when finding themselves beside the dying patriarch and leaving their tender hearts to the mercy of nature, did not suffer in having to separate from that faithful companion of their earthly pilgrimage, even if for a time? Mary could not forget the sacrifices, the pain, and the hardships that Joseph suffered for her sake during the difficult journeys of Bethlehem and of Egypt. Truly, Joseph ever found recompense for his sufferings in her presence; however, if this was a reason for comfort for him, it was not reason to dispense the most tender heart of Mary from sentiments of gratitude.
>
> And since Jesus (who was certainly not inferior to either in love) had arranged in the decrees of His divine providence for Joseph to be His custodian and protector on earth — protection that cost Joseph so much suffering and so great fatigue — Jesus must have also felt in His most loving Heart the most sweet awareness of grateful remembrance.[32]

Sacred Heart of Jesus, provident over all things, grant us final perseverance and the consolation of the last sacraments. St. John Bosco, pray for us!

February

February 1

Supreme pontiff between two world wars, Pope Pius XI (1857–1939) decried the rising tides of inhumane ideologies and anti-Christian forces, recommending that reparation be made to the Sacred Heart of Jesus. In his encyclical *Miserentissimus Redemptor,* Pius XI offered a comprehensive view of the Sacred Heart devotion. The "auspicious sign" of the Sacred Heart ever proclaims the condescension and mercy of God.

> For is not the sum of all religion and therefore the pattern of more perfect life, contained in that most auspicious sign and in the form of piety that follows from it inasmuch as it more readily leads the minds of men to intimate knowledge of Christ Our Lord, and more efficaciously moves their hearts to love Him more vehemently and to imitate Him more closely? It is no wonder, therefore, that our predecessors have constantly defended this most approved form of devotion from the censures of calumniators, and have extolled it with high praise and promoted it very zealously. … Devotion of the faithful towards the Most Sacred Heart of Jesus has made great increase in the course of time; hence pious confraternities to promote the worship of the Divine Heart are everywhere erected, hence too the custom of receiving Holy Communion on the first Friday of every month at the desire of Christ Jesus.[33]

Sacred Heart of Jesus, summary of charity, I surrender to you! May the full weight of Your love descend upon my soul that I may imitate Your gracious self-gift.

February 2 | *Feast of the Presentation of the Lord*

Today's feast marks the revelation of the Messiah to those souls of dedicated prayer, Simeon and Anna, whose hearts were set on the Lord. The following account, composed by St. Margaret Mary Alacoque, records her mystical exchange of hearts with Christ. Here, Christ removes her heart so as to impart to her the very the fire of His love.

> He demanded my heart, and I begged Him to take it. He did so, and put it into His own Adorable Heart, in which He allowed me to see it as a little atom, being consumed in that fiery furnace. Then, drawing it out like a burning flame in the form of a heart, He put it into the place whence He had taken it, saying: "Behold, My beloved, a precious proof of My love. I enclose in your heart a little spark of the most ardent flame of My love to serve you as a heart and to consume you until your last moment." He added, "Until now, you have taken only the name of My slave; henceforth, you shall be called the well-beloved disciple of My Sacred Heart."[34]

Sacred Heart of Jesus, sign of salvation, I consecrate myself to Your service. Let me never rely upon myself, but only upon You. Saints Simeon and Anna, souls of hope and longing, pray for us!

February 3

Bl. Elisabeth Canori Mora (1774–1825; memorial Feb. 4) was a Trinitarian tertiary, favored with the mystical gifts of bilocation and the stigmata. Her spiritual encounters with Christ, set down by her own hand, reveal a life of intimate dialogue with the Lord. In the following excerpts, Christ speaks of the importance of intercessory prayer and its power to obtain grace. The first saying references the conversion of a great sinner, whereas the second concerns the poor souls in purgatory.

> My daughter, your prayer does violence to My Heart. Do you wish that he should be saved? Very well, be it so.
>
> I grant you the grace which you ask, according to the measure of your desires. … Beloved daughter, place your hand in the wound of My Heart, and bring out an abundance of Blood.

In this final saying, Christ speaks of Elisabeth's own heart, which He desires to conform to His own.

> My daughter, receive the impression of My love. This is not done by the ministry of an angel, but it is I who desire to wound you with My own hand. May the favor that I have shown you be a special proof of the love that I bear you.[35]

Sacred Heart of Jesus, radiant with love, purify me from all stain of sin. Give me the courage to approach You with a docile heart and contrite spirit, confident in Your tender mercy. Bl. Elisabeth Canori Mora, pray for us!

February 4 | *St. Catherine de' Ricci*

St. Catherine de' Ricci (1522–1590), whose memorial is February 2, was a Dominican mystic who for twelve years endured the stigmata and visible wounds suffered by Christ in His passion. In a revelation transcribed by a religious companion, Jesus encouraged their monastic community to enter His Sacred Heart, abandoning earthly attachments, that they may drink deeply from this wellspring of grace.

> When will you determine, once for all, to give your hearts perfectly to Me — to come and hide yourselves in this wound in My side, finding pure joy and lasting happiness there? You say that to receive My gifts and graces the soul must be rightly disposed for them, and you speak truly. You say, again, that this disposition of soul is given by Me, and you are right. … Therefore, if you would have My grace and My gifts to take possession of your hearts, tear from them all earthly affections. Remember that the things of this world quickly pass away, never to return; while I shall never be wanting to My faithful spouses! Practice holy humility, be grateful to the favors of God, obey your superiors, keep peace and mutual love among yourselves, and profit by the words of My well-beloved spouse Catherine, in whom I show you a living image of the sorrowful mysteries of My own passion.[36]

Sacred Heart of Jesus, break all my attachments to sin, and hasten my steps to Your side. St. Catherine de' Ricci, sharer in Christ's passion, pray for us!

February 5

In his encyclical *Haurietis Aquas*, Venerable Pope Pius XII (1876–1958) offered a summary of the devotion to the Sacred Heart of Jesus. Here the pontiff explains that the Sacred Heart is a veritable sign of the Christian Faith.

> When we adore the Sacred Heart of Jesus Christ, we adore in it and through it both the uncreated love of the divine Word and also its human love and its other emotions and virtues, since both loves moved our Redeemer to sacrifice himself for us and for His Spouse, the universal Church, as the apostle declares: "Christ loved the Church and gave himself up for her, that he might sanctify her, having cleansed her by the washing of water with the word, that he might present the Church to himself in splendor, without spot or wrinkle or any such thing, that she might be holy and without blemish" (Eph 5:25–27).
>
> Just as Christ loved the Church, so He still loves it most intensely with that threefold love of which we spoke, which moved Him as our advocate who "always lives to make intercession for [us]" [Heb 7:25] to win grace and mercy for us from His Father. The prayers which are drawn from that unfailing love, and are directed to the Father, never cease.[37]

Sacred Heart of Jesus, revelation of love and source of redemption, I place my whole trust in You. Wound me with Your love, granting me a spirit of heartfelt repentance. Venerable Pius XII, pray for us!

February 6

A gifted and fluent writer, St. Alphonsus Liguori (1696–1787) flourished in a legal career before responding to God's call to enter the priesthood and religious life. Here, the saint recalls that solemn moment when Christ gave himself to man in the Holy Eucharist, a gift that proceeds from His Heart at each Holy Sacrifice of the Mass.

> "Jesus knew that his hour had come" (Jn 13:1). … Behold how He spoke that night to His disciples: "I have earnestly desired to eat this Passover with you" [Lk 22:15]; by which words He would express to us the desire and anxiety that He had to unite himself with us in this Sacrament of Love. "With desire I have desired"; these words, said St. Lawrence Justinian, were words which came from the Heart of Jesus, which was burning with infinite love: "This is the voice of the most ardent charity." Now, the same flame which burned in the Heart of Jesus, burns there at present, and He gives the same invitation to all of us today to receive Him as He did to His disciples: "Take, eat; this is my body" (Mt 26:26). And to entice us to receive Him with affection, He promises paradise to us: "He who eats this bread will live forever" (Jn 6:58).[38]

Sacred Heart of Jesus, source of life and unity, grant that all may be one in You. Look upon us with love, and bless us with Your Sacrament of charity. St. Alphonsus Liguori, pray for us!

February 7 | *Blessed Pius IX*

Blessed Pius IX (1792–1878), elected to the papacy as a liberalizing force, altered his posture when grave threats to religious and civil stability were leveled against the Church and state. In response, he recommended that the faithful have recourse to the all-powerful remedy of prayer. Whereas humanity is quick to seek political solutions to its problems, Pius IX understood that Christ alone can unite the human race in His Heart of burning charity.

> It is before all things necessary to go with faith to the throne of God, to obtain mercy and find grace in timely aid. We have therefore judged it right to excite the piety of all the faithful, in order that, with us and with you all, they may pray without ceasing to the Father of lights and of mercies, supplicating and beseeching Him fervently and humbly, and in the plentitude of their faith they may seek refuge in Our Lord Jesus Christ, who has redeemed us to God with His Blood, that by their earnest and continual prayers, they may obtain from that most dear Heart, victim of burning charity for us, that it would draw all to himself by the bonds of His love, that all men being inflamed by His holy love may live according to His Heart, pleasing God in all things, and being fruitful in all good works.[39]

Sacred Heart of Jesus, make of us a civilization of love, gathered around Your kindly Heart. Blessed Pius IX, champion of the Sacred Heart, pray for us!

February 8

A son of the Rabbi of Saverne, Ven. Francis Libermann (1802–1852) found his faith's fulfillment in the Messiah, Jesus. After entering the Church, he became a priest. Writing to his brother — a father of six and fellow convert — he notes that paternal love flows from, and returns to, its source in the Heart of Jesus.

> If Our Lord came into the world, lived and died to procure the salvation of these little children, why should you not endeavor to cooperate with that divine grace He merited for you, to promote and accomplish His Heart's most ardent desire — the salvation of your children? Remember well, you hold for them the office of priest, missionary, and guardian angel, in order to lead them to a happy eternity. … The six children whom God has given to you are six talents, committed to your care; it rests with you to make them fructify. They are an admirable treasure that you will have to return to Him in heaven, and you shall be rewarded a hundredfold, even in this world, if you turn this treasure to advantage. What happiness it will be for you to see yourselves one day in heaven in the midst of six elect! Every ray of glory God shall shed on them will be reflected on you, and will render you more resplendent than the sun.[40]

Sacred Heart of Jesus, assist earthly fathers in their noble vocation. Help them to reflect the Father's love to their children! Ven. Francis Libermann, pray for us!

February 9 | *Bl. Anne Catherine Emmerich*

Bl. Anne Catherine Emmerich (1774–1824) was a German nun whose extraordinary mystical gifts — including ecstasies, visions, and the stigmata — provoked an onerous episcopal inquiry. The commission found Anne Catherine to be sincere, and her visions were posthumously published by the poet Clemens Brentano. In the following excerpt from *The Dolorous Passion of the Lord Jesus Christ,* Bl. Anne Catherine recounts the touching moment when Jesus foretold His death to His mother, Mary. Pressing her to His Sacred Heart, this tender exchange reveals Christ's solicitous care of all those who mourn.

> When Our Lord announced to His Blessed Mother what was going to take place, she besought Him in the most touching terms to let her die with Him. But He exhorted her to show more calmness in her sorrow than the other women, told her that He should rise again, and named the very spot where He should appear to her. She did not weep much, but her grief was indescribable, and there was something almost awful in her look of deep recollection. Our Divine Lord returned thanks as a loving Son for all the love she had borne Him, and pressed her to His Heart.[41]

Sacred Heart of Jesus, devoted Son of Mary, You descended into the valley of shadow for love of me. Be with me at the hour of my death, bearing me to everlasting life. Bl. Anne Catherine Emmerich, pray for us!

February 10

The mystic and priest Johannes Tauler (c. 1300–1361) lived a contemplative life motivated by his fervent desire for union with God. In this sermon, he describes the disposition of a soul purified from all temporal attachments.

> Now, when the Bridegroom sees this whole and faithful will in the Bride, and her deep and thorough humility, what does He then do? His Heart yearns over the Bride and gives her a very costly, noble, sweet cup to drink. What is this cup? It is that she suffers far more from all manner of temptations and tribulation than she has ever suffered before. And when the Bride perceives this, and sees the Bridegroom's earnestness and good pleasure concerning her, she suffers all these things willingly and gladly for the Bridegroom's sake, and bows humbly before Him, saying, "Ah! Dear Lord and Bridegroom, it is right and just that You should not will as I will, but I desire and ought to will as You will." …
>
> Then, He looks upon her with infinite, mighty divine love. To this joyful high tide comes the Father of the Eternal Bridegroom and says to the Bride, "Rise up, my lovely, chosen beloved, it is time to go to Church," and He takes the Bridegroom and the Bride and leads them to the Church, and marries them to each other, and binds them together with divine love.[42]

Sacred Heart of Jesus, abundant in love, complete the work of Your hands, preparing me to receive You as King.

February 11 | *Our Lady of Lourdes*

Juan de Castañiza (d. 1589), a Spanish Benedictine, wrote *The Spiritual Conflict and Conquest,* which was later adapted by the Italian priest Lorenzo Scupoli. Both are true authors, as Scupoli expanded the work, making it his own. As the Church celebrates the feast of Our Lady of Lourdes, de Castañiza here speaks of the Sacred Heart as that source of living water that springs unto everlasting life.

> O wound of the precious side of my sweet Savior. … In You do all those who are heavy and sad find comfort; by You are the sick cured; through You do sinners enter into heaven.
>
> O open side! O Heart of Jesus! O furnace of love! O house of peace! O treasure of the Catholic Church! O fountain of living water that springs up unto everlasting life!
>
> Open, O most loving Lord, I beseech You, this gate unto me, receive my heart into this most delightful dwelling place! Through this passage let me draw closer to Your Divine Heart. Let me drink of its sweet fountain; let me be inebriated with its most Precious Blood. Here, let my soul rest in this harbor. Here, let it sleep. Here, let it eat. Here, let it sing sweetly with the prophet: "This is my resting place for ever; here I will dwell, for I have desired it" (Ps 132:14).[43]

Sacred Heart of Jesus, safeguard me from the storms of this world, securing me in the recesses of Your side. Our Lady of Lourdes, pray for us!

February 12

The renowned Flemish Jesuit Fr. Cornelius à Lapide (1567–1637) was buried in a distinctive spot, that he might easily be found upon his hoped-for beatification. Here Father Lapide offers a moral interpretation of Christ's teaching: "Learn from me; for I am gentle and lowly in heart" (Mt 11:29).

> Learn how great and dear humility is to Christ. It is as if He said: "Learn of Me not to create a world, not subtlety to dispute concerning God and the Holy Trinity, not to perform Herculean labors, but that I am meek and lowly in heart."
>
> Humility is the secret of peace. There is no rest for the mind, save in humility. Do you wish for rest? Embrace humility, a lowly place, a lowly office, humble food, clothing, and so forth. It is impossible for the proud to have peace of soul, because they always desire great things and often are unable to attain them.
>
> Humility is the virtue of Christ. Learn of Me, He says. This is My own special virtue, dear to Me above all others, which, by descending from Heaven to this lower world, and by stooping to the shameful death of the cross, I manifested in such a manner that none should be more illustrious and more wonderful in My life and in My death.
>
> On the contrary, pride is the sin of Lucifer. Humility, therefore, makes us most like Christ.[44]

Sacred Heart of Jesus, lowliest of hearts, may I never set myself above others. Make my heart like Yours!

February 13

Ven. Fulton Sheen (1895–1979) served as an archbishop, professor, and media evangelist. Here he teaches that Christ understood human suffering with all the perfect knowledge of the Godhead, yet the cross afforded Him direct human experience of pain. God has therefore shared in our griefs.

> Shall we not say this, and find in the cross of Calvary the perfect expression of love by an all-perfect being? ... If we do say this, that He is very God of very God, and love is now reaching its climax in the redemption of mankind, then no longer can men say, "Why does God send men into the world to be miserable when He is happy?" — for the God-man is miserable now. No longer can men say, "God makes me suffer pain while He goes through none" — for the God-man is now enduring pain to the utmost. No longer can men say that God has a Heart that cannot understand, for now His own Sacred Heart understands what it is to be abandoned by God and man as He suffers — suspended between the kingdoms of both, between heaven and earth, rejected by one and abandoned by the other. Now it is true to say of love itself that it is really dying for us, for greater love than this no man hath that a man lay down his life for his friend.[45]

Sacred Heart of Jesus, conform us to Your cross of charity by which You revealed Your love for humanity. Ven. Fulton Sheen, pray for us!

February 14 | *Saint Valentine*

Today the Church honors the third-century bishop known for his steadfast love of Christ. Here, Bl. Mary of the Divine Heart writes of the Divine Spouse, whose lively presence she felt in the Blessed Sacrament.

> He made himself my companion, my friend, my confidant. The mere thought of being the spouse of His Heart sweetened every bitterness, every privation and mortification. He gave himself entirely to me in the Blessed Sacrament, and sometimes only to think of Him set me on fire with His Love. At times, I felt so intimately united to Him that I could not leave Him: He was with me and I with Him. …
>
> Oh, how I envied that [sanctuary] lamp, burning day and night before the Blessed Sacrament! It increased my desire of being, not the spouse only of the Sacred Heart of Jesus, but also its victim. When lighting it, I always begged Our Lord never to allow the light of His grace to be extinguished in my heart. I entreated Him to burn and consume me by His love. He has heard my prayer. The oil of my life which is my lamp, is now being consumed by bodily sufferings; and assuredly it is the fire of His divine love which He has enkindled within it that is consuming my heart, because I offered myself to Him as a victim, and He has accepted the sacrifice.[46]

Sacred Heart of Jesus, consume our sins in the fire of Your love. Bl. Mary of the Divine Heart, pray for us!

February 15 | *St. Claude de la Colombiére*

St. Claude de la Colombiére (1641–1682) served as spiritual director to St. Margaret Mary Alacoque, discerning the content of her revelations and faithfully spreading their message. In this sermon, Saint Claude praises the Sacred Heart of Jesus as the exemplar of meekness and humility, being free of all pride.

> Let us enter into the Heart of the Son of God and see what His dispositions were with regard to His enemies. … He sees that what they do is very much in ignorance; and although envy, human respect, interest, hatred, pride, and injustice are involved; nevertheless, His Heart, full of sweetness, looks rather at that which diminishes the sin than at that which increases it.
>
> We should have much greater cause to do the same when people provoke us. … In general, we do just the contrary: We exaggerate trifles and magnify them into crimes and acts of the grossest injustice, while very often they are not even venial sins. We rejoice over the misfortunes of those whom we look upon as our persecutors, and we are vexed at their prosperity. Oh how pitiable is all this! How humbled we ought to be when we are conscious of such feelings! How mean it is! How unworthy of a reasonable creature! O my God! If You were to judge us in this manner, we should all be lost![47]

Sacred Heart of Jesus, soften my heart that I may ever seek after reconciliation and peace. St. Claude de la Colombiére, pray for us!

February 16

Fr. Jean Pierre de Caussade (1675–1751) was a Jesuit priest and the author of the classic text *Abandonment to Divine Providence.* This simple yet formidable work urges souls to profit from every circumstance of life, recognizing each event as the result of God's providence. In the following extract, Father Jean Pierre exhorts Christians to cast themselves upon the Heart of God, whose love directs all things.

> Let us fly then, dear souls, and plunge ourselves into that sea of love which invites us. What do we await? Why do we tarry? Let us hasten to lose ourselves in God, in His very Heart, that we may inebriate ourselves with the wine of His charity. In this Heart, we shall find the key to all heavenly treasures. Then let us proceed on our way to heaven, for there is no secret of perfection that we may not penetrate: Every avenue is open to us, even to the garden, the cellar, the vineyard of the Bridegroom. If we would breathe the air of the fields, we have but to direct our steps in that direction. In a word, we may come and go at will armed with this key of David, this key of knowledge, this key of the abyss which contains the hidden treasures of divine wisdom.[48]

Sacred Heart of Jesus, perfect wisdom, help us to recognize Your providence in all things, accepting both the bitter and sweet as proceeding from Your loving hand. Sacred Heart of Jesus, have mercy on us!

February 17

An Augustinian prior and mystic, Walter Hilton (c. 1340–1396) wrote and taught in a familiar and accessible way. This excerpt from *The Scale of Perfection* treats the gift of meditative prayer.

> When this meditation is made by the help of the Holy Ghost, then it is right, profitable, and gracious, and you shall know it by this token: When you are stirred to a meditation in God, and your thoughts are suddenly drawn out from all worldly and fleshly things, and you think that you see in your soul the Lord Jesus in a bodily likeness as He was on earth; and how He was taken and bound as a thief, beaten and despised, scourged and judged to death. Also of the crown of thorns upon His head, and of the sharp spear that sticked Him to the Heart.
>
> And you, in this spiritual sight, feel your heart stirred to so great compassion and pity of your Lord Jesus that you mourn and weep, and cry with all your might of body and soul; wondering at the goodness, love, patience, and meekness of your Lord Jesus, that He would, for so sinful a wretch as you are, suffer so much pain. Nevertheless, you see so much goodness and mercy to be in Him that your heart rises up into a love, joy, and gladness in Him, with many sweet tears.[49]

Sacred Heart of Jesus, grant us perfect contemplation, that we might be ever drawn to You. Sacred Heart of Jesus, have mercy on us!

February 18

St. Jean Vianney (1786–1859) was a French priest whose humble service transformed the forgotten town of Ars into a place of worldwide pilgrimage. This text, taken from his *Catechism,* reveals the curate's thoughts on the dignity of priests. Their vocation, he writes, is the love of the Sacred Heart.

> If I were to meet a priest and an angel, I should salute the priest before I saluted the angel. The latter is the friend of God, but the priest holds His place. Saint Teresa kissed the ground where a priest had passed. When you see a priest, you should say, "There is he who made me a child of God, and opened heaven to me by holy baptism; he who purified me after I had sinned; who gives nourishment to my soul." At the sight of a church-tower, you may say, "What is in that place?" "The Body of Our Lord." "Why is He there?" "Because a priest has been there, and has said Holy Mass."
>
> What joy did the apostles feel after the Resurrection of Our Lord at seeing the Master whom they had loved so much! The priest must feel the same joy at seeing Our Lord whom he holds in his hands. The priesthood is the love of the Heart of Jesus. When you see the priest, think of Our Lord Jesus Christ.[50]

Sacred Heart of Jesus, by Your Holy Eucharist, let Your perfect Heart mold my imperfect heart, and Your all-pure Blood cleanse mine. St. Jean Vianney, pray for us!

February 19

St. Bridget of Sweden (c. 1303–1373) was a mystic and mother of eight children, including St. Catherine of Sweden (c. 1331–1381). Upon widowhood, Bridget established a dual monastery devoted to the Passion. The "Fifteen O Prayers," whose thirteenth and fourteenth entries invoke the anguished Heart of Jesus, has long been attributed to her.

> O Jesus, most valiant lion, immortal and unconquered King, remember the pain that You endured when all the powers of Your Heart and Body entirely failed You. And inclining Your head, You exclaimed, "It is consummated." By that anguish and pain, remember me in the last consummation of my departure when my soul shall be in anguish and my spirit troubled. Amen. *Our Father. Hail Mary.*
>
> O Jesus, only-begotten Son of the Most High Father, splendor and figure of His substance, remember the commendation whereby You commended Your spirit to the Father, saying, "Into Your hands, O Lord, I commend my spirit," and then, with lacerated Body and broken Heart, and with a loud cry, the bowels of Your mercy exposed, You did expire to redeem us. By this precious death, I beseech You, O King of saints, comfort me to resist the devil, the world, and flesh and blood; that dead to the world, I may live unto You. And in the last hour of my departure, receive my exiled and wandering spirit, returning unto You. Amen.[51]

Sacred Heart of Jesus, crushed by sorrow, grant me heartful repentance and final perseverance. Saint Bridget, pray for us!

February 20 | *Sts. Francisco and Jacinta Marto*

Sibling visionaries of Fatima, Sts. Francisco (1908–1919) and Jacinta Marto (1910–1920) fell to the Spanish flu pandemic. Their cousin and fellow visionary, Ven. Lúcia de Jesus Rosa dos Santos, here recalls their encounter with an angel.

> We had enjoyed the game for a few moments, only, when a strong wind began to shake the trees. We looked up, startled, to see what was happening, for the day was unusually calm. Then, we saw coming towards us, above the olive trees ... a young man, about fourteen or fifteen years old, whiter than snow, transparent as crystal when the sun shines through it, and of great beauty.
>
> [He said] "Do not be afraid! I am the Angel of Peace. Pray with me." [He] bowed down until his forehead touched the ground, and made us repeat these words three times: "My God, I believe, I adore, I hope and I love You! I ask pardon for those who do not believe, do not adore, do not hope and do not love You." Then, rising, he said: "Pray thus. The Hearts of Jesus and Mary are attentive to the voice of your supplications." His words engraved themselves so deeply on our minds that we could never forget them. From then on, we used to spend long periods of time, prostrate like the Angel, repeating his words.[52]

Sacred Heart of Jesus, may You forever be adored! Humble my heart that I might give You endless glory. Saints Francisco and Jacinta, pray for us!

February 21 | *St. Peter Damian*

St. Peter Damian (1007–1072), a Doctor of the Church, suffered from grave neglect in his youth and was subsequently adopted by his brother, Damian, an archpriest in Ravenna whose name he added to his own. His delicate soul and religious zeal led him to the monastery at Fonte Avellana. In his poetic hymn, *Of the Glory of Paradise,* Saint Peter describes the transcendent joys of heaven, drawing upon Saint Paul's declaration: "I shall understand fully, even as I have been fully understood" (1 Cor 13:12). He here describes this intimate union in terms of a merging of hearts, alluding to those early Christians who were "of one heart and soul" in Christ (see Acts 4:32).

> Beholding the All-Knowing One, nothing can be hid;
> For the inward heart of each penetrates the other:
> Oneness in willing, oneness in refusing, unity of mind.
> And to each who variously works for reward,
> Charity shares what is loved in the other,
> and the gift of each becomes common to all.
>
> Where the Body is, there the gathering of eagles.
> With angels and saints, souls are there refreshed
> By that one bread upon which they live, each citizen of heaven:
> Desiring, yet ever full — filled with desire.
> Neither satisfied in satiety, nor hungering with strain,
> They long to eat, and in consuming, long.[53]

Sacred Heart of Jesus, inheritance of the saints, unite all hearts in yourself. Grant us a share of the hidden manna that we may live unto You. St. Peter Damian, pray for us!

February 22 | *St. Margaret of Cortona*

St. Margaret of Cortona (c. 1247–c. 1297) lived a life of open scandal as mistress to an unmarried man before a radical conversion led her into the Franciscans of the Third Order. Living as a penitent, Margaret experienced an abundance of mystical visions, which were set down by her spiritual director, Father Giunta. The following dialogue illustrates the unity of mind and will that the saints enjoy with the Lord. Saint Margaret's only desire was to be conformed to the spirit of sacrificial love that characterizes Christ.

> "My daughter, do you love Me?"
>
> "Not only do I love You, O Lord, but I would wish, if it was pleasing to You, to be in Your Heart."
>
> "Eager as you are to enter into My Heart, why do you not try to penetrate the wound on My side?"
>
> "O my Lord Jesus Christ, if I was in Your Heart I would be in the wound on Your side, in the depths of Your nails, in the crown of thorns, in the gall and vinegar, and in the bandage covering Your venerable eyes."
>
> "My daughter, do you love Me?"
>
> "No, my Lord."
>
> "When will you love Me?"
>
> "I shall love You when I shall so cruelly feel in my body the sufferings You endured for me, that I can join my hands to die."[54]

Sacred Heart of Jesus, pierced for love, permit me to enter Your side. Form me in Your self-giving love, teaching me to suffer for Your sake. Saint Margaret, pray for us!

February 23 | *St. Robert Southwell*

St. Robert Southwell (c. 1561–1595; memorial, February 21) was a Jesuit poet and martyr. His poem "Saint Peter's Complaint," excerpted here, describes Peter's repentance and struggle to accept God's mercy.

> Ah! tongue, that didst his praise and Godhead sound.
> How wert thou stain'd with such detesting words,
> That every word was to His Heart a wound,
> And lanced Him deeper than a thousand swords?
> What rage of man, yea what infernal sprite,
> Could have disgorged more loathsome dregs of spite?
>
> But oh! how long demur I on His eyes,
> Whose look did pierce my heart with healing wound!
> Lancing imposthumed sore of perjured lies,
> Which these two issues of mine eyes have found;
> Where run it must till death the issues stop,
> And penal life hath purged the final drop.
>
> Christ! health of fever'd soul, heaven of the mind,
> Force of the feeble, nurse of infant loves,
> Guide to the wandering foot, light to the blind,
> Whom weeping wins, repentant sorrow moves;
> Father in care, mother in tender heart,
> Revive and save me, slain with sinful dart.[55]

Sacred Heart of Jesus, protect me from self-reliance that I may depend on You alone. St. Robert Southwell, pray for us!

February 24

Adam of Saint Victor (c. 1080–c. 1146) was a canon regular of the Abbey of Saint Victor and a celebrated composer of liturgical hymns. The following hymn, composed for the feast of St. John the Apostle, acclaims the spiritual vision of the beloved disciple.

Though all flesh pines and strains,
waned by season's passing,
throughout every age,
the word of John stands,
proclaiming that Word, true and substantial.

Reclined upon the Master's breast,
He drank of wisdom's fountain,
whence forth teachings flowed;
and in that heaven of heart's embrace,
the word of faith, speech and hearing,
the soul and God, together rested.

Whence the mind rises up,
above the flesh and senses strides,
above the mists of deception, ascending;
brilliant beyond sun's light,
that sharpened sight of heart,
pierces as the eagle.[56]

Sacred Heart of Jesus, paradise of the saints and repose of the beloved, permit me to rest upon You. Restore my soul in Your Heart's embrace, and impart to me the secrets of its love. Sacred Heart of Jesus, with all my heart, I love You!

February 25

Fr. Lorenzo Scupoli (1530–1610) is often credited as the sole author of *The Spiritual Combat*, but this classic text is actually adapted from Juan de Castañiza's earlier work (see February 11). Fr. Scupoli translated, elaborated on, and impressed his own spirit upon this piece. This excerpt describes God's love as entirely selfless, seeking only the good of others.

> [His pure love for us] is in no way blended with self-interest like friendships of this world. … Therefore, when He showers His blessings upon us, He has no other view but our advantage.
>
> With this thought, let each one say in himself: Who could have imagined, O Lord, that a God, infinitely great, should place His affections on so vile and abject a creature as myself? What could be Your design, O King of glory? What could You expect from dust and ashes? That ardent charity in which You are encircled, that fire which at once enlightens and inflames me, convinces me that You had but one design, and consequently that Your love is void of all interest: Your design in giving yourself entirely to me in this sacrament is to transform me into You; that I may live in You, and You in me; and that by so intimate a union I become one with You, and change an earthly heart, such as mine, into a heart entirely spiritual and divine, as Yours is.[57]

Sacred Heart of Jesus, graciously sustain me with Your holy Presence! Abide in me, O Lord, that I may ever abide in You!

February 26

In this homily, St. John Chrysostom (347–407) demonstrates Christ's humility of heart. Possessing unrestricted power to silence His enemies; He instead offered humanity the sublime example of patient suffering, forbearance, and charity.

> Christ himself said, "Learn of me, for I am meek and lowly in heart." At one time, the Pharisees sent servants to take Him, and at another time they sent plotters against Him. They continued insulting Him, even when they had no fault to find, but were continually benefiting. After such conduct, He still did not cease to do well to them, both by words and deeds. And when a certain domestic struck Him on the face, He said, "If I have spoken wrongly, bear witness to the wrong, but if I have spoken rightly, why do you strike me?" (Jn 18:23).
>
> But this was to those who hated and plotted against Him. Let us now see how He acts toward the disciples, or rather, what actions He shows toward the traitor. The man whom most of all there was reason to hate — because being a disciple, having shared the table and the salt, having seen the miracles and been deemed worthy of such great things, he acted more grievously than any, not by stoning indeed, nor insulting Him, but by betraying and giving Him up — observe in what friendly a manner He receives this man, washing his feet.[58]

Sacred Heart of Jesus, inexpressible love, help us to forgive those who hurt us, ministering to them for Your glory. St. John Chrysostom, pray for us!

February 27

Along with her entire immediate family, Ven. Mary of Ágreda (1602–1665) entered religious life, becoming a Franciscan nun. Her private revelations of Our Lady are recorded in *The Mystical City of God.* Here we read of the solemn events of Holy Thursday whereupon Jesus poured forth the full power of His love.

> On [Thursday] our Redeemer proceeded on His way to Jerusalem. During their conversation on the way, while He instructed them in the approaching mysteries, the apostles proposed their doubts and difficulties, and He, as the Teacher of wisdom and as a loving Father, answered them in words which sweetly penetrated their very hearts. For, having always loved them, He, like a divine swan in these last hours of His life, manifested His love with so much the greater force of amiable sweetness in His voice and manner. The knowledge of His impending passion and the prospect of His great torments not only did not hinder Him in the manifestations of His love, but just as fire is more concentrated by the frost, so His love broke forth with so much the greater force at the prospect of these sufferings. The conflagration of the love that burned in the Heart of Jesus issued forth to overpower by its penetrating activity those who were nearest about Him, and then also those who sought to extinguish it forever.[59]

Sacred Heart of Jesus, consume our faults in Your purifying fire, and grant us entrance to Your Eucharistic feast. Ven. Mary of Ágreda, pray for us.

February 28

A man of true longing, St. Augustine of Hippo (354–430) glimpsed the mysteries of God in his uncompromising search for Truth. In his *Commentary on John,* Augustine addresses Christ's maxim to "turn the other cheek."

> "When he had said this, one of the officers standing by struck Jesus with his hand, saying, 'Is that how you answer the high priest?' Jesus answered him, 'If I have spoken wrongly, bear witness to the wrong; but if I have spoken rightly, why do you strike me?'" [Jn 18:22–23]
>
> What could be more true, meek, and just than such an answer? Some will here say, "Why did He not do what He had commanded? He should not have answered, but turned the other cheek to him who struck him." Nay: Did He not answer truthfully, meekly, and righteously, and at the same time not only prepare His cheek, but His whole Body to be nailed to the tree? Thus He demonstrated what needed to be shown; namely, that these great precepts of His are to be fulfilled not by bodily pretention, but by the preparation of the heart. For, it is possible for an angry man to visibly hold out his cheek; yet, how much better is it for one with inward peace to give a truthful answer, and with a tranquil mind hold himself ready to endure heavier sufferings to come?[60]

Sacred Heart of Jesus, gentle and forgiving, grant us a spirit of compassion for those who offend us. St. Augustine, pray for us!

March

March 1

Julian of Norwich (c. 1342–c. 1416) was an English anchoress, well aquainted with suffering, who experienced sixteen visions of Christ's merciful love detailed in her *Revelations of Divine Love.* Here she describes Christ's Heart as a spacious dwelling of loving refuge.

> Then with a glad cheer Our Lord looked unto His side and beheld, rejoicing. With His sweet looking He led forth the understanding of His creature by the same wound into His side within. And then He showed a fair, delectable place, and large enough for all mankind that shall be saved to rest in peace and love. And therewith He brought to mind His dearworthy Blood and precious water which He let pour all out for love. And with the sweet beholding He showed His blessed Heart even cloven in two.
>
> And with this sweet enjoying, He showed unto mine understanding, in part, the blessed Godhead, stirring then the poor soul to understand the endless love that was without beginning, and is, and shall be ever. And with this our good Lord said full blissfully: "Lo, how that I loved thee," as if He had said: "My darling, behold and see thy Lord, thy God that is thy maker and thine endless joy, see what satisfying and bliss I have in thy salvation; and for My love rejoice with Me."[61]

Sacred Heart of Jesus, from which flowed our salvation, let my soul find its refreshment in You. Increase in me hope, that I may obtain its eternal reward.

March 2

En ut superba criminum is an eighteenth-century hymn of unknown authorship, which was adopted into the Roman Breviary for the feast of the Sacred Heart of Jesus. Its six stanzas offer a holistic view of the wounded Heart of Jesus, drawing upon scriptural themes from the Old and New Testaments.

Behold, the countless crimes
and malice of man's pride,
wounding that Heart most pure
of Him who merited glory.

The soldier's trembling spear
our misdeeds did direct,
and the fearful steel's sting
our gravest sins sharpened.

From this pierced Heart was born
the Church, Christ's espoused.
Lo, the threshold of that Ark
cast open for salvation!

Grace ever flows thence
as from a sevenfold fount
that our stained robes be cleansed
in the Blood of the Lamb.

Let no return to sin's shame
His blessed Heart rend.
Rather, let hearts emulate
those burning tongues of charity.

Grant this, O Christ; this, O Father;
this, O Holy Spirit!
Whose is the power and kingdom
and glory without end![62]

Sacred Heart of Jesus, treasury of grace, supply in me all that is lacking. Turn my heart from sin that I may become an instrument of Your honor and praise. Sacred Heart of Jesus, have mercy on us!

March 3 | *Bl. Concepción Cabrera de Armida*

Bl. Concepción Cabrera de Armida (1862–1937) was a Mexican laywoman whose prolific spiritual writings reveal a rich interior life carried out amidst ordinary circumstances. With Christ at the center of her life, she flourished in her vocation as a wife and mother of nine children. In the following prayer, Blessed Concepción spiritually reclines upon the breast of Jesus, professing His Heart to be her light, life, and love.

> Tell me that we both do not burn at the same time with the same desires … with equal pain, for the same ideal! Tell me that the tabernacle is not my delight, the subject of my envy, and that I do not live inside of it, leaning upon Your most pure chest, looking for Your glances of holy fire, just as the moth looks for light! Tell me that I do not burn there, remaining just like a poor worm of the earth.
>
> Tell me that I do not desire everything that has something to do with You, everything that is close to You!
>
> Tell me that those eyes that are always looking at me do not make me happy; that I do not wish to drown myself and be lost in tenderness in the depths of those eyes that are always blessing!
>
> Tell me that Your Heart is not my light, my life, my love![63]

Sacred Heart of Jesus, look upon me with kindness. Let my works echo Your will, fulfilling its just decrees. Bl. Concepción Cabrera de Armida, pray for us!

March 4

St. Margaret Mary Alacoque's written instructions to her novices offer practical advice for every season. Here, she urges them to trust in the providence of Christ; for in the shelter in the Sacred Heart is heavenly strength and a remedy for every ill.

> Try to please God in all that you do, and see only Him in all that happens to you. His good pleasure must suffice. Rest like a child without anxiety on His Heart: His love will take care of you. Be humble toward God and gentle toward your neighbor. Judge and accuse yourself alone, always excusing others. If you wish to honor the Sacred Heart of Our Lord Jesus Christ, make Him the depositary of all that you do or suffer. Offer Him all your actions, so that He may dispose of them according to His will, uniting yourself to Him in all that you do, and in all that happens to you. Dwell in this adorable Heart; to Him, take all your minor troubles and all that is bitter, He will sweeten it all; there you will find the remedy for all your evils, strength in your weakness, and refuge in every danger. Act toward Our Lord with entire simplicity. Do not amuse yourself with reflecting too much on your faults; that only leads to the flattery of self-love and to discouragement.[64]

Sacred Heart of Jesus, help me to discern Your providence in all things, lovingly leading me toward everlasting life. St. Margaret Mary Alacoque, pray for us!

March 5

Born to a wealthy family, St. Angela of Foligno spent the earliest years of her marriage pursuing worldly pleasures. A vision of St. Francis of Assisi inspired her profound conversion, causing her to become a Franciscan tertiary and penitent. Here Angela considers Christ's lowliness of heart.

> The Savior of the world has truly shown meekness and lowliness of heart to be the root and foundation of all virtue. Thus neither abstinence nor the hardship of fasting, nor poverty, nor vileness of raiment, nor the outward show of good works, nor the performing of miracles can avail anything without humility of heart. United with that, abstinence would be blessed and right, then would hardship and poorness of raiment be blessed, and living and stable would be the works built upon this foundation.
>
> This lowliness of heart is mother of all the virtues, from which springs even the exercising of these virtues, as the trunk and branches spring from the root. … And inasmuch as it is the root and safeguard of all virtues, the Virgin Mary, forgetful of all the other virtues of body and soul which she possessed, did trust only in this one, affirming that God was made man of her expressly because of her lowliness of heart, saying, "For he has regarded the low estate of his handmaiden. For behold, henceforth all generations will call me blessed" [Lk 1:47–48].[65]

Sacred Heart of Jesus, guard me from all pride that I may glory only in Your Name. Saint Angela, pray for us!

March 6 | *St. Colette of Corbie*

St. Colette of Corbie (1381–1447), a Poor Clare nun, reformed over a dozen monasteries in her lifetime, restoring them to the ascetic disciplines of St. Clare of Assisi. Her final letter to her spiritual daughters evidences her profound spiritual life as it speaks of their heavenly reunion.

> Oh! How I have need of His infinite mercy! The sight of my iniquities overwhelms me, and I have no support other than the merits of His passion and death. By your prayers, you will assist me in obtaining and applying their fruits so that, purified from every stain by His Blood, I may appear with confidence before His tribunal. Invoke Mary, who has ever protected me from all perils: Call upon her and her chaste spouse, Saint Joseph, to receive my soul and present it to their Divine Son.
>
> This day also awaits you, my beloved sisters; that day of rejoicing for the elect; the day that the Lord has made and which is without end. Then, we will find ourselves gathered upon the bosom of God in an ocean of peace and joy. Live in such a way that your names will never be blotted out from the Book of Life. If, despite my innumerable sins, the all-merciful God will receive me into His paradise as I hope, I will unceasingly pray for you.[66]

Sacred Heart of Jesus, graciously grant me Your pardon. Repair my faults, clothe me with Your merits, and conduct me into eternal life. Saint Colette, pray for us!

March 7 | *St. Siméon-François Berneux*

St. Siméon-François Berneux (1814–1866), a French missionary who suffered persecution and arrest in Vietnam, was ultimately martyred in Korea. In this letter, he praises his mother for her sacrificial heart of worship and affirms her devotion to the wounds of Christ — a sure means of advancing in holy surrender.

> What has filled me with joy in your last letter is the assurance that you have accepted the sacrifice which God has required of us, and are no longer so broken-hearted at my departure. This vocation of mine — this glorious mission to carry the gospel tidings to a people who know not God — this vocation (is) in reality the source of untold blessings to us both. Our faith has become more vivid, our confidence in God stronger, our love for Him more ardent. …
>
> You say that your favorite meditation is now on the wounds of Our dear Lord. I am so glad of it, for I feel that in no other way will you so readily learn conformity to His will. Following the example of the Blessed Virgin, dearest mother, you will offer your sacrifice not only with courage and resignation, but with joy, when you think of the high honor God has granted me, despite my unworthiness, of being permitted to work for the sanctification of the souls whom He died to save.[67]

Sacred Heart of Jesus, consolation in trials, grant me a love of sacrifice, even to my life, for your sake. Saint Siméon, pray for us!

March 8

St. Ambrose of Milan (c. 340–397) here teaches the Old Testament sacrifice of Gideon (see Jgs 6:11–24) as foreshadowing the sacrifice of Christ, the God-man whose humanity is a life-giving fountain, offering the drink of everlasting life.

> When so moved by hearing that message, Gideon offered a kid goat, and according to the word of the angel, laid its flesh and the leavened cakes upon the rock, pouring broth upon them both. And as soon as the angel touched them with the end of his staff, fire burst forth from the rock, and so the sacrifice was consumed. By this, it seems clear that that rock was a figure of the Body of Christ. …
>
> Even at that time, it was declared in a mystery that the Lord Jesus in His Flesh would, when crucified, do away with the sins of the whole world — and not only the deeds of the body, but desires of the soul. For the flesh of the goat refers to sins of deed, whereas the broth refers to the enticements of desire. … That the angel then stretched forth his staff, and touched the rock from which fire went out shows that the Flesh of the Lord, being filled with the Divine Spirit, would burn away all the sins of human frailty. Wherefore, the Lord says, "I came to cast fire upon the earth" [Lk 12:49].[68]

Sacred Heart of Jesus, receive my heart upon Your altar, offered in union with Your self-gift. St. Ambrose, pray for us!

March 9 | *St. Catherine of Bologna*

Originally an Augustinian tertiary, St. Catherine of Bologna (1413–1463) founded a Poor Clare monastery, desiring to live a more radical religious life. In this excerpt from her seminal work, *The Seven Spiritual Weapons,* she entreats her sisters to overcome the pomp and pride of the world by imitating the humble Heart of the Master.

> I do not say, however, that a person should wish to walk the way of obedience in order to do miracles, because Christ said, "Learn from Me not to do miracles, but to be humble and meek of heart" (see Mt 11:29). Christ's servants, male or female, neither seek nor desire any miracle except to finish their lives virtuously, persevering in that state to which God has called them. And this will be such a great and wondrous miracle, she will want that it not be known by the ignorance of worldly persons who have no experience of the combat waged by God's servants, male and female, with those enemies, that is, against the deceiving world which always appears to mortal creatures as if it were covered with flowers, and against their own flesh which rebels against the spirit and attacks it constantly with natural weapons, and against the countless infernal enemies who, with much malice and treachery, like wicked traitors, always seek to deceive and kill the souls disposed for divine service.[69]

Sacred Heart of Jesus, let me not seek wonders or signs, save that of the cross. St. Catherine of Bologna, pray for us!

March 10

Ven. Alfred Pampalon (1867–1896), a Redemptorist, died of tuberculosis at an early age. Here, Pampalon submits his heart to Christ, ardently longing that he be enclosed within the Sacred Heart and thus conformed to Christ.

> O my most loving Redeemer; life, hope, and love of my soul! I thank You for all the graces that You have bestowed upon me during this retreat. I understand. O Lord, You desire that I love You. You desire all my heart. I hear You say to me, "My son, give me your heart. It is for this heart that I have suffered; for it I have died; and it is for you that I remain in My Sacrament of Love. Give to me then, this heart" (see Prv 23:26). Ah! Yes. Lord, here! It is for You and no longer belongs to me.
>
> O my most loving Redeemer, make my heart like unto Yours! Unite my heart with Your Heart, and never permit it to be separated from You. My well-beloved Savior, penetrate it with Your holy love, with Your holy fear, with a love and filial fear that would make me avoid the smallest faults and imperfections. Yes, O Jesus! I desire to live in union with You — in union with Your adorable Heart.
>
> Heart of my Savior, open to receive me, and then close yourself upon me, that I forever remain in this blessed refuge.[70]

Sacred Heart of Jesus, impress yourself upon my heart, wounding it with Your merciful love. Ven. Alfred Pampalon, pray for us!

March 11

Franciscan Fr. Francisco de Osuna (c. 1492–c. 1540) had a lasting impact on Spanish schools of prayer, influencing even the Doctor of Prayer, St. Teresa of Ávila. In his *The Third Spiritual Alphabet,* he preaches *love* to be the driving force behind all of Christ's actions.

> There are no arms as strong as those of love, not only in its tender embracing, but in its conquering. Wherefore this more excellent love is named *Israel,* as it is said: "If you have been strong against God, how much more will you prevail against men?" [see Gn 32:28] The love against God was strong; for this and only this cast Him down from heaven to earth so as to become man. And He endured the passion as meekly as a lamb; for such nails would not have sufficed to hold Him had love not fastened Him tight; love which is strong as death and more so; for it brought death to the Immortal One; and the same slayed our death.
>
> Whoever does not love God is a great thief, because there is no lord on earth who can so justly claim something as his own as God can claim man's heart. [He] made it for himself, and He gave His own for us. Indeed, He redeemed it, asks for it, and does not permit it be taken from Him and given to another.[71]

Sacred Heart of Jesus, let Your love, stronger than death, inspire new devotion! Sacred Heart of Jesus, I love You!

March 12

The anonymous fourteenth century English text "An Epistle of Discretion" is reminiscent of *The Cloud of Unknowing* and other medieval texts that express the obscure nature of contemplative prayer. Here, the author beautifully reflects on union with Christ, referencing the Song of Songs.

> Though a seeking soul sees nothing that may be conceived with the spiritual eye of reason, in this life it suffices that God be thy love and meaning, the choice and the point of thine heart. Such a blind shot with the sharp dart of longing love may never fail of the prick, the which is God, as He says in the book of love, where He speaks to a languishing soul and a loving, saying thus: "You have ravished my heart, my sister, my bride, you have ravished my heart with a glance of your eyes" (Sg 4:9).
>
> Eyes of the soul they are two: reason and love. By reason we may trace how mighty, how wise, and how good He is in His creatures, but not in himself; but ever when reason fails, then listen, love, live, and learn to practice love. For by love we may feel Him, find Him, and hit Him, even in himself. It is a wonderful eye, this love. For of a loving soul, it is only said of Our Lord: "You have ravished my heart with a glance of your eyes."[72]

Sacred Heart of Jesus, guard my heart and turn my will from all transgression. Sacred Heart of Jesus, defend and protect us!

March 13

St. Claude de la Colombiére advocated for that spiritual freedom found in Christ. In the following prayer, he offers all his prayers and practices for the glory of the Sacred Heart.

> Most adorable and amiable Heart of Jesus, in reparation for so many outrages and for such cruel ingratitude — and to avoid such a misfortune as far as I can — I offer to You my heart with all its movements. I give myself entirely to You and henceforth most sincerely declare my desire to forget myself, and all that relates to me, in order to remove any obstacle that might impede an entrance into this Divine Heart, which You have the goodness to open to me, and into which I hope to enter, to live and die there with Your most faithful servants, penetrated and inflamed with Your love.
>
> To this Heart, I offer all the merit and satisfaction of all the Masses, prayers, acts of mortification, religious practices, acts of zeal, humility, obedience, and all the other virtues that I shall practice until the last moment of my life. I do this not only to honor the Heart of Jesus and its admirable dispositions, but I also humbly beg Him to accept the entire oblation that I make to Him, to dispose of it in the manner that shall please Him, and in favor of whom He pleases.[73]

Sacred Heart of Jesus, receive my works as a sacrificial gift, joined to Your perfect sacrifice. St. Claude de la Colombiére, pray for us!

March 14

"Restore all things in Christ" was the motto of Pope St. Pius X (1835–1914). In his first encyclical, *E Supremi,* he wrote that the renewal of society must be worked charitably, in imitation of Christ's lowly Heart.

> On the contrary, harm is done more often than good by taunting men harshly with their faults, and reproving their vices with asperity. True the Apostle exhorted Timothy: "Accuse, beseech, rebuke," but he took care to add: "with all patience" (2 Tm 4:2). Jesus has certainly left us examples of this. "Come to me," we find Him saying, "come to me all ye that labor and are burdened and I will refresh you" (Mt 11:28). And by those that labor and are burdened he meant only those who are slaves of sin and error. What gentleness was that shown by the Divine master! What tenderness, what compassion towards all kinds of misery! Isaiah has marvelously described His heart in the words: "I have put my Spirit upon him … a bruised reed he will not bend, and a dimly burning wick he will not quench" (Is 42:1-3). This charity, "Patient and kind" (1 Cor 13 13:4), will extend itself also to those who are hostile to us and persecute us.[74]

Sacred Heart of Jesus, help us bring about Your kingdom, fostering reconciliation and peace. Pope St. Pius X, pray for us!

March 15 | *St. Louise de Marillac*

After the death of her husband, St. Louise de Marillac (1591–1660), at age thirty-four, founded the Daughters of Charity, a religious order dedicated to serving the poor. In this reflection, Saint Louise considers the parable of the sower and finds fertile ground only in the Heart of Jesus. Trusting not in her own merits, she commends her works to Christ, allowing Him to be the source and end of her actions.

> Having read in the Gospel the parable of the sower, and not being able to recognize any good grain in myself, I desired to sow in the Heart of Jesus all the productions of my soul, and my bodily actions, so that I may benefit by the hundredfold increase of His merit, and may work no more except in Him and by Him.
>
> My dear Savior! Our Master and model, Jesus crucified! All these wonders come to us from and originate in You. It is Your love which, directed to the hearts of Your dear servants, has kindled fire and flame in them for the exercise of charity — a fire which does not consume so much as burn with the zeal of Your love and the desire that all creatures should share in this love after they have felt its effects in their own hearts in the good You have caused them to perform.[75]

Sacred Heart of Jesus, produce in me a harvest of charitable works, bringing forth an abundance of good fruit. St. Louise de Marillac, pray for us!

March 16

Bl. Mary of the Divine Heart joined the Sisters of the Good Shepherd with the unspoken desire that the Sacred Heart be affixed to her religious name. Her desire was answered, thus confirming her personal charism. This epistolary excerpt reveals a life lived wholly in reference to the Sacred Heart of Jesus.

> Let us love the Sacred Heart of Jesus more and more! You will help me, Father, to thank the good God for so many favors, as my weakness and misery prevent me from thanking Him as I ought and would wish to do. Be so good Father, as to offer the Holy Sacrifice of the Mass tomorrow in honor of the Sacred Heart of Jesus, in thanksgiving for so many tokens of love.
>
> As tomorrow is the first Friday of the month, I send you the first part of the notes you desired me to write in order that you may offer them to the Divine Heart of Jesus as a pledge of my love and gratitude. May He deign to accept this offering with that infinite mercy which He has always manifested towards me! … You know well how unworthy I am of so many favors received from my Divine Spouse, the remembrance of which profoundly humbles me. I relate them in order that you may thank the Sacred Heart of Jesus, in my name.[76]

Sacred Heart of Jesus, let my tongue declare Your mercies and my soul forever praise Your Name. Bl. Mary of the Divine Heart, pray for us!

March 17 | *Saint Patrick*

Born in England, Saint Patrick (c. 385–461) was captured and enslaved by Irish marauders as a youth, but eventually managed an escape. In his *Confessio,* Patrick describes the tremendous mercy of God that drew him out of darkness and into the light, enabling him to serve his former captives.

> Before I was afflicted, I was like a stone lying in the deep mire, and He that is mighty came, and in His mercy, lifted me up and verily raised me aloft and placed me on the top of the wall. And, therefore, I ought to cry aloud that I may also render somewhat to the Lord for His benefits which are so great both here and in eternity, the value of which the mind of man cannot estimate.
>
> Wherefore then, be astonished you that fear God, both small and great, and you clever men, you rhetoricians, hear therefore and search it out. Who was it that called me up, fool though I be, out of the midst of those who seem to be wise and skilled in the law, powerful in word and in everything? And me, moreover, the abhorred of this world, did He inspire beyond others — if such I were — only that with reverence, godly fear, and without blame I should faithfully be of service to the nation to whom the love of Christ conveyed me.[77]

Sacred Heart of Jesus, set me high upon a parapet. Safeguard me with Your grace, never permitting me to be moved. Saint Patrick, pray for us!

March 18 | *St. Cyril of Jerusalem*

St. Cyril of Jerusalem (c. 313–386) was a Father of the Church and author of the famed *Catechetical Lectures* for catechumens. Here, he regards the staff of Moses, which had turned the waters of the Nile into blood, as the means of Moses' begetting the nation of Israel. Similarly, the cross of Christ, upon which Blood and water flowed from the side of Christ, begat the Church.

> But someone will say to me, "These are views of your own; show me from some prophet the wood of the cross; unless you give me a testimony from a prophet, I will not be persuaded."
>
> Throughout, life comes by means of wood. In the time of Noah the preservation of life was by an ark of wood. In the time of Moses, the sea, beholding the emblematical rod, shrunk from him who smote it; is then Moses' rod mighty, and is the cross of the Savior powerless? I pass by the greater part of the types, to keep within compass. The wood in Moses' case sweetened the water; and from the side of Jesus the water flowed upon the wood. The beginning of signs under Moses was blood and water; and the last of all Jesus' signs was the same. Moses begat by changing the river into blood; and Jesus at the end gave forth from His side water with Blood.[78]

Sacred Heart of Jesus, draw all men to Your saving sacraments, which You plenteously pour out in holy Church. St. Cyril, pray for us!

March 19 | *Solemnity of Saint Joseph*

Today we honor the foster father of Jesus, spouse of the Blessed Virgin Mary, and patron of the universal Church, Joseph the Just. St. Alphonsus Liguori here considers the deference Christ gives to priests administering the sacraments. He praises the Sacred Heart of Jesus, marveling at Christ's condescension to his Church.

> Saint Luke says that while He dwelt on earth, He obeyed the Most Blessed Virgin Mary and St. Joseph; but in this Sacrament, He obeys as many creatures as there are priests on earth, "and I do not resist" [Is 1:4]. Permit me now to address You, O most loving Heart of my Jesus from which all the Sacraments indeed flowed forth, but principally this Sacrament of Love. I would gladly give You as much glory and honor as You give in the Holy Sacrament in our churches to the Eternal Father.
>
> I know that on this altar, You still love me with that same love with which You loved me when You closed Your Divine Life in the midst of so much anguish on the cross. O Divine Heart, enlighten all those who know You not with the knowledge of yourself! ... I know that I, indeed, owe You much; and that You have, indeed, placed me under great obligations: It will be but little if I consume and wear myself out for You.[79]

Sacred Heart of Jesus, teach me holy obedience. Incline my heart to Your just decrees. Saint Joseph, pray for us!

March 20

In his most famous work, *The Sinner's Guide*, Ven. Luis de Granada (1504–1588) addresses the gratuitous gift of Christian election. He renders thanks for the unmerited grace of baptism, given to us His creatures, foreknown and beloved by God.

> What, in fact, can be a greater happiness than to have been from all eternity the object of God's love and choice; to have had a privilege place in His Heart throughout the eternal years; to have been chosen as the child of His adoption before the birth of His Son according to nature; and to have been always present to His Divine Mind, clothed in the splendor of the saints!
>
> Weigh all the circumstances of this election, and you will find that each of them is an extraordinary favor, a new motive to love and serve God. Consider first the greatness of Him who has chosen you. It is God himself, who, being infinitely rich and infinitely happy, had no need of you or any other creature. Next consider the profound unworthiness of the object of this election. … Consider further, how generously and gratuitously this favor is bestowed. It preceded all merit on our part and sprang solely from the good pleasure and mercy of God and, according to the apostle, turns "to the praise of his glorious grace" [Eph 1:6].[80]

Sacred Heart of Jesus, direct my paths through the darkness and night. Prepare my heart to receive You and to behold Your glory. Ven. Luis de Granada, pray for us!

March 21

In *Christ the Life of the Soul*, Bl. Columba Marmion contemplates the Heart of Jesus, particularly the mystery that the Son of God is fundamentally oriented toward the Father. This self-giving love is expressed before all men, sacrificially offered upon the cross.

> The Heart of Christ is an immense furnace of love. The great love of Christ is that which He bears towards His Father. All His life can be summed up in these words: "I do always the things that please My Father."
>
> Let us meditate upon these words in our prayers; only thus shall we be able to penetrate a little into their secret. This unspeakable love, this tending of the Soul of Christ towards His Father's is the necessary consequence of His hypostatic union. The Son is altogether *ad Patrem*, as the theologians say: This is, if I may thus express it, His essence: The holy humanity is carried along by this divine current; having become, by the Incarnation, the humanity of the Son of God, it therefore belongs entirely to the Father. The fundamental disposition, the primary and habitual sentiment of the Soul of Christ is necessarily this: I live for My Father, "I love My Father." …
>
> All that His Father had decreed for Him, He fulfilled to the least detail. Lastly, it was out of love for His Father that He was made obedient to the death of the cross.[81]

Sacred Heart of Jesus, teach us perfect devotion and commend us to the Father. Bl. Columba Marmion, pray for us!

March 22

The English foundress of the Sisters of the Little Company of Mary, Ven. Mary Potter (1847–1913) was dedicated to the care of the sick and dying. In *The Brides of Christ,* she speaks of Christ's spirit of self-giving and our obligation to make a return for such sacrifice.

> It may be sometimes we are left cold with few thoughts, because, perhaps, we depended too much upon our own devotion. We might think we were getting very angelic in prayer, whereas we are losing humility even in the presence of the Blessed Sacrament. Rather should we approach Him in all our spiritual poverty, relying on the dispositions of Our Lady, and truthfully acknowledging that our highest dispositions cannot honor or worship God like those of His Blessed Mother, who was favored above all. Ah! Mother bring your children to Jesus! Keep us at His feet! Mother, draw your favored ones close up to His Sacred Heart! Hearken to our Mother's answer: "Only those of my children who will be crowned with thorns; whose hands and feet will be pierced with nails; whose flesh shall be scourged and whose heart pierced with the lance — only those shall have a special place near to the Heart of my Jesus!" Sisters dear, will we have that special place or will we refuse it?"[82]

Sacred Heart of Jesus, mystery of mercy, You give yourself in the sublime gift of Holy Communion. Desiring to return this favor, I consecrate myself to You! Ven. Mary Potter, pray for us!

March 23

Guilielmus Parvus (d. 1208), known in English as William Little of Newbury, composed a now-lost commentary on the Song of Songs. Portions of this work still exist in quotation, such as this passage. In the voice of Christ, William declares that the soul who reclines upon the Heart of Jesus will be impressed with His image as from a seal.

> "Who is that coming up from the wilderness, leaning upon her beloved? Under the apple tree I awakened you. There your mother was in travail with you, there she who bore you was in travail. Set me as a seal upon your heart, as a seal upon your arm; for love is strong as death" (Sg 8:5–6).

> Be thou printed by Me, as by a seal,
> clinging closely to Me by love,
> that you may receive My image as from a seal,
> and derive likeness unto Me from that clear-cut impression.
> And as forcible as is the impress of love,
> so distinct will be the expression of the likeness.
> And the more eagerly you cling to Me in love,
> the more you shall be like unto Me.
> The more forcibly you press yourself unto Me,
> the more clearly shall I, Christ, be formed in you,
> and you be transformed and reformed in Me.[83]

Sacred Heart of Jesus, draw me close to Your holy wound. Melt my heart with charity's flame, and impress Your image upon me. I surrender myself to You!

March 24 | *St. Óscar Romero*

St. Óscar Romero (1917–1980) served as the archbishop of San Salvador during a time of civil and political unrest and suffered martyrdom while celebrating the Holy Sacrifice of the Mass. Here, Saint Óscar criticizes those social movements that are purely human in their motive and means, thereby failing to proceed according to the Heart of God. For him, all such social movements are mere ideologies that will fail; for God alone can bring about true human flourishing.

> The Church's social teaching tells everyone that the Christian religion does not have a merely horizontal meaning, or a merely spiritualized meaning that overlooks the wretchedness that surrounds it. It is a looking at God, and from God at one's neighbor as a brother or sister, and an awareness that "whatever you did to one of these, you did to Me."
>
> Would that social movements knew this social teaching! They would not expose themselves to failures, to shortsightedness, to a nearsightedness that sees no more than temporal things, the structures of time. As long as one does not live a conversion in one's heart, a teaching enlightened by Faith to organize life according to the Heart of God, all will be feeble, revolutionary, passing, violent. None of these is Christian.[84]

Sacred Heart of Jesus, King of nations, You order all things according to Your love. May all mankind acknowledge Your sovereign authority and work to build a society centered around Your merciful Heart. St. Óscar Romero, witness to Christ, pray for us.

March 25 | *Solemnity of the Annunciation*

Having a lifelong devotion to the Blessed Virgin, Pope St. John Paul II (1920–2005) claimed the papal motto *totus tuus* — "totally yours." In *Ecclesia de Eucharistia,* he meditates upon the Eucharist in light of the mystery of the Incarnation.

> The Eucharist, while commemorating the passion and resurrection, is also in continuity with the incarnation. At the Annunciation Mary conceived the Son of God in the physical reality of his body and blood, thus anticipating within herself what to some degree happens sacramentally in every believer who receives, under the signs of bread and wine, the Lord's body and blood.
>
> As a result, there is a profound analogy between the *Fiat* which Mary said in reply to the angel, and the *Amen* which every believer says when receiving the Body of the Lord. … What must Mary have felt as she heard from the mouth of Peter, John, James, and the other apostles the words spoken at the Last Supper: "This is my body which is given for you" (Lk 22:19)? The Body given up for us and made present under sacramental signs was the same Body which she had conceived in her womb! For Mary, receiving the Eucharist must have somehow meant welcoming once more into her womb that heart which had beat in unison with hers and reliving what she had experienced at the foot of the cross.[85]

Sacred Heart of Jesus, make me Your dwelling place. Let my every breath proclaim Your praise. Holy Mary, Mother of God, pray for us!

March 26

St. Mechtilde of Hackeborn's mystical work *The Book of Special Grace* was renowned throughout medieval Europe and instrumental in spreading devotion to the Sacred Heart. In this excerpt, Jesus offers Mechtilde practical instruction on making a daily oblation of oneself, listing five methods: as an espousal, as a renunciation of created things, as a renunciation of oneself, as a vessel, and as a festal dish.

> Offer your heart in five different ways, and this will be a very agreeable offering to Me.
>
> First, offer it as the pledge of espousals, with all the fidelity of which it is capable, and beg of Me by the love of My Heart to purify it from all its stains of unfaithfulness.
>
> Offer it also as a jewel; joyfully presenting it as if you enjoyed all happiness and renounced it for Me.
>
> Offer it as a crown, adding all the honor you might acquire both in this world and the next so as to have Me alone for your glory and crown.
>
> Offer it as a golden cup from which I may drink My own sweetness.
>
> Finally, offer it as a dish upon which exquisite food is served for Me to feed upon myself. This offering ought to be frequently renewed.
>
> The Sacred Heart expects it at least daily. On rising in the morning, give Me your heart, that I may pour My love into it.[86]

Sacred Heart of Jesus, object of my affections, receive my heart, and purify it from all attachments. St. Mechtilde of Hackeborn, pray for us!

March 27

In his *Commentary on the Gospel of John,* Saint Augustine offers mystical insights, gleaned from Scripture, on the piercing of Christ's side.

> A fitting word was used by the evangelist by not saying, "pierced his side," nor "wounded," nor anything else, but "opened"; that thereby, the gate of life might be thrown open, from which the sacraments of the Church flowed forth, without which there is no entrance to the life that is true. That Blood was shed for the remission of sins; that water makes up the health-giving cup, and also supplies the laver of the baptism and water for drinking. This was previously announced when Noah was commanded to make a door in the side of the ark, whereby those animals destined not to perish in the flood might enter, prefiguring the Church. Because of this, the first woman was formed from the side of the man asleep and was called, "life," and the "mother of all living." Truly, it pointed to a great good, prior to the great evil of the transgression. This second Adam bowed His head and fell asleep on the cross, that a spouse might be formed for Him from that which flowed from this sleeper's side. O death, whereby those dead are raised anew to life! What can be purer than such Blood? What more health-giving than such a wound?[87]

Sacred Heart of Jesus, raise me from the tomb of sin. Pour upon me that Precious Blood and water which enlivens and sustains the Church. Saint Augustine, pray for us!

March 28

O Esca viatorum is a Eucharistic hymn, commonly attributed to Thomas Aquinas for its poetic likeness to *Panis angelicus* and *Adoro te devote,* but which only dates to the seventeenth century. The anonymous author extols the glories of the Blessed Sacrament and identifies its sacred source as the Heart of Jesus. From this wellspring of grace, man finds purification, solace, and the love for which he longs. This alone satisfies man, for no other fount dispenses that drink of everlasting life.

> O food of wayfarers and bread of angels!
> O manna from the heavens!
> Satisfy us of our hungering,
> and deprive us not this sweetness;
> for our hearts long for You.
>
> O crystalline spring, font of love,
> from the Savior's Heart outflowing!
> Give drink to the thirsting.
> This alone is our prayer.
> This alone satisfies.
>
> O Jesus, Your hidden face we honor
> beneath the form of bread.
> When, at last, this veil is torn in heaven,
> solace us with Your sight.[88]

Sacred Heart of Jesus, my God and my all, look upon me from Your Eucharistic throne. Remove my heart of stone, and place in me Your Heart of love. Sacred Heart of Jesus, hidden in the Blessed Sacrament, I adore You!

March 29

From his *Meditations on the Life of Christ,* Thomas à Kempis here recommends placing one's heart deeply into the Heart of Jesus, the great source of protection and rest.

> As far as can be, draw out your own heart and place it near the Heart of Jesus so that He may guard, rule, and have possession of it. ... When you have given your heart entirely to Jesus — to forever keep it and dwell therein — you shall then, in great peace, not be easily disturbed, nor oppressively grieved.
>
> O Jesus most pure, Creator of all things hidden who dwells in the hearts of those that love You! O You who are to the contemplative a cruciform image! O divine treasure of gifts and graces! O Christ, our King and Redeemer of the faithful, who caused Your most sacred side to be opened by the point of a dreadful spear: Open to me, I pray You, the gate of Your compassion. Suffer me to enter, by the great and open door of Your side, the secret recesses of Your most loving Heart, that my heart may be united to You by the inseparable bond of love, and vehemently inflamed thereby; so that You may dwell in me, and I in You; and that I may remain one with You forever.[89]

Sacred Heart of Jesus, my truest friend! Listen to the cry of my soul and grant Your merciful aid. Restore all that is broken, as only You can. Enclose my heart into Yours!

March 30 | *St. John Climacus*

St. John Climacus (c. 579–649) sought a life of prayer and penance on Mount Sinai. His *The Ladder of Divine Ascent,* emphasizes the excellence of humility.

> Humility is a grace of the soul without a name, being named by those alone who have made trial of it, an inexhaustible treasure, having obtained a name from God, a singular gift of God. Learn, He says, not of an angel, not of a man, not out of a book, but from Me, that is, from My dwelling in you, and working in you, because I am meek and lowly in heart, and in thought, and in sense, and you shall find rest from internal conflicts in your souls.

Sixteenth-century commentator, Cornelius à Lapide, extols humility above all virtues, pairing his remarks with Climacus's.

> "Learn of Me," that is, "do not fear to come to Me and to take the yoke of My Gospel on your neck; for if you come and receive it, you shall indeed learn that I am no tyrant, nor a severe and rigid King, but a lowly, meek, clement, and benign Lord." Moreover, Christ was of such great humility and meekness in bearing with the scribes, His disciples, and the multitude … that even if He had wrought no miracle He would, by such meekness, have proved [sufficiently] that He was the man from heaven and the true prophet sent from God.[90]

Sacred Heart of Jesus, clothe me with the garment of humility, forbearance, and kindness. St. John Climacus, pray for us!

March 31

In *The Pricke of Conscience*, Richard Rolle (c.1300–1349), an English hermit, restated the tenets of the Faith into a poetic rhyming scheme. Here, he contemplates the second coming.[91]

When our Lover'd shall come to doom
That is to say above in the air
That till good men shall show bright and fair.
This token, also I know, shall not be
the same cross, nor the same tree,
on which God was nailed, foot and hand
but a token of that cross to attend.
Yet, some know, and so may well be
That the token of the spear men shall then see,
That sticking of Christ till the Heart root
And nails that Him through hand and foot
To the hard rood tree fast presséd
And of the crown of thorns that was thrested.

On His head fast, that Blood did out fall
When the thorns Him pricked unto the skull,
And of the scourges also that burst His hide
That the Blood ran down that side.
All these tokens shall then be shewed
before all men, both learn'd and crude.
But the wicked, that damned shall be
To their shame then shall them see,
Christ shall show then His wounds wide
In hand, and foot, and side.
That shall now seem and all bled and
Till the sinful, that before Him shall stand.

He shall show, to their confusion
All the signs of His hard passion.[92]

Sacred Heart of Jesus, let all humanity fall silent, plunged into adoration before Your cross. Your kingdom come!

April

April 1

Dignare me, O Jesu, rogo te is a seventeenth-century Latin hymn of unknown authorship. Its austere verses impressively depict the Sacred Heart of Jesus as a bulwark against all evils. Within this divine dwelling place, the world, the flesh, and the devil prove powerless to ensnare the soul. The poem culminates with a request to "live and die" within the Heart of Christ.

Deign, O Jesus, I beseech Thee:
in the wound of Thy Heart, hide me!
Permit me there to ever live,
and take my rest within Thy side.

If stratagems demons plot,
and the world should boast its wealth,
within Thy Heart is refuge found,
safeguard in Thy side.

More treacherous the flesh inconstant,
the heart to tempt in flattery.
Fearing naught, here in security,
in Thy side, my sanctuary.

If eyes and breath should fade,
and life give way to death,
O Jesu! Cast me not from Thy side:
but let me here to live and die![93]

Sacred Heart of Jesus, my home and the place of my belonging, let me forever dwell in You. Defend me from all enemies, safe within Your gracious Heart. Sacred Heart of Jesus, I trust in You.

April 2

In his *Little Book of Divine Wisdom,* Bl. Henry Suso records the following locution in which God speaks of His goodness. So ineffable is God that Suso is exhorted to employ all his powers to describe His infinite perfections.

> I am in myself the incomprehensible good, which ever was and is, and which never was and never will be uttered. I may indeed give myself to men's hearts to be felt by them, but no tongue can truly express Me in words. And yet, when I, the supernatural immutable good, present myself to each creature according to its capacity to perceive Me, I bind the sun's splendor, as it were, in a cloth, and give you spiritual perceptions of Me and My sweet love in bodily words thus. I set myself tenderly before the eyes of your heart. …
>
> Lo! all and everything that you and all men could possibly imagine of form, of elegance, and grace, is in Me far more ravishing than anyone can express. And in words like these do I choose to make myself known. Now, listen further; I am of high birth, of noble race; I am the Eternal Word of the Fatherly Heart, in which, according to the love-abounding abyss of My natural Sonship in His sole Paternity, I possess a gratefulness before His tender eyes in the sweet and bright-flaming love of the Holy Ghost.[94]

Sacred Heart of Jesus, raise up a host of saints, who will forever praise Your Name. Bl. Henry Suso, pray for us!

April 3

Saint Margaret Mary here counsels a novice experiencing interior trials. The saint recognizes that God permits spiritual tribulations and urges her sister to surrender herself to the Sacred Heart, relying on Him alone.

> I beg the Sacred Heart of Our Lord to be himself your support as it is not His will to calm the storm within you. Then will you be steadfast and peaceful in the midst of the tempest, which you must not be troubled about so long as you remain close to Jesus through loving confidence and calm strength; no matter how you feel, nor however much your enemy disturbs you. It is a good sign when the devil makes a noise — he does not have what he is aiming for as long as he clamors for it. ... The Sacred Heart of Jesus knows well what passes within yours, and this is why He allows you to suffer. Keep calm, and abandon yourself to all His designs for your soul. ... Look upon yourself as a tree planted by the riverside and bearing fruit in due season: The more it is swayed by the winds, the deeper it strikes its roots into the ground. [So] the more the winds of temptation surround you, the deeper must you bury yourself in the Sacred Heart of Jesus by profound humility.[95]

Sacred Heart of Jesus, shatter the darkness of my soul. Illumine my paths, guiding me to eternal life. Saint Margaret Mary, pray for us!

April 4 | *St. Isidore of Seville*

St. Isidore of Seville (c. 560–636) succeeded his older brother, Bishop Leander, as the archbishop of Seville, ruling alongside his younger brother, Saint Fulgentius, the bishop of Astigi. In teaching on the Sacrament of Penance, Saint Isidore describes the seventh-century celebrations of this cleansing rite, acknowledging the frailty of man and underscoring that he must never despair of God's gracious pardon.

> The Catholic Church confidently imposes the exercise of the remedy of penance in the hope of pardon. Of this remedy all should acknowledge that they stand in need for the daily trespasses of human frailty, without which it is impossible to pass this life.
>
> Let it be with the priest standing solemnly in front of them in the presence of God so that a faithful confession may cover the stain which a headstrong appetite or the neglect of ignorance is noted as having been incurred. That, as in baptism all sins are remitted, or as we believe that to none of those who pass through martyrdom are sins imputed, so we confess that by the fruitful compunction of penance all sins are done away. For the tears of penitents are accounted with God as in the place of baptism. Whence, however great are faults, however grave, yet even for these the mercy of God is not to be despaired of.[96]

Sacred Heart of Jesus, unequaled in splendor, matchless in mercy, pour Your healing balm upon me, bathing me in the light of Your redemption. St. Isidore of Seville, pray for us!

April 5 | *St. Maria Crescentia Höss*

The humble origins of St. Maria Crescentia Höss (1682–1744) occasioned scornful mistreatment from her Franciscan sisters. Persevering, she eventually became novice mistress. Here, she contemplates the primacy of love in the spiritual life.

> Love gives me wings that, like a bee, I may approach every creature and extract from it the honey of love. Love, too, is the best teacher; it instructs me how to conquer myself, how to obey, how to suffer, and how to keep silence. For this reason, I surrender myself entirely to love. If I love You, O my God, by that very love I am as strong as death. By love, I can draw You, the Supreme Good, down from heaven into my heart. And with You I can pass through every wall. By love, I can soften the obdurate hearts of sinners; I can break the chains made through sin. By love, I can redeem the captives of purgatory. By love, I can conquer my evil wishes, my vicious nature, my wicked self-will. By love, I can defeat all the attacks and temptations of hell. By love, I can endure all hardships and pains. By love, I can constantly love God more and more … I offer You, therefore, my heart and all the hearts of the whole human race, and place them in Your Divine Heart, O Lord, for an eternal love.[97]

Sacred Heart of Jesus, establish me so deeply in Your Heart that we may never be parted. St. Maria Crescentia Höss, pray for us!

April 6 | *St. Juliana of Liège*

The mystical visions of St. Juliana of Liège (c. 1192–1258) led Pope Urban (1195–1264) to promulgate the Solemnity of the Body and Blood of Christ (Corpus Christi). Here, Pope Urban describes that magnanimity of heart in which Christ instituted his Eucharistic feast.

> In His great generosity, He has bestowed himself on us, and surpassing all fullness of rich gifts, exceeding every way of love, He has made himself our food. O unique and wonderful generosity, when the Giver comes as the Gift, and that which is given is the same as He who gives. … He has given himself for food, that, as man fell through by death, by food also he may be restored to life. Man fell through the food of deadly wood; man has been raised through the food of life-giving Wood. In the one was the means of death; in the other was the nourishment of life.
>
> If anyone shall eat of this bread, he shall live forever. This is the food which fully refreshes, which really nourishes, which highly sustains, not the body but the heart, not the flesh but the spirit, not the belly but the mind. For man, therefore, who needed spiritual nourishment, the merciful Savior himself in the goodness of His mind provided for the refreshment of the soul from this noble and powerful sustenance.[98]

Sacred Heart of Jesus, prune away the thorns of sin upon our hearts, making us fit to receive You. St. Juliana of Liège, pray for us!

April 7 | *St. Jean-Baptiste de la Salle*

St. Jean-Baptiste de la Salle (1651–1719) was dedicated to improving the religious formation of children. Here he proposes the pierced Heart of Jesus as the exemplar of suffering. Because Jesus permitted His Heart to be wounded for love, Saint Jean-Baptiste believes that it ought to inspire souls to embrace one's cross with courage.

> The wounds of Jesus Christ can grant us the further benefit of animating us with a love of suffering; for His wounds reveal how greatly this Divine Savior was moved to suffer for us. In His glorified Body, He retains these wounds as solemn decoration and as marks of honor. As members of Jesus Christ, you must likewise accept the honor to suffer like Him and for Him; and after the example of Saint Paul, you must glory only in the cross of your Savior.
>
> Prostrate yourself often before these divine wounds, and look upon them as the source of your salvation. Place your hand in that wound of His side with Saint Thomas — not to strengthen your faith, but to penetrate, if possible, unto the very Heart of Jesus. Endeavor to draw from that adorable Heart the sentiments of complete Christian patience, of total resignation, of perfect conformity to the will of God, and of courage to seek occasions of suffering, that these sentiments may pass into your own heart.[99]

Sacred Heart of Jesus, fill me with such faith in Your Resurrection that suffering will ever be sweet to me. St. Jean-Baptiste de la Salle, pray for us!

April 8 | *St. Julie Billiart*

St. Julie Billiart (1751–1816) founded the Congregation of the Sisters of Notre Dame de Namur. Prefiguring the spirit of St. Thérèse of Lisieux, Saint Julie speaks of resting in the merciful arms of Jesus and upon his Heart.

> I cast myself into His merciful arms and into His adorable Heart. Put me deep into it, my dear friend. This is my one prayer: "My Jesus, fasten me tight to Your blessed cross and hold me there, for I am nothing but misery." … My heart and my soul rest in God in spite of all the fogs of the Somme. God alone!
>
> I must tell my daughters a little secret — it is that this time of waiting gains me happy moments with my good God. As much as I can, I remain in the bishop's chapel. I am there with the good God and all my dear daughters. I give them all to Him one after another, and I hope that they in their turn see in God's presence their poor little mother in the adorable Heart of her good Jesus. Ah! Yes, the Heart of Jesus: How sweet it is to make our dwelling there; for the love of God let us never leave it; let us live there by love, let us die there of love, each and all of us.[100]

Sacred Heart of Jesus, refuge of sinners, be our justification, that we may pass from death to life, living on Your love. St. Julie Billiart, pray for us!

April 9

Inspired by his fellow Jesuit, St. Edmund Campion, St. Henry Walpole (1558–1595; memorial, April 7) left his missionary travels to minister to recusant Catholics in Anglican England, where he was torturously martyred. In a letter to his friend, Father Richard, he writes of God's mercy in permitting him the martyr's crown.

> Your reverence's letters give me great comfort: But if I could but see you, though it were but for one hour, it would be of greater service to me than I can possibly express. I hope that what is wanting, my sweet Lord Jesus will supply by other means, whose heavenly comfort and assistance has always hitherto stood by me in my greatest necessities, and I am persuaded will continue so to do, since His love for us is everlasting.
>
> I am much astonished that so vile a creature as I am should be so near, as they tell me, to the crown of martyrdom: But this I know for certain, that the Blood of my most blessed Savior and Redeemer, and His most sweet love, is able to make me worthy of it ... I sit here an idle spectator of the field; yet ... Our Lord, makes us mutually partakers of one another's merits: And what can be more closely united than we two, who, as your reverence sees, [are set apart for this ministry].[101]

Sacred Heart of Jesus, may we never fail to proclaim Your love by suffering for Your sake. St. Henry Walpole, pray for us!

April 10

Before St. Margaret Mary, the great advocate of the Sacred Heart devotion, was St. Gertrude the Great. Here, the mystical intimacy of the dialogue between Christ and Saint Gertrude characterizes the Incarnation as a divine espousal to all mankind.

> As I meditated on and compared Your mercy with my malice, I was filled with extreme joy, and even presumed to complain that You had not assured me of these favors by solemn contract. Your sweet and affable charity agreed to satisfy my objection, saying to me: "Do not complain of this. Approach and receive the confirmation of My promises." And immediately You opened to me, with both hands, the Ark of Your Divine Love and infallible Truth, namely, Your Deified Heart. You commanded me to extend my hand. … You said, "Behold, I promise to preserve inviolate the gifts which I have bestowed on you; however, if I suspend their effects for a time by way of dispensation, I oblige myself by the omnipotence, wisdom, and love of the Trinity in which I live and reign, true God through all ages, to recompense you afterwards threefold."
>
> After these most sweet words, as I withdrew my hand, I perceived thereon seven golden circlets in the form of rings, one on each finger, and three on the signet finger, which indicated that the seven privileges were confirmed to me as I had asked.[102]

Sacred Heart of Jesus, bind me to yourself that we might never be parted. St. Gertrude the Great, pray for us!

April 11 | *St. Gemma Galgani*

St. Gemma Galgani (1878–1903) was an Italian mystic and stigmatic. Acutely aware of Christ's Presence in the Blessed Sacrament, Saint Gemma here laments the insensibility of those who fail to hear His loving call.

> What gladness one feels abandoning herself into the arms of Jesus! How well we are, wholly alone with Jesus! The faithful soul becomes His cherished daughter: He opens His arms and presses her upon His Heart … Jesus! How I have need of Your love! Is it not true, Father, that one cannot find herself before Jesus in the tabernacle of His sanctuary, even for a moment, without sensing the greatest happiness? And when Jesus permits me to enter into this sacred tabernacle, where He is present in both Body and Blood, am I not then in paradise?
>
> Father, you may find my letter without sense; but no matter. Allow me to speak of Holy Communion. I can bear it no longer … that one finds souls who do not understand what the Most Holy Eucharist is! It is truly impossible that souls should remain insensible to the entreaties of their God, to the mysterious and ardent effusions of the Sacred Heart of my Jesus! How, O Jesus! do we not consecrate all the beatings of our hearts, all the blood of our veins, to You? Heart of Jesus, Heart of love![103]

Sacred Heart of Jesus, awaken us to your loving call. May we faithfully respond to Your voice, casting ourselves upon Your Heart. St. Gemma Galgani, pray for us!

April 12

Prompted by interior inspiration, Bl. Mary of the Divine Heart wrote to Pope Leo XIII, requesting he consecrate the world to the Sacred Heart of Jesus. Convinced of the divine origins of her request, the pope agreed. Here, Blessed Mary thanks the pope, promising the triumph of the Sacred Heart.

> What treasures are contained for me in this decree which your holiness has sent me! The Vicar of Jesus Christ condescends to remember a poor religious, and by sending her his blessing he, as it were, confirms the favors which the Divine Spouse has in His infinite mercy conferred on me! Ah! Truly I am not worthy of so great a grace. … The Divine Heart of Jesus has inspired your holiness with this holy and grand determination, to correspond to His ardent desire by consecrating the whole world to Him. May He be forever praised! …
>
> Lately, when your holiness was so dangerously ill, my want often caused me to tremble lest this consecration should not take place. I poured out my complaint to my Divine Spouse, and He deigned to console me by affirming that He would preserve the life of your holiness in order that the desires of His Heart should be accomplished, telling me that the realization of the consecration was now on the right road. Then He added: "Trust in Me; My Heart will reign; My Heart will triumph."[104]

Sacred Heart of Jesus, reign over me, bringing about the triumph of Your will. Bl. Mary of the Divine Heart, pray for us!

April 13

Servant of God Abbot Prosper Guéranger (1805–1875) was abbot of Solesmes Abbey for over forty years. Inspired to renew devotion to the liturgy, he published a fifteen-volume companion to the Mass and Office, *The Liturgical Year.* This excerpt considers Christ's resurrected appearance to the inconstant Peter, whom he approaches with gentleness and mercy.

> Suddenly, then, in the course of this afternoon, the apostle sees standing before him that Divine Master who, three days previously, he had seen bound and led away by the servants of Caiaphas. This Jesus is now resplendent with light — He is the conqueror, the glorious Messiah. And yet, what most affects the apostle is the ineffable goodness of this his Lord who comes to console him, rather than to show him the splendors of His Resurrection. Who could describe the interview between the penitent and his offended Master; the sorrow of Peter, now that he finds himself treated with such generosity; the loving pardon that comes from Jesus' lips and fills the apostle's heart with paschal joy? Blessed be Your Name, O Jesus! who raised up from his fall him who You are to leave for our chief pastor and father when You ascend into heaven! It is just indeed that we adore the infinite mercy that dwells in the Heart of our risen Jesus, and which He shows with the same profusion and power as during His mortal life.[105]

Sacred Heart of Jesus, clothe us in the light of Your Resurrection; fill our hearts with joy. Sacred Heart of Jesus, I love You!

April 14 | *Saint Lydwine*

Saint Lydwine (1380–1433) was a Dutch mystic whose difficult life was marked by poverty, spiritual trials, and grave illness. Thomas à Kempis recorded her spiritual biography and here speaks of Saint Lydwine's daily meditations on the passion. Though she endured a life of extraordinary sufferings, she savored the sweetest consolations, drinking from the opened side of Christ.

> While then the sick virgin earnestly occupied herself every day in exercises of the Lord's passion, sometimes she was rapt by a holy angel to the places of the holy land in which Our Savior by His birth, life, and suffering wrought the mysteries of man's redemption. When, therefore, on Mount Calvary, where the Lord was crucified, or at the other holy places, she was admitted to kiss the Lord's cross or His wounds, and for the refreshment of her tribulations sucked honey out of the rock and oil from the hardest stone, and attained to the embrace of the transfixed feet, and to the expiring of her Spouse crucified for love; then also after the example of Him whom she sought and loved, she commended her spirit into His hands. And through the rapture of contemplation, she often passed from the wounds of the flesh to penetrate the open abyss of His divinity so that she ceased to feel the sufferings of her body due to the abundance of spiritual graces and sweetness.[106]

Sacred Heart of Jesus, let us penetrate the blessed veil of Your humanity that we may contemplate Your divinity. Saint Lydwine, pray for us!

April 15

Bl. Pauline von Mallinckrodt (1817–1881; memorial, April 30) founded the Sisters of Christian Charity. In her journal, she quotes John's Gospel, seeing herself as the similarly faithful soul who leans upon the Beloved: "One of his disciples, whom Jesus loved, was lying close to the breast of Jesus" (Jn 13:23).

> The complete detachment from all earthly things, everything required by the vows of poverty, chastity, and obedience, passed before the eyes of my soul, and I was glad to offer all to the Heavenly Bridegroom. How different is He from all others! He, being infinitely rich, requires no dowry — nothing but my heart, my heart alone. Yes, Lord, You shall have it. I will love You; I will keep my eyes on Yours and be quick to follow every one of Your beckonings; my whole ambition tends only to Your pleasure. What does the whole world concern me, if only I please You — You, my sole Beloved!
>
> God is infinitely faithful, and He loves us with an inexpressible love. … He asks nothing more but that the soul deliver itself to Him; that it love Him. He gave it the counsel to throw aside all the dross of wealth, all earthly love, and self-will, and to confide itself to Him. He will know how to guide it safely through this world to a blessed eternity.[107]

Sacred Heart of Jesus, I give you my memories, that you may heal them, my mind that you may enlighten it, my will to guide it. Blessed Pauline, pray for us!

April 16 | *St. Bernadette Soubirous*

St. Bernadette Soubirous (1844–1879) lived in grim poverty in the forgotten village of Lourdes, before she was thrust upon the world's stage by a series of apparitions of the Blessed Virgin Mary. At the age of twenty-two, Saint Bernadette entered religious life with the Sisters of Charity at Nevers and there embraced a life of hiddenness and obscurity for Christ. In the following exclamatory prayer, Saint Bernadette begs those masters of prayer, Mary, Joseph, and St. John the Apostle, to instruct her in the ways of contemplation and charity.

> O Immaculate Mary! O glorious Saint Joseph! And you, Saint John, beloved disciple of the Divine Heart, teach me the great science of love! May it draw me powerfully! May I soar at last, may I take flight and hasten to lose myself, unite myself and disappear with you in the adorable Heart of Jesus, and Jesus crucified, the Divine Heart of charity, purity, self-denial and perfect submission.
>
> I must die to myself continually and accept trials without complaining. I work, I suffer, and I love with no other witness than His Heart. Anyone who is not prepared to suffer all for the beloved and to do His will in all things is not worthy of the sweet name of friend, for here below, love without suffering does not exist.[108]

Sacred Heart of Jesus, all-consuming fire, You transform mankind in Your love. Look upon us from Your tabernacle throne, blessing us with Your beneficent gaze. St. Bernadette of Soubirous, simple of heart, pray for us!

April 17

An Anglican priest whose conversion to Catholicism ignited great controversy, St. John Henry Newman (1801–1890) is remembered primarily as an intellectual, but his meditations reveal his piety. Here, Newman meditates upon the Heart of Jesus, breaking under the weight of its own love.

> The anguish was such that it, as it were, burst open His whole Body. … The Blood, rushing from His tormented Heart, forced its way on every side, formed for itself a thousand new channels, filled all the pores, and at length stood forth upon His skin in thick drops, which fell heavily on the ground. He remained in this living death from the time of His agony in the garden; and as His first agony was from His Soul, so was His last. As the scourge and the cross did not begin His sufferings, so they did not close them. It was the agony of His Soul, not of His Body, which caused His death. His persecutors were surprised to hear that He was dead. How, then, did He die? … He gave the word, and His Heart broke. O tormented Heart, it was love, and sorrow, and fear, which broke Thee. It was the sight of human sin, it was the sense of it, the feeling of it laid on Thee; it was zeal for the glory of God, horror at seeing sin so near Thee.[109]

Sacred Heart of Jesus, inundate my soul with compassion that I may console those who suffer and mourn. St. John Henry Newman, pray for us!

April 18

Hugh of Saint Victor (c. 1096–1141), in his insightful and highly useful commentary on the Augustinian Rule, here reflects on Augustine's command: "Let there be among you one heart and one soul in God."

> The heart and soul here spoken of are the first fruits of the Spirit that we are to offer to God at the very outset of our conversion to the interior life, as wisdom herself has bidden us where it is said, "My son, give me your heart" (Prv 23:26). Through the heart and the will, we are first drawn to God. If we are cut off from this world in body, let us see that we are united to God in heart and soul so that we may say in all truth: "For me it is good to be near God" [Ps 73:28]. "He who is united to the Lord becomes one spirit with Him" [1 Cor 6:17].
>
> Let us then cling to Him that we may be strong through Him, that we may be one with Him, that we may be content with Him, and say to Him, "My soul clings to you" [Ps 63:8]. The love of God tears us away from the world, and this same love will link us to God. So will there be among us but one heart and one soul in God.[110]

Sacred Heart of Jesus, turn our hearts from love of this world, setting them firmly upon You. Sacred Heart of Jesus, make us one in You!

April 19

A convert to Catholicism along with her husband, Ven. Cornelia Connelly (1809–1879) experienced the dissolution of her marriage, eventually founding a religious community. Cornelia's marriage and vocation story is a complicated and harrowing one, but in the way of providence, her unspeakable sufferings became the source of her holiness.

> Do not allow your heart to be wounded, and if it is wounded in spite of your efforts, stitch up the wound with the love of God. … We do not renounce our good sentiments and heart throbbings, though we try to supernaturalize them and unite them with those of the Heart of Jesus. And oh, how much we may console His Heart by our acts of self-renunciation, in accepting all for His sake and in remembering that He wishes us to console Him for the ingratitude of mankind! Is it not a wonderful thought that He condescends to show us the love of His Heart, pointing to it and saying, "Learn of Me, for I am meek and humble of heart"? Oh, what deep humility in condescending to wish for our love, and in allowing us to console Him and make reparation for the ingratitude of sinners! …
>
> Open to me, O Jesus, Thy Sacred Heart. Unite me to it forever, that each breath, each palpitation of my heart [says] without ceasing, "Yes, Lord, I am all Thine."[111]

Sacred Heart of Jesus, I offer You all the hardships I shall suffer today that hardened hearts may turn to You. Ven. Cornelia Connelly, pray for us!

April 20

Origen was an early theologian who had a marked influence on the ancient Church. Though he developed some unorthodox views from his intense study of Platonic philosophy, he was eminently capable of defending the Faith against early critics of the Church. In his treatise *Against Celsus,* Origen martials all his philosophical powers to demonstrate the intellectual integrity of the Faith. Here, he offers a touching portrait of Jesus and His lowly Heart of service.

> Moreover, let them show where there may be found even the appearance of arrogant speech proceeding from Jesus. For, how could an arrogant man express himself thus: "Learn from me; for I am gentle and lowly in heart, and you will find rest for your souls" [Mt 11:29]? Or how can He be styled arrogant who, after supper, laid aside His garments, girded himself with a towel, poured water in a basin, and in the presence of His disciples, washed the feet of each? And He rebuked him who was unwilling to allow his feet to be washed with the words: "If I do not wash you, you have no part in me" [Jn 13:8]. Or, how could He be called such who said, I "came not to be served but to serve" [Mt 20:28].[112]

Sacred Heart of Jesus, strained by love, You could not rest until You had wholly divested yourself, even stooping to wash the feet of sinners. Let heaven and earth confess Your mercies and my soul ever imitate Your lowliness. Sacred Heart of Jesus, I adore You!

April 21 | *St. Anselm of Canterbury*

St. Anselm of Canterbury (c. 1033–1109) was a Benedictine abbot who served as the archbishop of Canterbury for over fifteen years. His meditation here ponders the dread ironies of the passion.

> His tunic is not rent, but passes by lot to one of them. His dear hands and feet are bored with nails, and He, stretched upon the cross, is hung up between thieves. Of God and man, the mediator, He hangs in the midst between heaven and earth; joining the lowest things and highest, earthly things and heavenly; and heaven is bewildered, and earth condoles.
>
> And what of you? No wonder if, while the sun mourns, you mourn also; if, while the earth shakes, you tremble; if, while rocks rend, your heart is torn; if, while the women beside the cross are all in tears, you cry aloud with them.
>
> And O! Amidst it all, think of that sweetest Heart of His; how pitifully still it kept itself, reckoning not contumely, heeding no pain, refusing to feel insults and reproaches. Nay, rather, at whose hands He suffers, He has compassion on them; those by whom He is wounded. He heals them: by whom He is slain, He procures them life. O with what sweetness and self-devotion of Heart and Soul, with what abundant overflowing charity He cries, "Father, forgive them!"[113]

Sacred Heart of Jesus, teach me to carry the cross! Let me humbly fulfill the office of Simon the Cyrene, for love of you. St. Anselm of Canterbury, pray for us!

April 22

Abbot Louis de Blois (1506–1566) became a Benedictine of Liessies in adolescence and, as abbot, oversaw a widespread renewal. Here Abbot Louis counsels Christians to offer their works to God the Father in and through the Heart of the Son.

> Commend your good works and exercises to the Most Sacred and sweet Heart of Jesus Christ to be amended and perfected; for, this is what the same most loving Heart greatly desires and it is ever ready excellently to complete your imperfect works. Rejoice and exult, because however poor you may be in yourselves, you are exceedingly rich in your Redeemer who has willed you to be a partaker of His merits; who for you was made man, and for you fasted, labored, endured torments, shed His Blood and laid down His life. In Him is laid up for you a truly immense treasure if you are truly humble and of goodwill.[114]

…

> Jesus has opened His Heart to us as His secret chamber, to introduce into it pure souls as His dear spouses. … He has given us His Heart so cruelly wounded for us to make our abode therein. … "Come, my sister, into the clefts of the rock. My Heart is open to you. Draw near, and I will give you to drink of this new wine, which is nothing but the Precious Blood that flows from My Heart."[115]

Sacred Heart of Jesus, may Your Precious Blood intoxicate my spirit, transporting it with love. Sacred Heart of Jesus, Your kingdom come!

April 23

Ven. Frederic Baraga (1797–1868) emigrated from Slovenia to the United States as a missionary priest. A polyglot, he ably ministered to the many nationalities present in Ohio and Michigan, becoming the first bishop of Sault Sainte Marie, now the Diocese of Marquette. Baraga's letter below reveals the tenderness and mercy of his priestly heart.

> [The] greatest and most awful offense is the sin of despairing in the infinite mercy of our Eternal Father. O that I could imprint with angelic words upon the heart of the miserable sinner, who with a contrite heart wishes to return to his offended Father, but who, under the sense of the immense outrage committed against God, cannot imagine how the eternal, just God can forgive him; O that I could impress upon his heart these words: My friend! In the everlasting justice of God is also at the same time the love of an infinite mercy, though we cannot understand this with our poor, limited intellect. By your offense you indeed outraged the divine justice so much that all mankind combined could not sufficiently atone for this outrage, but the eternal Son of God gave himself for you, sinner, as a just reconciliation. He reconciled you with the Eternal Justice and made it possible for you to be reunited again with the Eternal Love, through love. See, God demands nothing else from you but your goodwill.[116]

Sacred Heart of Jesus, I thank You for Your merciful pardon and beg for perseverance in Your grace. Ven. Frederic Baraga, pray for us!

April 24 | *St. Mary Euphrasia Pelletier*

St. Mary Euphrasia Pelletier (1796–1868) reorganized the Order of Our Lady of Charity of the Refuge, which was founded by St. John Eudes. Addressing her religious sisters, she underscores the central role of humility in the spiritual life, which pleases the Heart of God.

> Humility, my dear daughters, is the key of the treasure of God, for nothing is dearer to the Heart of God than the truly humble soul, utterly devoid of all feelings of self-love. And yet how rarely is this virtue met with; for it is fundamentally opposed to human nature — a nature steeped in pride, so to speak, from its very birth. This is why Holy Scripture says, "Pride is the beginning of all sin" [Sir 10:15].
>
> If Our Lord had known any surer way to heaven than that of humility, He would have taught it to us. Never shall we reach the point to which He attained. Who among you was, like Him, cradled in a manger? Who has been calumniated as He was? Who has been condemned to the ignominious death of the cross? "A disciple is not above his teacher" [Mt 10:24]. I have often told you, my dear daughters that humility alone, apart from all other mortifications which your Rule enjoins on you to practice, is sufficient for the attainment of a high degree of virtue.[117]

Sacred Heart of Jesus, help us to reject all pretension of pride and enter that cruciform gate of humility, leading to everlasting life. St. Mary Euphrasia, pray for us!

April 25

So great was his compassion for those publicly fallen from grace that St. John Eudes (1601–1680) founded the Congregation of Our Lady of Charity of the Refuge, offering penitents entrance to the religious life. In this *Contract of Alliance*, Saint John extolls the Holy Hearts of Jesus and Mary.

> Oh, why have I not the hearts of all men and angels. … [But] it needs the Heart of a God to love worthily, a Man-God and a Mother of God. Thanks be to God that I have one at my disposal. Having given himself entirely to me, Jesus' Heart is consequently mine. Yes, the Heart of Jesus is my heart. It is with the love of this Heart that I love my good Savior and His Holy Mother and that I wish to love them strongly, ardently, and tenderly. Them only and forever. I wish to love nothing except what they love, to hate nothing except what they hate, to rejoice in nothing except what pleases them, nor to sorrow for anything except what is displeasing to them. I wish to place all my consolation and delight in thinking of them, in conversing with them, in speaking of them and hearing them spoken of, in serving them, in suffering for their love, and to die ten thousand times, if it were possible, for Jesus and Mary.[118]

Sacred Heart of Jesus, I offer You my heart that You might present it to the Father and obtain every grace. St. John Eudes, pray for us.

April 26

Likely composed by the Franciscan friar Jean Tisserand (d. 1494), *O filii et filiae* memorializes the events of Christ's Resurrection leading up to Saint Thomas's confession.

And when the disciples had gathered,
Christ stood in their midst
proclaiming: "Peace be with you." Alleluia!

And when Thomas heard
that Jesus had risen
in doubt did he remain. Alleluia!

"Behold Thomas: behold My side!
See My hands, see My feet!
Do not remain in unbelief!" Alleluia!

When Thomas beheld Christ,
His hands, his feet, and side,
Then did he declare: Thou art my God! Alleluia!

Blessed are those who do not see,
yet believe most firm,
eternal life for them awaits. Alleluia!

At this most holy feast,
let there be praise and jubilation.
Bless the Lord! Alleluia!

Before God we give thanks
in whose debt we remain
in devoted prostration.
Alleluia![119]

Sacred Heart of Jesus, help us to live the resurrected life, mindful of our new creation in You. Your kingdom come!

April 27

Favored with mystical vision from youth, St. Marie of the Incarnation (1599–1672; memorial, April 30), an Ursuline nun, discovered in Teresa of Ávila a kindred spirit. In this letter, she summarizes her spirituality of sacrifice, centered on the Sacred Heart. There, she offers all her affections, intentions and works.

> Become accustomed to admiring the beauty of the Son of God, and make perpetual homage to Him. Since you have devoted your heart to Him, it must have been touched by His divine beauty. Then, often say to Him that verse of the Psalm, *Speciosus forma præ filiis hominum* (the most beautiful of the sons of men), etc. I advise you to have a psalter in both French and Latin. There, you will find a spiritual meal that will satisfy the soul; yet with a satiety free of repugnance; and which continually fills the soul with those good sentiments of God.
>
> You must also have a love of sacrifice. But upon what altar will you offer sacrifice? With the greatest reverence, take the Heart of the Son of God, and after presenting it to the Father, offer upon this Divine and Most Sacred Heart, as upon an altar, all of your oblations, which are your intentions, affections, desires, actions, and friends: There, offer me with the rest, my beloved daughter, even as I also offer you each day.[120]

Sacred Heart of Jesus, receive my works, sufferings, and prayers. Present them to the Father, and bless those dearest to me. St. Marie of the Incarnation, pray for us!

April 28 | *St. Louis-Marie de Montfort*

St. Louis-Marie de Montfort (1673–1716) developed a method of total consecration to Jesus through the Blessed Virgin Mary. In this excerpt from *True Devotion to the Blessed Virgin,* Saint Louis argues that devotion to Mary is the key to penetrating the Heart of God.

> The more you gain the favor of that august Princess and faithful Virgin, the more you will go by pure faith in all your conduct; a pure faith that will make you scarcely care about the sensible and the extraordinary; a lively faith animated by charity, which will enable you to perform all your actions from the motive of pure love; a faith firm and immovable as a rock, through which you will rest quiet and constant in the midst of storms and hurricanes; a faith active and piercing, which, like a mysterious pass-key, will give you entrance into all the mysteries of Jesus, into the last ends of man, and into the Heart of God himself.
>
> [You will proceed with] a courageous faith, which will enable you to undertake and carry out, without hesitation, great things for God and for the salvation of souls; a faith which will … overthrow, by your meek and powerful words, the hearts of marble and the cedars of Lebanon, and finally, to resist the devil and all the enemies of salvation.[121]

Sacred Heart of Jesus, bequeathing to us Your mother, may her entreaties obtain for us an unshakable faith and trust in You. St. Louis-Marie Grignion de Montfort, pray for us!

April 29 | *St. Catherine of Siena*

A Doctor of the Church, St. Catherine of Siena (1347–1380) was a Dominican tertiary whose bold letters inspired Pope Gregory XI to leave Avignon for Rome. In this passage from her *Dialogues,* Christ explains that His finite sufferings possessed an infinite character, which fruits we receive in the sacraments.

> [Catherine:] "Your side was opened. Why then did You want to be struck and have Your Heart divided?"
>
> He said: Because My desire toward the human generation was ended, and I had finished the actual work of bearing pain and torment; however, I had not been able to show by finite things how much more love I had as My love was infinite. Thus I wished you to see the secret of the Heart, showing it open that you might behold how much more I loved than could be shown by finite pain.
>
> Though My works — that is, the pains of the cross — were finite, the fruit of them, which you receive in baptism, through Me, is infinite. … Had it not been infinite, the whole human generation could not have been restored to grace, neither the past, the present, nor the future. This I manifested in the opening of My side, where is found the secret of the Heart, showing that I loved more than I could show with finite pain. I showed to you that My love was infinite.[122]

Sacred Heart of Jesus, may we recognize Your boundless love, manifested on the cross of Calvary. St. Catherine of Siena, pray for us!

April 30 | *Pope St. Pius V*

Pope St. Pius V (1504–1572), a Dominican prelate elected to the papacy after the Council of Trent, faithfully implemented the Council's reforms at every level, promulgating a universal catechism. Here, including verses taken from the Douay-Rheims (DR) Bible, *The Catechism of the Council of Trent* speaks on the preeminence of love.

> But as Our Lord and Savior has not only declared, but has also shown by His own example, that the law and the prophets depend on love, and as also, according to the confirmation of the apostle, "the end of the commandment" and the fulfillment of the law "is charity" (1 Tm 1:5; Rom 13:8, DR); no one can doubt that this, as a paramount duty, should be attended to with the utmost assiduity, that the faithful people be excited to a love of the infinite goodness of God towards us; that, inflamed with a sort of divine ardor, they may be powerfully attracted to that supreme and all-perfect good, to adhere to which is solid and true happiness as he will clearly perceive, who can say with the prophet, "What have I in heaven? and besides thee what do I desire upon earth?" (Ps 72:25, DR). This is assuredly that "more excellent way" (1 Cor 12:31, DR) which the same apostle pointed out, when he referred the whole purport of his doctrine and instruction to charity.[123]

Sacred Heart of Jesus, inspire us to labor for love, accomplishing everything for Your sake. St. Pius V, pray for us!

May

May 1 | *St. Joseph the Worker; St. John-Louis Bonnard*

St. John-Louis Bonnard (1824–1852) was a French missionary priest and martyr who labored in northern Vietnam. Among his private notes was this "Act of Consecration to the Sacred Heart of Jesus," wherein John-Louis prays that his heart be buried within the Heart of Jesus.

> Jesus, I consecrate my heart to You; place it within Your Heart. Yes, it is within Your Heart that I desire to dwell, and through Your Heart that I desire to love. It is in Your Heart that I desire to live, unknown to the world and known only to You. It is from this adorable Heart that I will draw the ardent flames of charity that will consume mine. It is in Him that I will discover strength, light, courage, and true consolation. When I am languishing, He animates me; when sad, He gives me joy; disquieted and troubled, He reassures me.
>
> O Heart of Jesus, that my heart may be the altar of Your love! That my memory would forever preserve the precious remembrance of Your mercies! That my eyes be ceaselessly fixed upon Your sacred wound; that my tongue proclaim Your goodness, my mind meditate upon Your infinite perfections. That everything in me express my love for Your Heart, O Jesus; and that I am ever prepared to please You by every sacrifice! ... *Amen.*[124]

Sacred Heart of Jesus, remove from me the vanity of self-reliance, and teach me to wholly trust in You. St. Joseph and St. John-Louis Bonnard, pray for us!

May 2 | *St. Athanasius of Alexandria*

Saint Athanasius (c. 296–373) was the bishop of Alexandria whose unwavering adherence to the Catholic Faith merited him the title "Father of Orthodoxy." In the following letter, he describes the Heart of Jesus as the pattern of self-emptying love and urges Christians to imitate its example.

> First, there were Our Savior's own words, who from the heights of His divinity said to His disciples, "Learn from me; for I am gentle and lowly in heart, and you will find rest for your souls" [Mt 11:29].
>
> Oh, my brothers! How shall we admire the loving kindness of the Savior? With what power, and with what a trumpet should man cry out, exalting these His benefits! That not only should we bear His image, but should receive from Him an example and pattern of heavenly conversation. As He has begun, we should continue: In suffering, we should not threaten, and when reviled, we should not revile in turn. Rather, we should bless them that curse and in everything commit ourselves to God who judges righteously. For those who are thus disposed and form themselves according to the Gospel will be partakers of Christ and imitators of apostolic conversation. On this account shall they be deemed worthy of that praise from him with which he praised the Corinthians: "I commend you because you remember me in everything" [1 Cor 11:2].[125]

Sacred Heart of Jesus, root me in faith and charity that I may never be caught in the snares of pride. Saint Athanasius, pray for us!

May 3

Cor, arca legem continens is an anonymous eighteenth-century hymn, composed for the feast of the Sacred Heart of Jesus. It surveys the Old and New Testaments, revealing the sacred humanity of Jesus to be the new and definitive Temple of God.

O Heart! Ark of the New
Covenant!
Not the ancient law of servitude,
but the New Law of grace,
pardon, and mercy.

O Heart most pure!
Sanctuary of the New Covenant!
More sacred than the temple
of old,
and more blessed its veil
rending.

Your love graciously willed
a wound be struck wide
that Your unseen love,
spurned,
be manifest and honored.

Beneath this sign of love,
suffering in Blood and in
mystery,
Christ the High Priest
offered sacrifice of both.

Who could fail to return such
love?
Who would not cherish his
Redeemer,
choosing in that propitious
Heart
an eternal sanctuary?

Glory be to the Father and
Son,
and the Holy Spirit,
to whom be power, glory,
and kingdom, forever and
ever.[126]

Sacred Heart of Jesus, living temple of the Holy Spirit, fill my heart with love. Animate my works with charity that I may ever fulfill Your holy law. Sacred Heart of Jesus, I praise and bless You!

May 4

Tyburn Convent is a Benedictine monastery established on the field where more than one hundred English Catholics were martyred in the sixteenth and seventeenth centuries. In reparation, the Benedictines practice perpetual adoration of the Sacred Heart of Jesus, hidden in the Blessed Sacrament. Below is a portion of their annual consecration and promise.

> Jesus, immortal King of ages, Sovereign of nations, who envelops all mankind in the Love of Your Divine Heart. … This Convent of Tyburn, devoted to the great ends of our religious family, has received as its own and most special mission that of representing England unceasingly before Your adorable Heart, and the community has vowed itself to offer its adorations and prayers by night and day, in a special manner for England, and particularly for the return to the Holy Church of the children of this great nation, who are yet separated from the One True Fold. Lord Jesus, we renew today this vow and this offering, and we present them to Your Sacred Heart through the Blessed Virgin Mary, our holy father Saint Benedict, whose children brought the Faith to this country, and the glorious martyrs who shed their blood at Tyburn.
>
> O Jesus, may the day soon come when all England shall sing: "Praise be to the Divine Heart through which salvation has come to us! To Him be honor and glory for ever and ever. Amen."[127]

Sacred Heart of Jesus, inspiring a multitude of martyrs, strengthen my adherence to the Faith. Forty Martyrs of England and Wales, pray for us!

May 5

St. Claude de la Colombiére's discerning intellect made him the ideal director to guide St. Margaret Mary, the great visionary of the Sacred Heart. His meditation on the passion considers Christ's calm amidst the tempest of His arrest.

> Amidst all this disturbance and all these temptations, the Heart goes straight to God, does not make one false step, does not hesitate to act as the highest virtue suggests. This is a miracle which the Spirit of God can alone perform in a heart, to harmonize war and peace, storm and calm, desolation and a certain manly fervor, which nothing can shake, neither nature nor devils, nor God himself, who seems to be armed against us, or at least to abandon us.
>
> [Also,] the disposition of that Heart towards Judas who was betraying Him, the apostles who had forsaken Him in so cowardly a manner, the priests, and the other authors of the persecution He underwent. It is certain that all this could not excite in Him the slightest feeling of hatred or indignation; that it in no wise diminished His love for His disciples and for His persecutors; that He was sincerely and extremely grieved at the injury which they were doing to themselves, and that what He suffered, far from troubling Him, sweetened His sorrow to some extent, because He saw that His sufferings [were the remedy].[128]

Sacred Heart of Jesus, teach me to forgive as You forgave without counting the cost. St. Claude de la Colombiére, pray for us!

May 6

St. Dominic Savio (1842–1857) showed extraordinary signs of holiness from his earliest years, studying under St. John Bosco at the Oratory of St. Francis de Sales. In the following excerpt from Don Bosco's *Life of Dominic Savio,* Saint John speaks of Dominic's devotion to the Sacred Heart, which nurtured his Eucharistic piety.

> In regard to his actual reception of Holy Communion, he used to say a special prayer of preparation the night before. … But his thanksgiving cannot be said to have ever terminated. It was quite an ordinary occurrence that, if not specially called, he would not remember breakfast time or even school time, remaining in prayer, or rather in a sort of contemplation and adoration of the goodness of Our Divine Lord, who communicates with souls in His own ineffable manner.
>
> If he could spend an hour during the day in the presence of the Blessed Sacrament, it was his utmost delight; but he always found time for a visit every day, and got someone to go with him if possible. His favorite prayers were a series of acts in reparation to the Sacred Heart of Jesus — they were a well-known devotional practice, and to be found in most prayerbooks — in order that his Communions might be more fruitful and meritorious; and that there might be a motive of renewed fervor every day, he always had a definite intention in view.[129]

Sacred Heart of Jesus, hold fast our hearts, never permitting us to stray from Your side. St. Dominic Savio, pray for us!

May 7

The *Ancrene Riwle*, a medieval text for English anchoresses offering instructions on the eremitic way of life, here considers the mystical sufferings Christ endured during His passion; namely, the threefold wounding of His Heart. Jesus suffers for His sorrowful Mother, the infidelity of His disciples, and the loss of those souls who would reject Him. Christ's torments, then, include those of the innermost Soul.

> Our Lord in this sense had pain, not in one place only, but in all; not only over all His Body, but inwardly, in His Blessed Soul. In this, He had the sting of sorrow and of grievous pain; and grief made Him sorely to sigh. This sting was threefold, which, as it were three spears, smote Him to the Heart. One was the weeping of His mother and the other Marys, who flowed and melted all in tears. Another was that His own beloved disciples no longer believed Him, nor held Him for God, because He did not help himself in His great suffering, and they all fled from Him and deserted Him as a stranger. The third sting was the great sorrow and pity that He felt for the lost condition of those who dragged Him to death; in that He saw, in regard to them, all His labor lost that He labored on earth. These three things were in His Soul.[130]

Sacred Heart of Jesus, break through my heart of stone and breathe into it Your Spirit of Love. Sacred Heart of Jesus, I love You!

May 8

John Justus Lanspergius (1489–1539) was a Carthusian monk and an outstanding advocate of the Sacred Heart of Jesus. In this exhortation, Lanspergius recommends an integrated spirituality of the Sacred Heart, counseling Christians to offer their works to God the Father in and through the Heart of the Son.

> Take great care to animate yourself by frequent acts of devotion to honor the loving Heart of Jesus, so full of love and mercy for you. By means of it, and in it, you must offer to the Eternal Father all that you do. For, this Sacred Heart is the treasury of all supernatural gifts and graces. [It is] the way by which we unite ourselves more closely to God and by which Almighty God communicates himself more liberally to us. I advise you, therefore, to place some devout image of the Sacred Heart of Jesus wherever you may frequently pass. The sight of it will ever serve to remind you of your holy practices of devotion toward this adorable Heart and will move you to love Him more and more. When you feel yourselves touched with a more tender devotion, you may kiss the picture as though you were kissing the Sacred Heart of Our Lord Jesus Christ. To this Sacred Heart, you must continually endeavor to unite your own, wishing to have no other desires or sentiments but those [of Jesus Christ].[131]

Sacred Heart of Jesus, may I wholly be Yours, locked in Your love, that we might never be divided! I consecrate myself to You!

May 9 | *St. Pachomius*

St. Pachomius (c. 292–c. 346) ranks among the most illustrious of the Desert Fathers, having founded the first cenobitic (monks-in-community) monastery at Tabbenisi. Here, Pachomius relates a vision pertaining to the mercy of God. Recognizing that all things are founded upon God's mercy, Pachomius beseeches the Lord for this gift and discovers that it is nothing other than the Incarnate Word.

> Abba Pachomius heard a voice saying, "You boast of yourself, O Pachomius. You are a man. Ask mercy for yourself, because everything stands on compassion." When the blessed man heard these things, he immediately threw his face upon the ground and asked God for mercy, saying, "O Lord who sustains the universe, send Your mercies to me and never take them away from me; for, I know that without Your mercy nothing can possibly exist." And having said these words, two angels of God suddenly stood by his side. With them was a young man whose face was unspeakable, an appearance which cannot be described, and upon His Head was a crown of thorns. Then, the angels made Pachomius stand and said unto him, "Because you have asked God to send you His mercy, behold, this is His mercy, the Lord of glory, Jesus Christ, the only one, His Son, whom He sent into the world, and whom you crucified; and you set a crown of thorns upon His head."[132]

Sacred Heart of Jesus, let all come to recognize Your superabundant love, revealed on Mount Calvary. Saint Pachomius, pray for us!

May 10 | *St. John of Ávila*

St. John of Ávila (c. 1499–1569) was a Spanish priest of great austerity, spiritual discipline, and charity. In this letter, he writes of Christ's ardent love of man, expressing bewilderment that anyone could remain cold and insensible to Christ's Eucharistic gift.

> If you could enter into the very Heart of Our Lord, and if He would grant you to see that the reason for His coming down upon the altar is an impassioned and strong affection, which will brook no separation between the Lover and His beloved, your soul would swoon before the very sight of such a marvel. The mind is greatly moved by realizing Christ's presence on the altar [longing to cry out] with Saint Augustine: "Lord, what am I to You, that You should bid me to love You? What am I to You?"
>
> Oh, blessed may You be — who being what You are, have nonetheless set Your Heart upon such a creature as me! Can it be that You, King as You are, come and place yourself in my hands, and seem to say: "I died once for your sake and I come to you now to show you that I do not repent of it, but on the contrary that, if there were need, I would give My life for you a second time?" Who could remain unmoved by such love?[133]

Sacred Heart of Jesus, open the door of my soul and assume Your place as King. St. John of Ávila, obtain for us hearts of true devotion!

May 11

Conformed to the Sacred Heart, St. Damien de Veuster (1840–1889; memorial, May 10) was a Belgian missionary priest who served the lepers of Molokai. These excerpts are from Father Damien's official report on his island ministry.

> Many a time, in fulfilling my priestly duty at their domiciles, I have been compelled to run outside to breathe fresh air. … At that time, the progress of the disease was fearful, and the rate of mortality very high. The miserable condition of the settlement gave it the name of a living churchyard, which name I am happy to state is no longer applicable to our place. …
>
> As there were so many dying, [and] my exhortations were addressed to the prostrated, often they would fall upon the ears of public sinners who little by little became conscious of their wicked lives and began to reform, and thus with the hope of a merciful Savior, gave up their bad habits. Kindness to all, charity to the needy, a sympathizing hand to the sufferers and the dying, in conjunction with a solid religious instruction to my listeners, these have been my constant means to introduce moral habits among the lepers. I am happy to say that, assisted by the local administration, my labors here, which seemed to be almost in vain at the beginning, have, thanks to a kind providence, been greatly crowned with success.[134]

Sacred Heart of Jesus, seeking out the lost and forsaken, send forth missionaries conformed to Your Heart. Saint Damien, pray for us!

May 12

St. Margaret Mary Alacoque here teaches abandonment to the Sacred Heart of Jesus, which supplies for all that is lacking in us. Thus does an exchange of hearts takes place between Christ and the Christian: "A new heart I will give you" (Ez 36:26).

> If you can do nothing at prayer, content yourself by offering that which Our Savior makes for us in the most Blessed Sacrament of the Altar. … In each of your actions say, "My God, I wish to do or suffer this in the Sacred Heart of Your Divine Son, and according to His holy intentions, which I offer You in reparation for whatever is impure and imperfect in mine," and so of all the rest. When any pain, affliction, or mortification befalls you, say to yourself, "My soul, take what the Heart of Jesus sends you to unite you to himself." Try especially to preserve peace of heart, which is better than all imaginable treasures. The means of preserving it is to no longer have any will of our own, but to put that of the Divine Heart in its place, so that it may will for us whatever is most for its glory. This loving Heart will supply whatever is wanting on your part, for it will love God for you, and you will love in Him and through Him.[135]

Sacred Heart of Jesus, I offer You my heart, asking for Yours, that I might love with a perfect love. Saint Margaret, pray for us!

May 13 | *Our Lady of Fatima*

During the Easter season, the Church observes the "Sprinkling Rite," traditionally accompanied by the well-known chant *Vidi Aquam.* Adapted from the Book of Ezekiel, the chant recalls the prophet's vision of the sacrificial blood and water that flowed from the right side of the temple in Jerusalem, bringing new life to all that it touched. This prophecy was ultimately realized when the true temple, the Body of Christ, was pierced upon the cross, eliciting that outflow of sacrificial Blood and water. From this font, new life springs, restoring all that it touches to a new creation.

> I saw water flowing from the right side of the temple, alleluia; and all to whom that water came were saved, and they shall say: Alleluia, alleluia!
>
> Ps. Praise the Lord, because He is good: For His mercy endures forever.
>
> Glory be to the Father. I saw water flowing.
>
> V. Show us, O Lord, Your mercy, alleluia.
>
> R. And grant us Your salvation, alleluia.
>
> Let us pray:
>
> Graciously hear us, O Holy Lord, Father Almighty, Eternal God: And vouchsafe to send Your holy angel from heaven, who may keep, cherish, protect, visit, and defend all who are assembled in this place. Through Christ our Lord. Amen.[136]

Sacred Heart of Jesus, fountain of mercy, let flow those rivers of Blood and water, that they may inundate the earth. By this gracious watering, bring forth a new creation born of Your sacred side. Our Lady of Fatima, pray for us!

May 14

In her second letter to Pope Leo XIII, Bl. Mary of the Divine Heart testifies to the supernatural origin of the request to consecrate the entire world to the Sacred Heart. The reason she provides concurs with St. Thomas Aquinas's teachings on Christ's headship over the entire human race (see *Summa Theologiae,* III: Q.8, a.3).

> I understood the ardent desire He has that His adorable Heart may be glorified more and more, and better known, and to spread its gifts and blessing over the entire world. And He has chosen your holiness, prolonging your days in order that you might give Him this honor, [and] gave me a strict order to write again. …
>
> It may seem strange that Our Lord should ask for the consecration of the whole world, and not be satisfied with the consecration of the Catholic Church. But His desire to reign, to be loved and glorified, and to inflame all that He wills; that your holiness should offer Him the hearts of all those who, by holy baptism, belong to Him, in order to facilitate their return to the true Church, as well as the ones who have not been made partakers of the spiritual life, and yet for whom He has given His life and shed His Blood, and therefore has equally called them to be one day children of the Holy Church.[137]

Sacred Heart of Jesus, exalted throughout the earth, draw all nations to Your side, grafting them upon Your Heart. Blessed Mary, pray for us!

May 15

St. Vincent Strambi (1745–1824) was a Passionist bishop who was initially refused entrance into the order due to his frail health. In the following sermon, Saint Vincent contemplates the effusions of Precious Blood that flowed from the side of Christ and urges Christians to quench their thirst in those life-giving rivers of grace available in the sacraments.

> Inviting us to the fountain of mercy, He says: *Drink of it, all of you* [see Mt 26:28]. From His most holy wounds, as Saint Bernard says, He opens four founts: the fount of mercy, the fount of peace, the fount of devotion, and the fount of love. All souls are called to quench their thirst therein: *If any one thirst, let him come to me* [Jn 7:37]. And why did He institute the most holy sacraments, which are like channels of grace for His Precious Blood? Why does He continue to offer it to the Eternal Father in heaven, and desire that it be daily offered by His ministers upon the holy altar? Why has He awakened in the hearts of the faithful of our day devotions of this kind? Is it not because of the ardent yearning of His Heart that all draw from the fountain of His most holy wounds, and by the means of His Blood acquire grace?[138]

Sacred Heart of Jesus, send forth holy priests to slake the thirst of Your people with Your Precious Blood. St. Vincent Strambi, obtain for us a true devotion to the passion!

May 16 | *St. Simon Stock*

An early Carmelite prior, St. Simon Stock (c. 1165–1265) established monasteries throughout England and is associated with the giving of the Brown Scapular. His spiritual daughter, St. Thérèse of Lisieux, here speaks of the Sacred Heart, summarizing the logic behind her "Oblation to Merciful Love."

> O my God, must that love which is disdained lie hidden in Your Heart? It seems to me that if You found souls willing to offer themselves as holocausts to Your love, You would quickly consume them, pleased to release those flames of infinite tenderness imprisoned in Your Heart. If Your justice, which only extends to the earth, needs satisfied, how much more must Your merciful love desire to inflame souls, since "Your mercy reaches even unto the heavens?" O Jesus, permit that I may be that happy victim — consume Your holocaust with the fire of divine love. …
>
> [As an] act of perfect love, I offer myself as a victim of holocaust to Your merciful love, imploring You to consume me unceasingly, allowing the floods of infinite tenderness shut up within You to overflow into my soul, that I may become a very martyr of Your love, O my God! May this martyrdom, after having prepared me to appear in Your Presence, free me from this life at the last, and may my soul take its flight — without delay — into the eternal embrace of Your merciful love![139]

Sacred Heart of Jesus, consume me as a sacrificial vessel of love, offered for Your glory. Saint Simon, pray for us!

May 17

In his *Memoriale*, St. Peter Faber (1506–1546; memorial, August 2) details those movements of grace that led to his own life of ministerial service in the Society of Jesus. He recognizes here that Christ had laid His own Heart bare, even unto enemies.

> I was celebrating Mass and felt a sort of fear that I was not large enough in charity towards certain persons whose defects came before me. On this I heard the answer — if you shut your heart against your neighbors, God will shut His Heart against you, and if you open your heart wide to your neighbors, God will open His Heart wide to you. Seek first the love of God, and then you will easily find the love that you ought to have to enemy as well as to friend. And whenever there may be need of some actual reconciliation with your neighbor, either in word or deed, let it be done as soon as possible as a means of making your peace with God. [Be imitators of] Christ Our Lord … even after His death, when Longinus came with hatred to pierce His Heart with his lance and offend Him, not only did He not evade the blow, but with great love exposed His own Body and shed His Blood in order to heal him.[140]

Sacred Heart of Jesus, expand my heart to embrace my brothers and sisters; may their weaknesses and offenses only ever increase my love. St. Peter Faber, pray for us!

May 18

Saint Jerome (c. 347–c. 430, Doctor of the Church) was the greatest Scripture scholar of antiquity, renowned for producing the Latin Vulgate Bible. In the following letter to Abigaus, Jerome proves himself not only a doctor of the word, but a disciple, patterning himself on the meek and humble Heart of Jesus.

> Although I am conscious of many sins and daily pray on bended knees, "Remember not the sins of my youth, or my transgressions" [Ps 25:7]; yet, because I know that it has been said by the apostle, "let a man not be lifted up with pride lest he fall into the condemnation of the devil" [see 1 Tm 3:6], and that it is written in another passage, "God opposes the proud, but gives grace to the humble" [1 Pt 5:5], there is nothing I have striven so much to avoid from my boyhood as a swelling mind and a stiff neck — things which always provoke the wrath of God. For I know that my Master and Lord and God has said in the lowliness of His Flesh: "Learn from me; for I am gentle and lowly in heart" [Mt 11:29], and that before this, He sang by the mouth of David, "Lord, remember David and all his gentleness" [see Ps 132:1]. Again, we read in another passage, "Before destruction a man's heart is haughty, but humility goes before honor" [Prv 18:12].[141]

Sacred Heart of Jesus, do not deliver me over to pride, but adorn me with meekness and humility. Saint Jerome, pray for us!

May 19

Bl. Raymond of Capua (1330–1399) was master general of the Dominican Order and spiritual director to St. Catherine of Siena. In his firsthand account of Catherine's life, Blessed Raymond relates her mystical "exchange of hearts" with Jesus. Expressive of St. Paul's "It is no longer I who live, but Christ who lives in me" (Gal 2:20), Catherine here surrenders her heart to Christ, that His Heart may live within her.

> Some days later, she was in the chapel of the church of the Friar Preachers in which the Sisters of Penance of Saint Dominic assemble. She remained there alone so as to continue her prayer and was preparing to return home, when suddenly she saw herself surrounded with a light from heaven, and amid this light, the Savior appeared to her, bearing in His sacred hands a Heart of vermillion hue, radiating fire.
>
> Deeply affected with this presence and splendor, she prostrated herself on the ground. Our Lord approached, opened anew her left side, placed in it the Heart which He bore, and said to her, "Daughter, the other day I took your heart: today I give you Mine, and this will henceforward serve you." After these words, He closed her breast but, as a token of the miracle, He left there a scar, which her companions have frequently assured me they had seen.[142]

Sacred Heart of Jesus, abide in me, never permitting another to rest in me. Live in me, and let me live upon Your love. Bl. Raymond of Capua, pray for us!

May 20 | *St. Bernardine of Siena*

St. Bernardine of Siena (1380–1444) was a Franciscan priest and popular street preacher. His simple yet profound sermons state the dangers of sin, corruption, and vice. Here he exhorts the townspeople to reconcile with one another, lest they be separated from God.

> Oh! Fathers and brethren, love and embrace one another once again. And if some harm has been done to you in the past, pardon those injuries for the love of God, letting hatred abide with you no longer, lest you be hated by God. Love one another, proving your love by words and deeds and by the gift of your heart, as Christ did to those who had injured Him. Indeed, you know that while pinned to the wood of the cross, far from hating them, He showed how great was His love for them. … Who would be so cruel and wicked as to refuse forgiveness for God's sake? …
>
> I call on the women to help me for the love of God, and I solicit the assistance of all of you, both men and women, in the labors I have endured with such loving solicitude to secure your peace. … If you are reconciled with one another, you will enjoy peace here below and still more hereafter in the glory that I pray God to grant you by His merciful grace, *in sæcula sæculorum*. Amen.[143]

Sacred Heart of Jesus, teach us a radical love of humility that embraces those who offend us. St. Bernardine of Siena, pray for us!

May 21 | *St. Eugène de Mazenod*

Eugène de Mazenod (1782–1861) and his family were forced into exile during the terrors of the French Revolution. After eleven years, he returned to France and was eventually ordained a priest. In this letter, Saint Eugène recommends to his correspondent, Emanuel, a recurring spiritual rendezvous within the Sacred Heart.

> One of the most marvelous effects of Christian charity, dear Emanuel, is the sublime intercommunion that it creates between all who love one another in God. Members of the same Mystical Body, they participate in one another's joys and sorrows, combats and triumphs. Though at a distance from you, I was present with you in your heroic struggles by virtue of the communion of our mutual charity. …
>
> It seems to me that I should feel braver in combat and more certain of victory if I were near you and had an opportunity of witnessing your daily virtues. As this cannot be at present, I would suggest that we enter into an agreement to give one another a spiritual rendezvous in the Heart of Jesus every Sunday at half past ten o'clock. … At this spiritual rendezvous, we will seek by our united prayers to do a holy violence to the Sacred Heart of Our Lord and Savior, and obtain from Him the full application to our souls of the merits of His passion and death.[144]

Sacred Heart of Jesus, in whom all things are held together, gather us all within Your side, joining us in truth and charity. St. Eugène, pray for us!

May 22

Coming of age during the Reign of Terror, St. Madeleine Sophie Barat (1779–1865; memorial, May 25) had to wait for its self-destruction before she could enter the Society of the Sacred Heart. In this letter, Saint Madeleine, considering the evils of her time, sees renewed catechesis as a chance to serve Christ's Sacred Heart.

> We must prepare them by our teaching and by inculcating the devotion to the Sacred Heart. … Let us work then more zealously than ever; first, for our own perfection, next for that of our sisters, and then for that of the souls entrusted to us. The hope of the Church is in the young generation. The devil knows this only too well, and therefore strives so hard to deprive it of good education.
>
> …
>
> God, whose providence disposes all things with wisdom for the good of His Church, has at all times given her help proportioned to her wants, but it is especially in this latter age that He has manifested towards her His goodness and magnificence by revealing the immense treasures of grace contained in the Heart of His Son. It was His will, by this means, not only to secure to this Divine Heart the worship of love and of adoration [but to] revive the light of faith and the sacred fire of charity, which were being extinguished in all hearts by impiety.[145]

Sacred Heart of Jesus, fill us with the joy of the Gospel, and ignite our hearts with love. St. Madeleine Sophie Barat, pray for us!

May 23 | *St. John Baptist de Rossi*

St. John Baptist de Rossi (1698–1764) was known to hear confessions for several hours a day and to minister to souls in hospitals, prisons, and those homebound. Saint John here reasons that priests owe God an especially generous return of love, wholeheartedly expressed in deeds.

> If the love of God exacts a return from all men, how much more should be expected from priests who have received such celestial favors. And this love should not be a cold affection, but an active, moving principle, encouraging all that is good, arresting all that is evil, relieving the poor, consoling the sick, bringing the whole world to love our good God; in a word, to consume itself in the flames of charity.
>
> The Gospel of last Sunday tells us that we cannot serve two masters. [We ourselves] have only one Master to serve, and that is God whose ministers we are. Him only must we obey. We have not chosen Him, but He has chosen us. *Non vos me elegistis, sed ego eligi vos.* How great is this favor, how singular this preference, when so many others deserved it so much more than ourselves! But if He has deigned to choose us as His laborers, it is that we might really *work*, and that our work should bear lasting fruit.[146]

Sacred Heart of Jesus, who called me before I knew You, move me to abandon all other supports, that I may cast myself upon You alone! St. John Baptist de Rossi, pray for us!

May 24

Summi regis cor, aveto, attributed to St. Bernard of Clairvaux, is now credited as the work of St. Hermann Joseph (c. 1150–1241), a Norbertine priest and mystic. The hymn, excerpted here, movingly combines images of the passion with the spousal love reflected in the Song of Songs.

Heart of Christ my King! I
greet Thee:
Gladly goes my heart to meet
Thee;
To embrace Thee now it does
burn,
And with eager thirst it yet
yearns,
Spirit blest, to speak with
Thee.
Oh! What love divine compel-
ling!
With what grief Thy breast
was swelling!
All Thy Soul for us o'erflow-
ing,
All Thy life on us bestowing,
Sinful men from death to free!

Oh, that death! In bitter an-
guish,
Cruel, pitiless to languish!
To the inmost cell it entered,
Where the life of man was
centered,
Penetrating Thy sweet Heart
there.
For that death which Thou
has tasted,
For that form by sorrow
wasted,
Heart to my heart ever near-
est,
Kindle in me love the dearest;
This, O Lord, is all my
prayer.[147]

Sacred Heart of Jesus, open and expand my heart that I may receive the fullness of Your love, for I adore You!

May 25 | *St. Mary Magdalene de' Pazzi*

Extraordinary piety led St. Mary Magdalene de' Pazzi (1566–1607) to enter Carmel at fifteen, where her mystical revelations and ecstasies were recorded by her religious sisters. In this passage, God counsels a spirit of surrender of the saint.

> My words are like so many feathers, forming wings to fly up with the greatest ease, without feeling the least fatigue in the ascent. … And mark, My daughter, that this voice of My Spirit says that they shall walk and not faint from the fatigue of the journey; they shall run and not be weary, as it is easier and less fatiguing to go up quickly, as if flying, and to run very swiftly up this ladder of My words, than to go up slowly, because there is nothing more annoying on the road of the Spirit and of My counsels than slowness, or laziness, or cowardice. My daughter, you well know what My servant said, "The grace of the Holy Spirit knows not slow means," and that the man according to My Heart is he who — when he abandons himself wholly into My hands, and I enlarge his heart by charity — runs, as if it were nothing, over all the long and tedious road of the holy precepts: "I will run in the way of your commandments when you enlarge my understanding" (Ps 119:32).[148]

Sacred Heart of Jesus, fill me with Your Holy Spirit, that I might run in the way of Your Commandments. St. Mary Magdalene de' Pazzi, pray for us!

May 26 | *St. Philip Neri*

St. Philip Neri (1515–1595) was an Italian priest and Counter-Reformer who helped spiritually revive the decadent and corrupted city of Rome. Blessed with many mystical gifts, he received a radical dilation of the heart in prayer — breaking his ribcage — which overwhelmed him with the love of God. In the following series of maxims, Saint Phillip urges Christians to enclose themselves within the pierced Heart of Jesus, casting out every trace of self-love.

> Let us concentrate ourselves so completely in the divine love, and enter so far into the living fountain of wisdom through the wounded side of our Incarnate God, that we may deny ourselves, and our self-love, and so be unable to find our way out of that wound again.
>
> The greatness of our love of God must be tested by the desire we have of suffering for His love.
>
> The Holy Spirit is the Master of prayer who causes us to abide in continual peace and cheerfulness, which is a foretaste of paradise.
>
> We ought to apply ourselves to the acquisition of virtue, because in the end, the whole terminates in greater sweetness than before, and the Lord gives us back all our favors and consolations doubled.
>
> Let us throw ourselves into the arms of God, and be sure that if He wishes anything of us, He will make us fit for all that He desires us to do for Him.[149]

Sacred Heart of Jesus, cleanse me of all self-love, and direct my heart toward You! St. Philip Neri, pray for us!

May 27

St. Bede the Venerable (c. 673–735; memorial, May 25) was an English Benedictine priest and a great historian of the Middle Ages. His *Chronicle of the Six Ages of the World* details a sacred account of history, beginning with the creation of the world and ending in the eighth century. Here, Bede discusses the creation of Adam and Eve. As Eve was drawn from the side of Adam, so too was the Church drawn from the opened side of Christ.

> [God made Adam] from whose side, as he slept, He produced Eve, the mother of all living. And that day … is now called the twenty-third of March. Wherefore it is justly thought [that] Christ was crucified on the twenty-third of March as well, as has been written by the Blessed Theophilus in his disputation on Easter. … For thus it would seem fitting, that on the same day, not only of the week, but also of the month, the Second Adam, to redeem the human race, should die that He might rise again, and by the heavenly sacraments which He produced out of His own side, sanctify to himself His Bride, the Church. For on this same day, He had himself created the first Adam, the parent of the human race, and taking a rib out of his side, formed a woman to assist in propagating the human race.[150]

Sacred Heart of Jesus, sanctify me by Your passion, making me a new creation in You. St. Bede the Venerable, pray for us!

May 28

Fr. Alonso Rodriguez (1526–1616) was a Spanish Jesuit priest who authored *Practice of Perfection and Christian Virtue.* The following excerpt considers Christian humility in light of the first commandment.

> When, therefore, we seek to attract the esteem and praise of men, we pervert that order which God established and do Him injury, because in a manner we endeavor to make men, who should have no other employment than to praise and honor Him, employ themselves in praising and honoring creatures. And we endeavor to replenish with an esteem of ourselves, the hearts of creatures which God has made, as vessels to be filled with nothing else than with his own honor and praises. What is this, but to rob God of His creatures' hearts, and in a manner, to drive Him out of His own house? Can one commit a greater evil than this? …
>
> He who is truly humble desires not to live in the heart of any creature, but in the heart of God alone; he seeks not his own glory, but that of God alone; desires not that anyone should concern himself with him, but with God alone. In fine, he wishes that all the world should have God so in their hearts that no other object may ever have the least place in them.[151]

Sacred Heart of Jesus, empty my soul of vainglory, that I may always and everywhere magnify You! Sacred Heart of Jesus, I bless and glorify You!

May 29 | *Pope St. Paul VI*

Pope St. Paul VI (1897–1978) oversaw the worldwide implementation of the Second Vatican Council, affirming basic truths of the Faith, such as the value of human life in *Humanae Vitae* and the Real Presence of Jesus in the Eucharist in *Mysterium Fidei.* In this excerpt from *Mysterium Fidei,* he speaks of the Eucharistic Presence as the most efficacious means of sanctifying man.

> No one can fail to see that the divine Eucharist bestows an incomparable dignity upon the Christian people. … [In the Eucharist] He raises the level of morals, fosters virtue, comforts the sorrowful, strengthens the weak and stirs up all those who draw near to Him to imitate Him, so that they may learn from his example to be meek and humble of heart. … Anyone who has a special devotion to the sacred Eucharist and who tries to repay Christ's infinite love for us with an eager and unselfish love of his own, will experience and fully understand — and this will bring great delight and benefit to his soul — just how precious is a life hidden with Christ in God and just how worthwhile it is to carry on a conversation with Christ, for there is nothing more consoling here on earth, nothing more efficacious for progress along the paths of holiness."[152]

Sacred Heart of Jesus, Emmanuel, You nourish us with Your Eucharist as with honey from the rock. Let heaven and earth rejoice before Your tabernacle throne! Pope St. Paul VI, pray for us!

May 30

Ven. Mary Aikenhead (1787–1858) was born to a Catholic mother, but baptized into the Anglican tradition of her father. Eventually entering the Catholic Church, she founded the Sisters of Charity in Ireland. In this letter, Mary identifies the spiritual value of temptations as an aid to humility.

> Temptation is no real evil, but [actually helps] us to attain merit and plant great virtues. … Truly, if we profit by the lesson and really attain to self-knowledge, we shall be happy. This knowledge will, and it alone can, teach us real humility, and this precious virtue, most dear to the Sacred Heart, can alone secure our entrance into its altar of love and holy protection.

Elsewhere, Venerable Mary recommends imitating the Infant Jesus to learn self-abasement and charity.

> The labor is all for Him whose loving labors for us have purchased our dear vocation, with all other graces which will, I hope, be so cherished by us as to fructify in eternal life. … [Learn] to imitate the Sacred Babe of Bethlehem, and by loving adoration obtain the powerful graces necessary for each to be a practiced imitator of the humility and charity, and love of self-abjection, of which He gives us the perfect picture, and by which virtues alone we can become dear to His Sacred Heart.[153]

Sacred Heart of Jesus, help me to accept every humiliation as proceeding from Your providence, joining myself to Your holy will. Ven. Mary Aikenhead, pray for us!

May 31 | *Feast of the Visitation of the Blessed Virgin Mary; St. Camilla Battista da Varano*

Of Italian royalty, St. Camilla Battista da Varano (1458–1524) exchanged the riches of this world for a Poor Clare monastery at the age of twenty-three. Favored with the gift of mystical prayer, she here recounts a conversation between herself and Christ.

> I resolved then to employ my whole time of prayer in meditation on the passion of Jesus Christ, not wishing to occupy myself with anything else, so as to plunge with all the vigor and impetuosity of my soul into the sea of bitterness that inundated His Sacred Heart. … "How is it [that]," I once said to You, "You can love such a wicked creature?" "I cannot do otherwise," You replied, "for your name is written in My Heart!" and then lifting Your glorified arm, You made me read the words across the wound of Your Heart. O my soul, why did you not take courage and confidence at the remembrance of this goodness, this love of your beloved Jesus? I know that you will say to me that it is not possible. Alas! It is too true, that instead of encouraging me, this remembrance pierces my heart and forces me to cry out in lamentation, "O all you who pass by the way of divine love, attend and see if there be any sorrow like mine."[154]

Sacred Heart of Jesus, uphold me in my weakness, and fill my heart with joy. St. Camilla Battista da Varano, pray for us!

June

June 1 | *St. Justin Martyr*

The foremost Christian apologist of his day, St. Justin Martyr (c. 100–c. 165) employed both scriptural and philosophical arguments in defense of the Faith. In this excerpt from *Dialogue with Trypho,* he considers the anguished text of Psalm 22, demonstrating its fulfillment in Christ. As the Church observes the Month of the Sacred Heart, Saint Justin provides a sobering reminder of the sufferings of Christ.

> And this passage, "I am poured out like water, and all my bones are out of joint; my heart is like wax, it is melted within my breast" [Ps 22:14], foretold what happened to Him that very night in which they went out against Him; going to the Mount of Olives to take Him. For in those commentaries, which I say were written by His apostles and their disciples, it is recorded, "that sweat, like great drops of blood, fell from Him while He prayed and said, 'If it is possible, let this cup pass from me'" [see Lk 22:44, 41–42].
>
> And His Heart and bones trembled, and His Heart was made like melting wax in His belly that we might be fully assured that it pleased the Father that the Son should really and truly endure such great sufferings for our sake; and that we might not say that He, because He was the Son of God, was not sensible to those pains inflicted upon Him.[155]

Sacred Heart of Jesus, pour upon us a spirit of repentance, melting our souls with love. Saint Justin, pray for us!

June 2

Pope Leo XIII (1810–1903) approved the Scapular of the Sacred Heart, encouraged the First Fridays Devotion, and solemnly consecrated the world to the Sacred Heart of Jesus in 1899. In this consecration, he begs Christ to reign over all mankind as King.

> Most sweet Jesus, Redeemer … behold each one of us here today freely consecrates himself to Your Most Sacred Heart. … Be, O Lord, King not only of the faithful who have never departed from You, but also of the prodigal children who have turned their backs upon You. Grant that they may return to their Father's house, lest they perish of wretchedness and hunger. Be King of those who have been deceived by error, or whom discord keeps estranged. Bring them back to the haven of Truth and to the unity of Faith, that soon there may be one fold and one shepherd. Be King, moreover, of all those who continue in the ancient superstition of the Gentiles. Refuse not to deliver them out of darkness into the light and the kingdom of God. Grant, O Lord, to Your Church freedom and security; give peace and order to all nations; make the earth resound from pole to pole with one voice: "Praise to the Divine Heart through which our salvation has been accomplished: to the same be glory and honor forever. Amen."[156]

Sacred Heart of Jesus, enthroned by the cherubim, crowned by the seraphim, make our wills one with Yours, and reign over us as King. Amen.

June 3

St. Margaret Mary Alacoque cultivated a holistic view of the Sacred Heart devotion. In this letter to her novices, she offers her integrated vision of its endless assistance.

> The Sacred Heart of Jesus is an abyss of love in which we must lose all other love, especially self-love. … If you are in an abyss of privation and desolation, enter into this Divine Heart. There is all consolation, and we must plunge ourselves into this abyss, without, however, desiring to taste of its sweetness. If you are in an abyss of resistance and oppositions to the divine will, plunge yourself into the abyss of submission and conformity to the divine pleasure, which you will find in the Sacred Heart, and there losing your resistance, you will clothe yourself with conformity to His will in all that may happen to you. If you are in an abyss of dryness and weakness, go and bury yourself in the loving Heart of Jesus. If you are in an abyss of poverty and stripped of all things, go to the Heart of Jesus: He will enrich you. If you find yourself so weak that you fall at every step, go and bury yourself in the strength of His Sacred Heart: He will deliver you. If you are in an abyss of misery, go to the Heart of Jesus: He is full of mercy.[157]

Sacred Heart of Jesus, fulfill in me all that is wanting, stripping away all that is insincere. St. Margaret Mary Alacoque, pray for us!

June 4

In this passage from *Meditations on the Life of Christ,* Thomas à Kempis recalls the Lord's call, "My son, give me your heart" (Prv 23:26), and encourages all men to entrust their hearts to Christ.

> His desire is that you should have one heart with Him. "My son," He says, "give me your heart" [Prv 23:26]. Nothing more does God require of you: if you give Him this, you present an offering most acceptable. Give it, therefore, to Jesus, not to another. Give it to Christ, not to the world. Yea, give your heart to Eternal Wisdom, not to a vain philosophy. For this was the reason He caused His side to be opened so wide and pierced so deep: That a way to the Heart of the beloved might be clear to you; that you might penetrate the secret places of the Son of God and be joined with Him in true union of heart; that you might direct all your affections toward Him and, with singleness of heart, accomplish all your works for His honor. In sum, that your whole study may be to please Him alone and to cling to Him with a pure mind and with all your strength. For, where will you be able to rest more securely, dwell more safely, and sleep more sweetly, than in the wounds of Jesus Christ, who was crucified for you?[158]

Sacred Heart of Jesus, turn my heart from the wisdom of this world, grounding it in Your Spirit of Truth. May I rest in You!

June 5

Pseudo-Dionysius (fifth–sixth century), an enigmatic figure, pseudonymously wrote under the figure of Dionysius the Areopagite, who is mentioned in the Book of Acts. Here he writes that the one who loves is drawn out from himself so as to rest in another (*ekstasis*).

> But divine love is ecstatic, not permitting any to be lovers of themselves, but of those beloved. They show this too, the superior by becoming mindful of the inferior; and the equals by their mutual coherence; and the inferior, by a more divine respect towards things superior. Wherefore also, Paul the Great, when possessed by the divine love and participating in its ecstatic power, says with inspired lips: "It is no longer I who live, but Christ who lives in me" [Gal 2:20]. As a true lover and beside himself, as he says, to Almighty God, and not living the life of himself, but the life of the beloved as a life excessively esteemed. One might be so bold as to say [that the Lord] becomes out of himself ... beguiled by goodness and affection and love, and is led down from the Eminence above all, and surpassing all, to being in all, as befits an ecstatic superessential power centered in himself. Wherefore, those skilled in divine things call Him even jealous, as being that vast good love towards all beings, and as rousing His loving inclination to jealousy.[159]

Sacred Heart of Jesus, desiring with desire, may the angels prepare me to partake of Your Eucharistic gift. Amen.

June 6 | *St. Marcellin de Champagnat*

St. Marcellin de Champagnat (1789–1840) founded the Marist Brothers to provide for the educational needs of youths. In the following prayer, Saint Marcellin humbly confesses his lack of virtue and begs the Sacred Heart to destroy in him all vestiges of pride. Though determined to oppose his imperfections, he recognizes his utter dependence on Christ. Consequently, he asks for humility from that lowly Heart which has vanquished all pride.

> Lord, I confess that I do not know You, and that I am full of vice and imperfections. Grant me the grace to know my defects, and moreover, to make war upon them, never ceasing to fight and correct them. It is in the most profound annihilation of heart that I ask this favor. Divine Heart of Jesus — You who have by Your humility fought and vanquished human pride — it is to You that I chiefly address my prayer. I ask that You grant me humility, and destroy in me the very structures of pride; not because they are repugnant to man, but because they displease Your Divine Heart and offend Your holiness.
>
> Blessed Virgin, my good Mother, I, your unworthy servant, ask that You obtain from the adorable Heart of Jesus the grace of my knowing, fighting, vanquishing, and destroying my self-love and pride. At your feet, I resolve to make war upon these without ceasing.[160]

Sacred Heart of Jesus, renovate me in Your grace, grounding me in recognition of my dependence on You. St. Marcellin de Champagnat, pray for us!

June 7 | *Bl. Anne of Saint Bartholomew*

Bl. Anne of Saint Bartholomew (1550–1626) was the inseparable companion of the great Carmelite reformer and Doctor of the Church, St. Teresa of Ávila. Disturbed that her spiritual mother would be unappreciated by her confessor, the beata is here blessed with a vision of Saint Teresa in glory, united to the Heart of Christ.

> One day, I spoke to my confessor of one of my soul's secrets, but he did not take it well. He said to me, "That sounds like Mother Teresa. Go on now, do not be like her. Let those things alone." It seemed to me that he pronounced these words with little esteem for our holy mother. I was grieved because of this and sought a solitary spot in the garden. There, deeply pained [I began to pray]. Soon, I entered a state of supernatural recollection, and in this state saw the Divine Master [robed] in a most brilliant pontifical cope. When near me, He raised one side of the cope — it was the side next to His Heart — and showed me the saint resplendent in glory. He held her on His arm, as if she were no longer anything but a part of himself, and said to me, "Behold her, I have brought her to you here. Be not at all troubled; let them say what they will." After these words, He disappeared.[161]

Sacred Heart of Jesus, carry me upon Your arms and Heart, blessing me with constant devotion. Bl. Anne of Saint Bartholomew, pray for us!

June 8

Devoted to the Sacred Heart, Bl. Mary of the Divine Heart providentially died on the vigil of its feast, June 8, 1899. Here, she offers an examination of conscience suitable for the Month of the Sacred Heart, asking her sisters to consider where they might be lacking in fidelity and service to the Sacred Heart of Jesus.

> Let us often ask ourselves if we are not cowardly in His service; if we do not commit faults; if we do not fail in that generosity which is, however, the only proof of our love. This is the end I wish you to aspire to during this beautiful Month of the Heart of Jesus. Be generous toward our sweet Master, dear sisters. Give Him all, as He has given himself entirely to us, and you will console His Heart, procure happiness for yourselves, and perseverance in all religious virtues. Often ask yourself: Are my faults caused by my want of generosity? We are wanting in fervor and regularity in our spiritual exercises, the necessary attention. We fail in obedience, because it costs us to give up our own will. Failures in frankness, simplicity, and openness arise, because we fear a little humiliation and nevertheless, without humiliations we shall never become humble — and there can be no true and solid virtue without humility.[162]

Sacred Heart of Jesus, help me give of myself without reserve, living alone in You. Bl. Mary of the Divine Heart, pray for us!

June 9 | *Saint Ephrem*

Saint Ephrem (c. 306–373), Doctor of the Church, composed soaring hymns of exceptional catechetical value. The following contemplates the opened side of Christ, in which Saint Ephrem sees the fulfillment of Adam's rib, the overthrow of Dagon, and the door to paradise.

> With the rib that was drawn out of Adam, the wicked one drew out the heart of Adam. There rose from the rib a hidden power, which cut off satan as Dagon: for in that ark a book was hidden that cried and proclaimed concerning the Conqueror! There was then a mystery revealed, in that Dagon was brought low in his own place of refuge! The accomplishment came after the type, in that the wicked one was brought low in the place in which he trusted!
>
> Blessed be the merciful one who saw the weapon by paradise, that closed the way to the tree of life, and came and took a Body that might suffer, that with the door that was in His side, He might open the way into paradise. Blessed be that merciful one, who lent not himself to harshness, but without constraint conquered by wisdom. … Blessed is Your flock, since You are the gate thereof, You are the drink thereof, You are the salt thereof, yea, the visitor therefore. Hail to the only-begotten, that bears abundantly all manner of consolations.[163]

Sacred Heart of Jesus, teach us to embrace the cross, that we may participate in Your redemption. Saint Ephrem, pray for us!

June 10

Quicumque certum quææritis is an eighteenth-century hymn of unknown authorship, formerly included in the Roman Breviary for the feast of the Sacred Heart. Its poetic text encourages all those enduring hardships or persecution, or those suffering under the weight of sin, to approach the Sacred Heart.

All who seek solace
and consolation from sore trial,
from the bitter sting of conscience,
and the grave price of transgression:

Jesus, the Lamb, most innocent,
who gave himself in immolation,
cast open His pierced Heart.
Approach, then, this sanctuary!

Hear His sweet voice,
calling all to himself:
"Come, all you who labor
and who are heavy burdened."

Whose heart is meeker than His?
Jesus, fastened upon a cross,
who forgave, and to His Father implored:
Let not the sinner perish!

O Heart! Delight of the saints!
Faithful hope of men!
Lo, at Your loving call,
we approach with supplication.

By Your Blood poured out,
cleanse all our wounds.
Grant unto us a new heart;
we who call out to You![164]

Sacred Heart of Jesus, limitless love, You embrace the sinner as Your own and vest him with the mantle of life. Sustain us in grace, ease our consciences, and make us drink of the font of salvation. Sacred Heart of Jesus, I trust in You!

June 11

An Italian noblewoman, Ven. Mother Clare Mary of the Passion (1839–1904) renounced her privileges to join the Carmelites in Rome. There, she was favored with mystical gifts and intimate conversation with Christ. Venerable Clare here describes the manner in which Jesus took possession of her heart.

> Although Jesus Christ appeared all covered with wounds, His sacred Flesh was resplendent with great majesty. He made me understand that He wished to repose in my miserable heart, and this ravished my heart with joy … I perceived that God was drawing my heart to himself by His power, and I cannot express the peace and the sweetness I felt at that moment, seeing that the Divine Word, who is in the bosom of the Father, deigned to draw my heart to himself. There was, then, no need of my making any particular act in order to offer Him my heart, for my Divine Master was taking it as something that was His own, and already belonged to Him.
>
> Sometimes, I feel love for God suddenly arise within me, causing me outward agitation and trembling. At other times, it seems that my heart dilates and grows larger. … These last few days I have felt myself drawn to this state, which I continually feel more deeply. I have felt God very distinctly present in my heart, and I heard these words, "Heart to heart." [165]

Sacred Heart of Jesus, take captive my heart, which You knit together and then redeemed by Your Precious Blood. Venerable Clare, pray for us!

June 12

St. Gertrude the Great was a Benedictine nun who received a series of mystical revelations at the age of twenty-six, altering the course of her life. In this narrative, she relates an extraordinary grace received during serious illness, wherein she was met with a vision of the Sacred Heart of Jesus, radiating a crystalline stream.

> [When] I was left alone one morning, the Lord, who never abandons those who are deprived of human consolation, came to verify these words of the prophet: "I will be with him in trouble" (Ps 91:15). He turned His right side toward me and there came forth from His blessed and inmost Heart a pure and solid stream, like crystal. And on His breast, there was a precious ornament, like a necklace, which seemed to alternate between a gold and rose color. Then Our Lord said to me, "This sickness that you suffer will sanctify your soul so that each time you go forth from Me, like the stream which I have shown you, for the good of your neighbor — either in thought, word, or act — even then, as the purity of the crystal renders the color of the gold and the rose more brilliant, so the cooperation of the precious gold of My divinity, and the rose of the perfect patience of My humanity will render your works always agreeable to Me by the purity of your intention."[166]

Sacred Heart of Jesus, raise up the infirm, console the oppressed, and convert the hardened sinner. St. Gertrude the Great, pray for us!

June 13 | *St. Anthony of Padua*

St. Anthony of Padua (1195–1231), Doctor of the Church, was a learned Franciscan priest, commissioned by St. Francis of Assisi to instruct his brothers in theology. In the following sermon, Saint Anthony considers Christians seeking refuge within the Heart of Jesus, and the simplicity of the dove who seeks out the rocky cleft for its dwelling place, referencing the Song of Songs: "O my dove, in the clefts of the rock, in the covert of the cliff" (2:14).

> In her simplicity, [the dove] has a poorer nest than those of other birds. Be as the dove who makes her nest in the deepest cleft of the rock. This cleft, in which the soul should hide itself, is the wound in the side of Jesus Christ. There are many clefts in the rock … for His Immaculate Flesh bore many wounds, but the wound in His side leads to the Heart. And it is here He calls the soul, His spouse.
>
> The dove makes her nest with little bits of straw collected here and there. What are these scattered fragments that the world despises and treads underfoot? They are the virtues of Our Savior: humility, gentleness, poverty, patience, and mortification. The world despises them as useless, but it is with these that we shall build our nest, deep in the rock, in the Heart of Jesus.[167]

Sacred Heart of Jesus, grant me the virtues of austerity and kindness that invite entrance to Your adorable Heart. St. Anthony, pray for us!

June 14

A balanced Christological thinker and Doctor of the Church, Pope St. Leo the Great (c. 400–461) settled decades-long controversies between the theological schools of the East and West. Here, Saint Leo roundly declares that humanity is redeemed by the Body and Blood of Jesus Christ, who is both human and divine.

> Let him see what nature it was that was transfixed with nails and hung upon the wood of the cross. And let him understand from whence Blood and water flowed out, after the side of the crucified had been pierced by the soldier's spear; that the Church of God might be refreshed with the laver and with the cup. … Let him also not resist the testimony of blessed John the apostle, "And the Blood of Jesus the Son of God cleanses us from all sin." And again, "This is the victory which overcomes the world, even our faith." And, "Who is he that overcomes the world, but he that believes that Jesus is the Son of God? This is He who came by water and Blood, even Jesus Christ; not by water only, but by water and Blood; and it is the Spirit that bears witness, because the Spirit is Truth. For there are three that bear witness, the Spirit, the water, and the Blood; and the three are one."[168]

Sacred Heart of Jesus, torn open for love, let my heart be poured out for You; my tongue ever confessing Your blessed humanity and most high divinity. St. Leo the Great, pray for us!

June 15

St. Vincent de Paul (1581–1660) was a French priest and founder of the Congregation of the Mission, an association of priests and laity dedicated to serving the poor. Here, he teaches that missionaries will necessarily fail in their vocation if they lack humility. He recommends imitating the lowliness of Christ's Heart, seeking only the glory of God.

> Understand well this truth [and] let each one engrave it upon his heart, saying within himself: Though I had all virtue, if I have not humility, I only deceive myself; and believing myself virtuous, I am but a proud Pharisee and an abominable missionary. O my Savior, Jesus Christ, shed upon our minds those lights that tilled Your holy Soul and made You prefer contumely to praise! Inflame our hearts with those holy affections that burned and consumed Yours, and which caused You in Your own lowliness to seek the glory of Your heavenly Father. By Your grace, grant that we may begin to reject all that does not tend to Your glory and our reproach; all that reeks of vanity, ostentation, and self-esteem! Grant that, once for all, we renounce the applause of men — who are both deceived and deceivers — and all vain imaginations of the success of our works! In a word, O my Savior, by Your grace and Your example, grant that we may learn to be truly humble of heart.[169]

Sacred Heart of Jesus, shatter my illusions of power that I may glory in Your cross alone. St. Vincent de Paul, pray for us!

June 16

Fr. Peter Joseph Arnoudt (1811–1865), a Belgian priest, authored *The Imitation of the Sacred Heart of Jesus,* a work that alternates between the instructing voice of Christ and the attendant disciple. Here, Christ expresses astonishment that souls shrink from His healing hand.

> My child, if you feel yourself burdened with sins, or troubled with defects, hasten to My Heart. Here shall you be made free; here you shall breathe again. Let not the greatness of your sins hinder you, nor the grandeur of My majesty: I came not to call the just to repentance, but sinners. The greater the miseries to which you are subject, the greater the pity I feel for you: And the more you are ill, the greater need you have of a physician. I am not astonished at your infirmities; for I know your frame and your heart. That you did not fall into greater evils, you chiefly owe to My grace. But at this I wonder, that, when I present myself to heal you, you are unwilling to be healed; or, if you are willing, you seem to doubt My goodness. Ah! My child, do not offer this most bitter insult to My Heart. For My Heart loves to forgive, and does not grow weary of pardoning. Behold, with what kindness I treat truly repentant sinners, so that I have even been called the friend of sinners. [170]

Sacred Heart of Jesus, measureless in mercy, let my heart leap and take its strength from Your patience and pardon. Amen.

June 17

St. Lutgarde of Awyières (1182–1246; memorial, June 16) was a Cistercian mystic with a deep devotion to the Sacred Heart of Jesus. She lists no less than thirty-four mysteries of Christ's life, the twenty-ninth, thirtieth, and thirty-first of which are listed below.

> [I tender You thanks.] (29) For Your glorious Resurrection on the third day following Your sufferings; whereupon You appeared to Mary Magdalene, Your disciples and apostles, and then to many others; (30) For Your wonderful Ascension into heaven and glorious return to Your heavenly Father. … (31) For the wonderful fiery descent of the Holy Spirit upon Your apostles, disciples, and Your most beloved Mother on the holy days of Pentecost.
>
> For all these, and more especially for every beat of Your Heart and every act of love, for all Your thoughts and longings, for all the silent and the uttered prayers that You offered while on earth — and still offer in the Most Holy Sacrament of the Altar — for all these I tender You a thousand thanks. And I humbly ask that You would grant unto me, and unto all who have commended themselves to my prayers (or for whom I ought to pray) perfect contrition for our sins and a firm determination to never again offend Your divine majesty, together with the grace of final perseverance. Grant that we all may enjoy Your grace here.[171]

Sacred Heart of Jesus, let my heart sing of Your merciful love, forever exulting in Your Name. St. Lutgarde of Awyières, pray for us!

June 18 | *St. Elisabeth of Schönau*

St. Elisabeth of Schönau (c. 1129–1164) was a Benedictine nun whose mystical visions were recorded by her brother, Egbert, abbot of the Schönau monastery. This narrative recounts Elisabeth's vision of a dove descending from heaven during Mass at the recitation of the collect: "God to whom all hearts are opened … purify the thoughts of our hearts by the infusion of the Holy Spirit."

> [While the Office was being intoned,] I saw a dove descending from heaven, and it went to the right horn of the altar and sat. … And when the lord abbot said this collect among others, "God to whom all hearts are opened," and reached the words, "purify the thoughts of our hearts by the infusion of the Holy Spirit," it flew, and circling his head three times it returned to the place where it was sitting before. But when the *Sanctus* was said, it came and sat on the corporal and something like a ruby seemed to hang from its mouth. And when Mass was finished, I went to Communion among the sisters, and I bent the eyes of my flesh to it and was not able to see it. But my eyes being turned away, I saw it, and for the fear which I had of it immediately that I had communicated, I fell into an ecstasy presently I breathed.[172]

Sacred Heart of Jesus, dwelling place of the Holy Spirit, illumine my conscience with the bright light of Your grace. St. Elisabeth of Schönau, pray for us!

June 19

Spared from a serious illness, Fr. Joseph de Galliffet (1663–1749), a French Jesuit and friend of St. Claude de la Colombière, vowed to spread devotion to the Sacred Heart. Here he laments humanity's indifference to the glorious Eucharistic gift.

> Jesus Christ, the only Son of God, the Sovereign of angels and of men, the Creator of the universe; but more especially the God of Christians ... this same Jesus who, through excess of love, descended from heaven for them, became man and devoted every instant of His life to their salvation; who willed to die on the cross to deliver them from hell and open to them heaven; this Jesus, by another act of His immense love, has come a second time among them; made His abode in their midst; and that He may never be separated from them, has instituted the Sacrament of our altars, where He dwells actually, corporally, and perpetually. Behold Him in their city and often abiding under the same roof with them; and yet He is not loved, He is forgotten, abandoned, despised, insulted.
>
> O Jesus, whose Heart, the most tender and generous that ever lived, was also the most susceptible to ingratitude, what grief for You! Could a more cruel wound be inflicted upon this loving Heart? Make known Your complaints, O Sacred Heart! May they strike and penetrate our hearts![173]

Sacred Heart of Jesus, source of the sacraments, turn all hearts to You, that we might make a worthy return for Your kindness. Amen.

June 20 | *St. Methodius of Olympus*

St. Methodius of Olympus was an influential bishop and theologian, who was martyred under Emperor Maximinus. In his treatise *The Banquet of the Ten Virgins,* Methodius extols consecrated virginity, which captivates the Heart of Jesus.

> I will not bring forth praises of virginity from merely human testimony, but from Him who cares for us and has addressed this matter [in] the Song of Songs, where Christ himself praises those established in virginity, saying, "As the lily among thorns, so is my love among the daughters," comparing the grace of chastity to the lily on account of its purity, fragrance, sweetness, and joy. For chastity is like a spring flower, ever softly exhaling immortality from its white petals. Therefore, He is not ashamed to confess that He loves the beauty of its prime, saying, "You have ravished My Heart, my sister, my spouse; you have ravished My Heart with one of your eyes, with one chain of your neck. How fair is your love, My sister, My spouse! Your love is better than wine, and the scent of your ointments than all spices. Your lips, O My spouse, drop as the honeycomb; honey and milk are under your tongue, and the scent of your garments is like the fragrance of Lebanon. A garden enclosed is My sister, My spouse; a spring shut up, a fountain sealed."[174]

Sacred Heart of Jesus, let me drink of Your mystic cup that my heart may give You glory! Saint Methodius, pray for us!

June 21

While captive in the Tower of London, St. Thomas More (1478–1535) composed *A Dialogue of Comfort against Tribulation*, which extols the wisdom and necessity of suffering with Christ.

> Grievously pierced with nails, and in such torment, [Christ] suffered to be racked and pained the space of more than three long hours, till He willingly gave up unto His Father His holy Soul. After which, to yet show the mightiness of their malice, after His holy Soul departed, they pierced His holy Heart with a sharp spear, which issued out the holy Blood and water whereof His holy sacraments have inestimable secret strength. If we would, I say, remember these things in such wise as would God we would, I verily think and suppose that the consideration of His incomparable kindness could not in such wise fail to inflame our key-cold hearts, and set them on fire in His love, that we should find ourself not only content, but also glad and desirous, to suffer death for His sake, that so marvelous lovingly letted not to sustain so far passing painful death for ours.
>
> . . .
>
> [Consider] what heated affection many of these earthly lovers have borne, and daily do bear to those upon whom they doat! How many of them have not hesitated to jeopardize their lives, that by their death their lover should clearly see how faithfully they loved?[175]

Sacred Heart of Jesus, keep the image of Your cross before me always, driving away every worldly fear. St. Thomas More, pray for us!

June 22 | *St. John Fisher*

After refusing to bend to the state's Act of Succession under King Henry VIII, St. John Fisher (c. 1469–1535), imprisoned in the Tower of London, was beheaded. In his *Commentary on Psalm 130,* he contemplates God's endless mercies.

> Our sins are many times renewed after You have forgiven them; nevertheless, good Lord, Your mercy is limited to no certain time, but ever ready to be received by and by, of all who are penitent. For the mercy of God is infinite. He is not poor; He is most rich. In His treasure house are innumerable riches wherewith He may redeem all the world from the prison and captivity of the devil. The riches convenient for this redemption are no corruptible gold or silver, but as Saint Peter says, it is the very innocent and Precious Blood of the spotless Lamb, Jesus Christ. … The physician also commands a man to be let blood by a certain measure or quantity. Nevertheless, our blessed Lord shed His Blood so plenteously and without measure that no drop was left in His Body. And both Blood and water issued from His Heart; though, a single shedding was sufficient for the redemption of all sinners — though they be innumerable. Yet, He was not so content, but by His own will, suffered to have it issue from His most Precious Body many more times for our redemption.[176]

Sacred Heart of Jesus, receive my heart in ceaseless thanks for Your gracious self-gift. St. John Fisher, pray for us!

June 23

Bl. Columba Marmion's integrated approach to theology granted him profound insights into the mystery of Christ, evident in the following reflection. Here, Marmion concludes that Christ's human heart mysteriously reveals the Heart of God to man.

> Whence came this human love of Jesus, this created love? From the uncreated and divine love, from the love of the Eternal Word to which the human nature is indissolubly united. In Christ, although there are two perfect and distinct natures, keeping their specific energies and their proper operations, there is only one Divine Person. [The] created love of Jesus is only a revelation of His uncreated love. Everything that uncreated love accomplishes is only in union with the uncreated love, and on account of it; Christ's Heart draws its human kindness from the divine ocean.
>
> Upon Calvary, we see Him die a man like unto ourselves, one who has been prey to anguish, who has suffered, who has been crushed beneath the weight of torments, heavier than any man ever bore; we understand the love that this man shows us. But this love which, by its excess, surpasses our knowledge, is the concrete and tangible expression of the divine love. The Heart of Jesus pierced upon the cross reveals to us Christ's human love; but beneath the veil of the humanity of Jesus is shown in the ineffable and incomprehensible love of the Word.[177]

Sacred Heart of Jesus, flame of charity, help us to contemplate the depths of Your love, revealed in all Your works. Bl. Columba Marmion, pray for us!

June 24 | *Solemnity of the Nativity of St. John the Baptist*

Tibi dedo Jesu dulcissime contemplates the wound in Christ's side, describing the exchange of hearts that takes place between Christ and the Christian.

I give my heart to Thee
O Jesus most desired!
And heart for heart the gift
shall be,
For Thou my soul hast fired:
Thou hearts alone would'st
move;
Thou only hearts dost love.
I would love Thee as Thou
lov'st me,
O Jesus most desired!

What offering can I make,
Dear Lord, to love like Thine?
That Thou, the God, didst
stoop to take
A human form like mine!
"Give me thy heart, My son":
Behold my heart, — 'tis done!
I would love Thee as Thou
lov'st me,
O Jesus most desired!

Thy Heart is opened wide,
Its offered love most free,
That heart to heart I may
abide,
And hide myself in Thee:
Ah, how Thy love doth burn,
Till I that love return!
I would love Thee as Thou
lov'st me,
O Jesus most desired!

Here finds my heart its rest,
Repose that knows no shock,
The strength of love that
keeps it blest.
In Thee, the riven rock,
My soul, as girt around,
Her citadel hath found.
I would love Thee as Thou
lov'st me,
O Jesus most desired![178]

Sacred Heart of Jesus, let my life be an unending gift to You. St. John the Baptist, forerunner of Christ, pray for us!

June 25

While his attempts at mediating peace were rejected, Pope Benedict XV (1854–1922) assiduously worked to aid victims and refugees of World War I. On the feast of the Sacred Heart 1917, he delivered the encyclical *Humani Generis Redemptionem,* excerpted here.

> O that all [who] are engaged in the ministry of the Word were true lovers of Jesus Christ. Would that all could repeat these words of Saint Paul: "For [Christ's] sake I have suffered the loss of all things" [Phil 3:8], and "To me to live is Christ" [Phil 1:21]. Only those who glow with love themselves know how to set on fire the hearts of others. Wherefore Saint Bernard gave a preacher this counsel: "If you are wise, be a reservoir, not a conduit, be full yourself of what you preach and do not think it enough to pour it out for others" [*In Cant. Serm.* 18]. The Doctor then adds: "Today we have in the Church a profusion of conduits, but how few are the reservoirs!"
>
> We must strive with all our might and main, venerable brethren, to prevent such a state of things from occurring in the future. For it is your duty, by rejecting the unfit and by encouraging, training, and guiding the fit, to bring it to pass that there should now be no lack of preachers who are men after God's own Heart.[179]

Sacred Heart of Jesus, abyss of charity, fill us with a fresh outpouring of Your Spirit, that we may dispense Your mercy. Amen.

June 26

Meister Eckhart (c. 1260–c. 1328) was a German mystic whose works were censured by Pope John XXII, forcing him to publicly renounce their unorthodox elements. Eckhart's pious meditations on the passion, nevertheless, remain of enduring value. Here, Eckhart considers Christ's prophetic saying, "I, when I am lifted up from the earth, will draw all men to myself" (Jn 12:32).

> Our Lord Jesus Christ was inflamed and consumed on the cross; for His Sacred Heart burned like a fiery furnace from which flames issued forth on all sides. That the whole world might be redeemed, He was consumed on the cross in the fire of His love. It was by the fire of this love that He drew the world to Him; His love for mankind was so great that no one could conceal himself from those flames. … For nothing that Our blessed Lord ever did was accomplished with so great a love as the martyrdom He endured on the cross. There, He delivered himself for us, to wash away our sins in His Precious Blood and to offer himself up as a sacrifice to the living God. Therefore, it was principally by that love which He manifested for us on the cross that He drew us to himself, that all who compassionate His bitter sufferings and death may be happy with Him in the eternal bliss of heaven.[180]

Sacred Heart of Jesus, consume the defects of my soul in the fire of Your charity, that I may offer You a purified heart. Amen!

June 27

In *Dives in Misericordia,* Pope John Paul II contemplated God's self-revelation as *merciful love.* For him, the Sacred Heart of Jesus represents the incarnate fullness of this reality, signifying the divine-human love of Jesus.

> Everything that forms the "vision" of Christ in the Church's living faith and teaching brings us nearer to the "vision of the Father" in the holiness of His mercy. The Church seems in a particular way to profess the mercy of God and to venerate it when she directs herself to the Heart of Christ. In fact, it is precisely this drawing close to Christ in the mystery of His Heart which enables us to dwell on this point — a point in a sense central and also most accessible on the human level — of the revelation of the merciful love of the Father, a revelation which constituted the central content of the Messianic mission of the Son of Man.
>
> The Church lives an authentic life when she professes and proclaims mercy — the most stupendous attribute of the Creator and of the Redeemer — and when she brings people close to the sources of the Savior's mercy, of which she is the trustee and dispenser. Of great significance in this area is constant meditation on the word of God, and above all conscious and mature participation in the Eucharist and in the Sacrament of Penance or Reconciliation.[181]

Sacred Heart of Jesus, admit us to Your saving font, poured out in word and sacrament. Pope St. John Paul II, pray for us!

June 28 | *Saint Irenaeus*

Saint Irenaeus (130–202, Doctor of the Church) was the eminent successor to Saint Polycarp (69–155), the disciple of St. John the Apostle. As the heir of Saint John's teachings and ministry, Saint Irenaeus embodies the historical integrity of the Church. In his work *Against Heresies,* he speaks of the unity of the Church, teaching that all those joined to the Body of Christ are nourished by the teachings and life-giving sacraments that flow from Christ's side. The sacraments are, consequently, the divinely given means of entering into the Heart of Christ.

> "For in the Church" it is said, "God has set apostles, prophets, teachers," and all the other means through which the Spirit works; of which all those who do not join themselves to the Church are not partakers, but defraud themselves of life through their perverse opinions and infamous behavior. For where the Church is, there is the Spirit of God; and where the Spirit of God is, there is the Church, and every kind of grace; but the Spirit is Truth. Those, therefore, who do not partake of Him, are neither nourished into life from the mother's breasts, nor do they enjoy that most clear fountain which issues from the Body of Christ.[182]

Sacred Heart of Jesus, issuing forth torrents of grace, bless us with Your manifold gifts. Never permit us to stray from Your Body, the Church, but allow us to drink of the cup of unity. St. Irenaeus of Lyons, pray for us!

June 29 | *Solemnity of Saints Peter and Paul*

On the Solemnity of Saints Peter and Paul, the Church commemorates the martyrdoms of those two pillars of the Roman Church. In the following prayer, St. Claude de la Colombiére describes that central virtue acquired by both apostles: self-abandonment, founded upon a sure trust in Christ.

> O Holy Heart of Jesus, give me complete forgetfulness of self, since without that I cannot attain to You. And as for the future, as I would have all my words and deeds to be Yours, prevent me from such as are unworthy of You. Teach me how to acquire that purity of heart for which You have given me so great a longing. My heart burns with desire to serve You, but it is not possible for me to do so without such light and help as I can obtain from You alone. Fulfill Your will, O Lord, in me. That my will is often in opposition to Yours, I know only too well; but at least this opposition is hateful to me. You, my beloved Lord, can do all things. If I become a saint, to You be all the praise. It is as clear to me as the day that, my sanctification, being Your work, to You alone can be all the praise, and for that end alone do I desire it. Amen.[183]

Sacred Heart of Jesus, be my sole support! You are my rock and sure foundation: Help me to rely upon You alone! St. Claude de la Colombiére, pray for us!

June 30

In this letter, Bl. Antonio Rosmini-Serbati (1797–1855; memorial, July 1), priest and founder the Institute of Charity, also called the Rosminians, responds to a priest struggling with temptations to despair, advising him to turn his thoughts to the humanity of Christ and His Sacred Heart.

> With reference to what you say at the end of your letter concerning doubts about your eternal salvation, consider that of those who have confided in the Lord, not one has perished. Have full confidence therefore, and to this end meditate day and night on the humanity of Jesus Christ, His Sacred Heart, His sentiments, His unspeakable goodness and the merits of His Blood, so that you may have the image of Our crucified Lord and Savior always present to your mind. In order to confirm this confidence, the pledge of salvation, let us make great account of the Sacrament of Penance, accusing ourselves with great humility and childlike simplicity.
>
> Lest, however, we should entertain that fatal confidence in self which gives rise to negligence, we must offer to God frequent acts of humility, confessing our utter misery, poverty, nothingness, and wickedness, without ever growing weary or thinking we have humbled ourselves sufficiently. There are many beautiful verses in the psalms that can help us in this, especially those in which the soul speaks out of the depths of her abasement and rises to the greatest confidence.[184]

Sacred Heart of Jesus, still my trembling heart, that I may hear Your consoling voice of peace. Bl. Antonio Rosmini-Serbati, pray for us!

July

July 1

An Italian bishop, Gaetano Bonanni (1766–1848) founded the Missionaries of the Precious Blood along with St. Gaspar del Bufalo (1786–1837). As the Church enters the month of July, the month traditionally dedicated to the Precious Blood of Jesus, Bishop Bonanni's words are a stirring reminder that this life-giving Blood has its source in the Sacred Heart.

> O wound of love! O adorable Blood of eternal life! With Your devoted servant, Saint Bernard, I say unto You, O my Jesus, that I have found the most tender of hearts, opened and wounded for me: the heart of a most loving Father, the heart of a most attentive shepherd, the most faithful love, and the most tender Brother that one could want. Permit me, then, to approach Your sweetest Heart that I may be purified in the beneficent Blood that flows from it. Permit me to enter into this Ark of refuge that I may escape the shipwreck that my faults have brought upon me. For, in the adorable Blood pouring from Your Heart, You are able to quench the burning darts that divine justice has prepared against a sinner like me. It is there I wish to live, there I wish to die, with the most lively confidence that You will not suffer me to be torn from Your side and cast into the fires of hell.[185]

Sacred Heart of Jesus, in Your great mercy, be my satisfaction to the Father, offering perfect atonement to Him. Sacred Heart of Jesus, I thank and love You!

July 2

The Jesuit St. John Eudes' boundless love of the Sacred Heart of Jesus and the Holy Heart of Mary characterized his life's mission. Writing to an abbess who had forbidden devotion to these Holy Hearts, he here shows paternal concern for her spiritual well-being, even as he defends the glory of these venerable devotions.

> I take the liberty of [expressing] the sorrow I feel at hearing that you have not only forbidden the celebration of the feast of the most Holy Heart of Mary, but also of the Divine Heart of Jesus in your monastery. Oh, what are you thinking of? … The Sacred Hearts of Jesus and Mary were two impregnable towers, where the souls of the abbess and her daughters might always find safety from their enemies, and you destroy them.
>
> You strike and wound the Heart of the Mother of beautiful love, You excommunicate her venerable name and most Holy Heart, you drive them from your house. After that, how dare you appear before her? Do you not fear that her Son, who resents any insult offered to His mother, might send you some great misfortune and they should close the doors of their home against you? They had given you their Heart which is only one, by unity of disposition, to be your heart, your treasure, and your consolation, and you reject it. How will you live without a heart?[186]

Sacred Heart of Jesus, You overwhelm us with blessings. Make our hearts captive to Your own! St. John Eudes, pray for us!

July 3 | *Feast of St. Thomas the Apostle*

Today the Church honors the doubting apostle first bidden to enter within the sanctuary of Christ's side. In his *Commentary on the Gospel of John,* Fr. Cornelius à Lapide here expounds upon the visible wounds of Jesus and the invisible wounds of Saint Thomas.

> Behold the kindness of Christ in humbling himself to all Thomas's requests, and in all things complying with his wishes, in order to convert him. See, says Saint Chrysostom, how for one single soul He displays His wounds, and because he was somewhat dull of comprehension, seeks to give him proof by means of the dullest of his senses, I mean his touch.
>
> "Do not be faithless, but believing" [Jn 20:27]. "Do then as you have said: I offer you My wounded hands and side to touch and handle — nay more, that you may measure them with your hand; so that you may lay aside your unbelief and believe henceforth that I have risen, I, the very same that hung on the cross and no other." And in this way, Christ heals another wound of unbelief; for He shows that He knows all secrets, and is a searcher of hearts, and consequently God. He therefore radically cures the disease; for Thomas did not believe that Christ had risen, because he did not believe Him to be God.[187]

Sacred Heart of Jesus, place Your hand within my heart, healing it of every ill. Let me be conformed to Your opened side. Saint Thomas, pray for us!

July 4

Neither St. Margaret Mary Alacoque nor her spiritual advisor, St. Claude de la Colombiére, were spared trials, setbacks, and humiliations, but they mutually commended themselves to the Sacred Heart. Here, Saint Margaret Mary emphasizes the importance of abandoning oneself to the merciful Heart of Jesus with complete trust.

> Let your occupation be to love Him, and be careful not to resist Him or put any obstacle to His will. You will see how much progress He will allow you to make in a short time. What have you to fear, since He invites you to repose in His Heart? Is it not the throne of His mercy, where the most miserable are the best received, provided that they love? If we are cowardly, cold, sin-stained, and imperfect, His Heart is a burning furnace where we must be perfected and purified as gold in the crucible. Fear not, then, to abandon yourself without reserve to His loving providence, for the child will not perish in the arms of an all-powerful Father. … Since He loves you, what have you to fear, save not giving Him all the return of love He desires from you. This consists in a perfect abandonment and forgetfulness of self! Abandon self, and you will find God: Forget self, and He will think of you; bury yourself in your nothingness, and you will possess Him.[188]

Sacred Heart of Jesus, enlarge our hearts, that we might love as You love, placing no limits on our charity. Saint Margaret Mary, pray for us!

July 5

In his book *Jesus Christ the King of Our Hearts,* Alexis Cardinal Lépicier (1863–1936) summarizes the devotion to the Sacred Heart, affirming Christ's divine right to rule over the hearts of all, as King.

> This Divine Heart is the victim immolated for our sins, *Cor Jesu, Victima peccatorum;* it is the pattern we must copy in order to arrive at supernatural virtue, *Cor Jesu, virtutum omnium abyssus;* it is the delight of all the saints, *Cor Jesu, deliciae sanctorum omnium.* Beginning, middle, and end of our spiritual life and our eternal happiness — all this, the adorable Heart of Jesus is for us.
>
> Now, seeing that this Divine Heart is for us the fount of all good, it is only just that it should be the King of all our hearts. And this is the dignity to which the Eternal Father has predestined Jesus Christ, a dignity which Jesus himself exercised during His mortal life, and which He will exercise until the end of time. In the full sway of His regal power over our hearts, and in our entire submission to His strong and gentle rule, the practical meaning of devotion to the Sacred Heart of Our loving Savior consists. In this devotion … we give solemn homage to Him whose hands hold the keys of our hearts and proclaim, in the face of the world, His right to rule over us.[189]

Sacred Heart of Jesus, rule over mankind as King, inspiring in all hearts one adoration! Sacred Heart of Jesus, I adore You!

July 6

St. John of the Cross (1542–1591) a reformer of the Carmelite Order, describes the love between Christ and the soul.

On a dark night,
With anxious love inflamed,
O, happy lot!
Forth unobserved I went,
My house being now at rest. …

In that happy night,
In secret, seen of none,
Seeing nought myself,
Without other light or guide
Save that which in my heart
was burning,

That light guided me
More surely than the noonday
sun
To the place where
He was waiting for me,
Whom I knew well,
And where none but He
appeared.

O, guiding night;
O, night more lovely than the
dawn;
O, night that hast united
The lover with His beloved,
And changed her into her love.

On my flowery bosom,
Kept whole for Him alone,
He reposed and slept;
I kept Him, and the waving
Of the cedars fanned Him.

Then His hair floated in the
breeze
That blew from the turret;
He struck me on the neck
With His gentle hand,
And all sensation left me.

I continued in oblivion lost,
My head was resting on my
love;
I fainted away, abandoned,
And, amid the lilies forgotten,
Threw all my cares away.[190]

Sacred Heart of Jesus, You can change the night into day: Transform me into You. Sacred Heart of Jesus, make us one!

July 7

Salvete Christi vulnera is an anonymous hymn dating to the seventeenth century.

Hail holy wounds of Christ!
Marks of love, unmeasured,
letting forth that rubied Blood
in ever-flowing rivers. …

Through this open gate
stands the sanctuary of the soul
where no threat can steal
nor enemy trespass.

When stripped in the praetorium,
how great the lashes taken!
Stricken from all sides!
Rivers of Blood falling.

O bright brow, what sorrow!
A thornèd crown so pressed.
Blunted nails, dull and driven,
through hands and feet so kind.

Ah, after He was betrayed,
and lovingly gave His Spirit,
His Heart was opened by a lance,
and twin rivers poured forth.

To fulfill the redemption,
He was crushed in the winepress,
wholly forgetting himself,
withholding not His Blood.

Come! However touched by sin,
and poisoned by deadly deeds;
for, in this saving bath,
whoever washes will be clean.

All thanks be to the one who sits
at the Father's right hand,
who redeemed us by His Blood,
and strengthens by the Holy Spirit.[191]

Sacred Heart of Jesus, let me love without measure, pouring my life out for You! Sacred Heart of Jesus, have mercy on us!

July 8

The son of a Jewish rabbi, Ven. Francis Libermann pursued Talmudic studies only to fall into agnosticism. He eventually found the fulfillment of his first faith in the Messiah, Christ Jesus. Here Venerable Francis comforts souls suffering afflictions of every kind, explaining that the adorable Heart of Jesus cannot but rush to the aid of the anguished.

> This is what Jesus does every day for those souls who possess within themselves His divine love and who are, spiritually, in the same state as Lazarus through interior incapacity, troubles, afflictions, and temptations of every kind, which overwhelm and bind them so much that they feel as if they were dead. …
>
> Let such souls be of good courage! Jesus, their Lord, does not forget them. They cannot go to Him; they are constrained to remain buried in the dark sepulcher of their interior, unable to rise and go in search of Him who alone can cure them. But Jesus loves them and delights in them. He says to His angels and saints: "Our friend sleeps; but I go that I may awaken him from his sleep." He makes him wait for some time, as he made Lazarus wait in the tomb. But sooner or later, He will come with the great tenderness and infinite mercy which fill His adorable Heart; and by a new and even more perfect life than before.[192]

Sacred Heart of Jesus, divine tenderness, permit me to rest upon You, listening to the confidences of Your love. Look upon me with mercy, and awaken my soul to Your call. Ven. Francis Libermann, docile to grace, pray for us!

July 9 | *St. Veronica Giuliani*

St. Veronica Giuliani (1660–1727) was a Poor Clare whose life was intimately bound to the mystery of the cross — which sign was found imprinted upon her heart in death. In this prayer, she offers herself to God as a victim of love, united to the crucified Lord. She understands herself as consecrated to Christ, loving with His love, and interceding for sinners with His merits.

> O infinite love, I address myself with love to You who are my Spouse, my God, and my all. On my part, I am entirely Yours and I beg that I may be entirely Yours from this moment evermore. I intend to confirm all the protestations I have made to You with my blood and present myself anew in the quality of mediatrix between You and sinners. Behold, I am ready to give my life and my blood for their conversion and for the advancement of Your holy Faith. O my God, in union with Your Heart and Your love, I invite them thus: "O souls redeemed with the Blood of Jesus, I speak to you. O sinners, come all of you to the Heart of Jesus, to the fountain, to the immense ocean of His love; come sinners, every one of you; abandon your sins, and come to Jesus." Meanwhile, my beloved Spouse, let me love You with Your own love, now and forever.[193]

Sacred Heart of Jesus, let me burn before You as an offering of incense, spending itself in worship. Saint Veronica, pray for us!

July 10

Ven. Pope Pius XII protected an estimated 800,000 European Jews during World War II. In his encyclical on the Sacred Heart, *Haurietis Aquas,* the pontiff speaks of the threefold love exercised by the Sacred Heart of Jesus.

> The face of our adorable Savior was especially the guide, and a kind of faithful reflection, of those emotions which moved His Soul in various ways and like repeating waves touched His Sacred Heart and excited its beating. For what is true of human psychology and its effects is valid here also.
>
> For these reasons, the Heart of the Incarnate Word is deservedly and rightly considered the chief sign and symbol of that threefold love with which the Divine Redeemer unceasingly loves His Eternal Father and all mankind. It is a symbol of that divine love which [He alone] manifests through a weak and perishable Body. … It is, besides, the symbol of that burning love which, infused into His soul, enriches the human will of Christ and enlightens and governs its acts by the most perfect knowledge derived both from the beatific vision and that which is directly infused. And finally — and this in a more natural and direct way — it is the symbol also of sensible love, since the Body of Jesus Christ [possesses] full powers of feelings and perception, in fact, more so than any other human body.[194]

Sacred Heart of Jesus, in whom time and eternity meet, renew all things in Your love. May my works have enduring value, consecrated to Your service. Ven. Pope Pius XII, pray for us!

July 11

A Jesuit priest, Fr. Secondo Franco (1817–1893) composed the well-known *Devotion to the Sacred Heart of Jesus.* Here, he compares the majesty of creation to the greater manifestation of God's creative power in the Sacred Heart.

> Do you want a proof of the infinite power of God? In the beginning He made the heavens; He created the earth and the countless and varied beings that dwell on it; and by a simple act of His will, He could annihilate everything. You see from this fact that His power is infinite and wonderful. Yet, you will have a much grander idea of His power when you know that He has formed a heart so rich in gifts and so sublime in prerogatives that the Person of the Word has deigned to make it His own Heart. Would you understand the infinite wisdom of God? Look around you, and you will be struck by the truth of those words of the wise man: "You have made all things in wisdom." But if you wish to descend into the very depths of this wisdom, fix your eyes on the Heart of Jesus, and you will wonder at the baseness of man being united by the effect of an unspeakable miracle to the incomparable sublimity of God: There you will see [the mercy of the Lord] moved to compassion at the sight of our miseries.[195]

Sacred Heart of Jesus, help me to recognize Your surpassing love, manifest in Your Holy Heart. Sacred Heart of Jesus, I adore You!

July 12

Ven. Mary Potter was born with a delicate constitution, which delayed her entry into religious life. Upon founding the Little Company of Mary, she composed spiritual instructions, which here describe the importance of *hope.* Mary counsels all to draw near the Sacred Heart of Jesus, seeking strength and perseverance therein. Echoing those words of Job, "Though He slay me, still will I trust in Him" (see Jb 13:15), Mary advises complete confidence in Christ, no matter the circumstance.

> Yes — *Though He slay me, still will I trust in Him* — must be the cry of the soul that has anchored itself firmly to divine hope. Ah, what need of this divine hope have we not in these days, when the tempest-tossed Church, with its banners boldly unfurled, is tossed on the rude waves of a sea of indifference and unbelief. Even the crew of the good ship need to trust in divine power; for they see how truly vain is the help of man. Ah, they are a brave crew and grow braver in these times of trial. The world is fearful, distrustful, one dreads another, but Christians gather round the Sacred Heart and bind themselves more closely together by means of confraternities and communities. God's Spirit is renewed within them and they are happy in the hour of trial, confident that God can and will help them.[196]

Sacred Heart of Jesus, let me not shrink before the howling winds, but fix my gaze on You. Ven. Mary Potter, pray for us!

July 13

Born in Ireland, Bl. Columba Marmion became abbot of Belgium's Maredsous Abbey. His classic work, *Christ in His Mysteries,* canvasses the whole of Christ's earthly life and features a chapter on the Sacred Heart, declaring it a summary icon of the Christian message. He notes its general object is the Person of Jesus himself and His love of mankind.

> Hence you comprehend what is to be understood by devotion to the Sacred Heart. It is, in a general manner, devotion to the Person of Jesus himself, manifesting His love for us and showing us His Heart as a symbol of this love. Whom do we then honor in this devotion? Christ Jesus himself, in person. But what is the immediate, special, proper object of this devotion? The Heart of Flesh of Jesus, the Heart which beats for us in the bosom of the man-God; but we do not honor it apart from the human nature of Jesus, nor from the Person of the Eternal Word to whom this human nature was united in the Incarnation. Is this all? No; there is yet to be added: We honor this Heart as the symbol of love of Jesus toward us.
>
> Devotion to the Sacred Heart is then summed up in the worship of the Incarnate Word manifesting His love to us and showing us His Heart as the symbol of this love.[197]

Sacred Heart of Jesus, mystery of love, grant me the grace of perfect contemplation. Blessed Columba, teach us the secrets of the interior life!

July 14

Although it is uncertain whether he was a priest or Benedictine religious, Alcuin of York (735–804), a celebrated scholar, is generally agreed to have served as a deacon. Here, Alcuin draws a direct connection between the life-giving font of the Sacred Heart and the vivifying sacraments of the Church.

> Doubt not then, disown not, when you see the creature of bread and wine taken from the humble fruits of the earth. Regard the omnipotence of God and of Our Lord Jesus Christ, who by His mere will, without any delay, makes of them His Body and Blood. When you see water mingled with the wine, you are not to suppose that this is done without reason; for water came forth with the Blood from the side of Christ, who is the true vine, when His side was pierced with the lance. That Blood was shed for the sinner's pardon; that water tempers the saving cup. These are the sacraments of the Church. ... Draw nigh to them faithfully, without discussion, for it is the mystery of faith. Draw nigh in a peaceable disposition, for it is the sacrament of unity; in faith and work you are united to your mother, the Church; and this unity is denoted by the bread's being of many grains, and the wine of many grapes. Draw nigh with thanksgiving, for it is a mystery of charity.[198]

Sacred Heart of Jesus, source of all unity, unite us in Your sacraments, joining us in holy charity. Make us one in you.

July 15 | *Saint Bonaventure*

A Doctor of the Church, Saint Bonaventure (c. 1221–1274) secured the long-term success of the Franciscan Order of Friars Minor with his exceptional organizational gifts. Here he considers the Last Supper, and Saint John's unique access to the Sacred Heart.

> [While at supper, Jesus] revealed more clearly what was to follow. … "With desire have I desired to eat this Passover with you before I suffer, but one of you shall betray Me." His saying pierced them to the very heart, like a sharp sword, and made them cease eating. And looking at each other, they exclaimed, "Lord, is it I?"
>
> Consider them attentively and have compassion on both Our Lord and them; for they are in a most sorrowful position. … At the entreaty of Saint Peter, John then asked, "Lord, who is it that shall betray You?" And the Lord Jesus, with singular love, opened to him the secret, but John was struck dumb and wounded to the very heart, and turned himself towards Our Lord, and leaned upon His breast. …
>
> But Peter represents the *active life,* John the *contemplative.* [Realize] that the contemplative man does not interrupt the actions of the inner life, and even concerning offences, does not call down divine vengeance, but groans inwardly, and turns himself in prayer to God, and draws more closely to Him in contemplation, committing everything to His disposal.[199]

Sacred Heart of Jesus, permit me to recline upon Your Heart, sharing in the secrets of Your love. Saint Bonaventure, pray for us!

July 16 | *Feast of Our Lady of Mount Carmel*

At her mother's wish, St. Elizabeth of the Trinity (1880–1906) delayed entering the Carmel of Dijon until her twenty-first birthday. On the eve of her entry, Saint Elizabeth writes to her mother that she is already homesick — but for heaven.

> I have wished and waited so long for this day that I feel as if I were dreaming now. …
>
> You know that this good Master wants me for himself alone. I knew it, so I felt confident and was sure He would take me. Thank God for your little Elizabeth; He has given her so much, especially graces known to no one but himself; things which take place in the very depths of the soul. Oh, what love! But He knows well that I love Him, and that seems to me to include everything.
>
> Is it not to live by love — that is to say, to live no longer except with Him, in Him, by Him — to be already partly in paradise while still on earth? I will tell you a secret. If you only knew how homesick I sometimes feel for heaven, for I wish so intensely to go there to be near Him. I should be glad if He took me even before I entered Carmel, for Carmel in heaven is far better, and I should be a Carmelite just the same in paradise.[200]

Sacred Heart of Jesus, may I live as a praise of Your glory, wholly belonging to You. St. Elizabeth, pray for us!

July 17

The last pope to reside in Avignon, Pope Gregory XI (1329–1378), returned the See of Peter to Rome, encouraged by St. Catherine of Siena. The Latin hymn *Ave caput Christi gratum,* attributed to him, surveys the wounded Body of Christ.

Hail blessed head of Christ,
crowned with awful thorns!
From the price of sin, spare us,
graciously granting us pardon.

Hail right hand of Christ,
transfixed and bitterly wounded!
At that hand, command us to sit,
those whom You redeemed on the cross.

Hail left palm of Jesus,
cruelly fastened by a nail!
Lift us up, above all evil,
the mourning sons of Eve.

Hail pierced side of Jesus,
whence forth gracious tides flowed!
Draw us in faith's security,
to those shores of unending life.

Hail wound of the right foot,
tearing at tender heart's temple,
'til it hastens again to return.
Be our hope of reward.

Hail wound of the left sole,
root from which the virtues grow!
Go before and after us,
guarding us from deception's snare.

Hail blessed Body,
all stripped and scourged!
From every sin deliver us,
and grant us life without end![201]

Sacred Heart of Jesus, pierced for love, cast open the heavenly gate of Your Heart, that I might enter in. Have mercy on us!

July 18 | *St. Camillus of Lellis*

An Italian priest, St. Camillus of Lellis (1550–1614) founded the Order of the Ministers of the Sick. This pious exclamation, uttered during the elevation of the Eucharist, was recorded by witnesses.

> Behold, O brothers, your salvation. Behold, O you poor, your riches. Come forth to meet the Lord of heaven, who deigns to come to you in these impure places, to make peace with your faults. This is He whom you have so often offended, to make peace with your souls. Ask Him to pardon your faults. This is He whom you have so often offended. Be sure that if you ask Him to pardon you — with true penitent hearts, and with minds determined never to offend Him again — He will undoubtedly pardon you.
>
> Doubt not, for although it is bread to your taste, bread to your sight, bread to your touch, yet it is not in any way material bread, but under these sacred species there is the true Body, Blood, Soul, and Divinity of Christ the Son of God, who was born of the Virgin Mary, and who is to come to judge us. Adore Him, then, with all your heart; mourn bitterly for your sins. Pray Him to pardon you, and to save you, for this is what He comes to you for, to save you, and make you saints.[202]

Sacred Heart of Jesus, pillar of fire and cloud, warm our hearts in Your service and sustain us with the Bread of Life. St. Camillus of Lellis, pray for us!

July 19

In his soaring contemplations on charity, St. Robert Bellarmine (1542–1621) here depicts St. John the Apostle reclined upon the Sacred Heart, drinking from the very source of love.

> In all religion, there is no more significant picture than that of the evangelist John at the Last Supper reclining his head on the breast of the Savior. It indicates to us the source of all good things. It interprets Christ's words: "Whoever loves Me, dwells in Me and I in him," for if we have a Christ-like love in our hearts we need no more — we dwell in a celestial paradise surrounded with every luxury, with the King of Kings for our guest. Be we ever so wretched, ever so friendless, ever so sinful, we can feel that one great Heart throbs for us with the unreasoning love of a mother for her wayward child, of a father for his prodigal son; searches after us as perseveringly as the woman after the lost coin, goes after us as the shepherd after the lost sheep, and brings us home exultingly.
>
> We can best appreciate the love of the Sacred Heart for men from the love of men for the Sacred Heart. "I came," says Christ, "to cast fire upon the earth"; and what must have been the latent intensity of that fire that could enkindle and sustain such a mighty conflagration![203]

Sacred Heart of Jesus, help me to carry out Your commands in word and deed, offering them with grateful affection. St. Robert Bellarmine, pray for us!

July 20

In *A Little Book of Eternal Wisdom,* Bl. Henry Suso describes the glorified wounds of Christ as living fountains. Alluding also to Ezekiel's vision of water (see Ez 47:1), Suso recognizes in Christ the life-giving wellspring of restorative justice, making possible a new Eden.

> And is it not a paradise above every paradise in whom the dead again live if they only taste His fruit from whose hands, feet, and side the living fountains, which irrigate all the earth, flow; the fountains of inexhaustible mercy, unfathomable wisdom, overflowing sweetness, ardent love, the fountains of eternal life? Truly, Lord, whoever tastes of this fruit, whoever has drunk of this fountain, knows that these two gardens of paradise far surpass the earthly paradise. …
>
> Even as I present You before Your heavenly Father, so do I present Your pure tender mother before You. Look at her mild eyes … behold those fair cheeks which she so often affectionately pressed to Your infant face. Think, too, of the heart-rending woe that her maternal heart endured with You under the gibbet of Your miserable cross, where she saw You in the agony of death, and when her heart and soul so often died away in sorrow and distress with You. [For her sake] grant me every means of shaking off my sins, of acquiring Your grace, and never losing it again.[204]

Sacred Heart of Jesus, renew in us the grace of our baptism, that having died with You, we may live unto God. Bl. Henry Suso, pray for us!

July 21

St. Claude de la Colombiére served as a missionary preacher to Catholic members of the royal household of Great Britain. Despite these associations, he suffered persecution from the Anglican government and was exiled. Here Saint Claude confesses his own insensibility before the awesome gift of Christ's Presence in the Holy Eucharist.

> What will You do, O Lord, to overcome this obstinate insensibility? The Fathers of the Church tell us that You have exhausted yourself in this mystery of love; if the sacred contact of Your Body cannot break the spell which binds us to sin, what success can we hope for from any other remedy? In this, our evil plight, I can see but one resource. Give us, O my God, a new heart, pure and tender, neither of marble nor bronze; a heart in all things like to Yours. Give us, in fine, O Jesus, Your own Heart. Come, O sweet Heart of Jesus, to my breast, and if it be possible, light up a fire of love that shall burn with the ardent devotion I should pay to my Savior and my God!
>
> Come, O Sacred Heart, and love that Blessed Savior in me, even as You did love me in Him. May I live only in Him and for Him, so that at the last I may live with Him for ever and ever.[205]

Sacred Heart of Jesus, take away my heart of stone and grant me Your own Heart of Flesh. Help me love as You loved. Saint Claude, pray for us!

July 22 | *Feast of St. Mary Magdalene*

St. Mary Magdalene has traditionally been revered as the model penitent from whom Christ expelled seven demons. Her life of wholehearted service to Christ culminated in her discovery of the empty tomb, meriting her the exalted title "apostle to the apostles." Here, St. Robert Southwell illumines the meaning of Jesus' words to St. Mary Magdalene, "Do not hold me [*Noli me tangere*]" (Jn 20:17). Speaking in the voice of Christ, he explains that Saint Mary must now embrace Christ in faith, spiritually abiding in His Sacred Heart.

> Touch Me not, Mary, for if I deceive thy sight, or delude thy hearing, I can as easily beguile thy hand, and frustrate thy feeling. If I be true in any one thing, believe Me so in all. Embrace Me first in a firm faith, and then thou shalt touch Me with more worthy hands. It is now necessary to wean thee from the comfort of My external presence, that thou mayest learn to lodge in Me the secrets of My Heart, and teach thy thoughts to supply the offices of the outward senses: For in this visible shape I am not long to be seen here, being shortly to ascend unto My Father. But what thine eye then seeth not, thy heart shall feel, and My silent parley will find audience in thy inward ear.[206]

Sacred Heart of Jesus, illumine our minds with the light of the Resurrection, and free us from the snares of sin. St. Mary Magdalene, pray for us!

July 23 | *St. Bridget of Sweden*

St. Bridget of Sweden's mystical visions informed her writings on the life of Christ. The following example, narrated from the perspective of the Blessed Virgin Mary, movingly shows the Mother of God sharing in the tremendous pain of Christ's death. For her heart was buried with Christ, even as it rejoiced in the knowledge of His Resurrection.

> And so we three bore Him to a rock, which I had covered with the clean linen sheet in which we wrapped the Body; but I did not sew the winding sheet. For, I knew with certainty that He would not decay in the tomb. Afterwards, Mary Magdalene and the holy angels, like specks in the sunbeam, were present, paying reverence to their Creator. What grief I felt then, no one can tell. For, I was like a woman in childbirth, all whose limbs after delivery are tremulous; and although she can scarcely breathe for pain, yet rejoices inwardly as much as she can, because she knows that her child is born never to return to the misery from which he came.
>
> So, though I was incomparably sad for the death of my Son, yet as my Son was to die no more, but live forever, I rejoiced in soul. And so a certain gladness was mingled with my grief. … So my thoughts and heart were ever in the sepulcher of my Son.[207]

Sacred Heart of Jesus, inter my heart within Yours, that I may keep watch with You. St. Bridget of Sweden, pray for us!

July 24

The service of St. John Cassian (c. 360–c. 435; memorial, July 23), a Desert Father, moved between the monastic state in Egypt and his priestly ministry in Marseille. In his *Conferences,* Saint John speaks of those who have so advanced in the spiritual life as to possess the Lord's own Heart of compassion.

> When anyone has acquired this love of goodness of which we have been speaking, and the imitation of God, then he will be endowed with the Lord's Heart of compassion and will pray for his persecutors, saying in like manner, "Father, forgive them; for they know not what they do" [Lk 23:34]. But it is a clear sign of a soul that is not yet thoroughly purged from the dregs of sin who does not sorrow with pity at the offenses of others, but keeps the rigid censure of a judge. For how will he be able to obtain perfection of heart [who cannot, as the apostle has pointed out] "Bear one another's burdens, and so fulfil the law of Christ" [Gal 6:2]. … And so a monk is quite certain to fall into the same sins that he condemns in another with merciless and inhuman severity; for "a stern king will fall into misfortunes," and "he who closes his ear to the cry of the poor will himself cry out and not be heard" [Prv 21:13].[208]

Sacred Heart of Jesus, replicate Your life in me, that I may bear Your goodness to others. St. John Cassian, pray for us.

July 25

In Bl. Mary of the Divine Heart's second letter to Pope Leo XIII, she speaks of the great light that a world consecration to the Sacred Heart would shed upon the earth, citing the third Mass of Christmas Day: "For today a great light has descended upon the earth."

> Last summer, when your holiness was suffering from an indisposition which, taking into consideration your great age, filled the hearts of your children with anxiety, it was a great consolation to me to know from Our Lord that He would prolong the life of your holiness in order to bring about the consecration of the whole world to His Sacred Heart. …
>
> He left me the impression that, after making the consecration, your holiness would soon finish your earthly pilgrimage … [and that] by this fresh development of the cultus of His Heart, He will illuminate the entire world with fresh light, and these words of the third Mass of Christmas penetrated my heart: *Quia hodie descendit Lux magna super terram.* I seemed (interiorly) to behold rays descending from this light, the Heart of Jesus, that adorable sun, and shedding its rays upon the earth in a faint manner at first, then brighter and brighter till the world was illuminated. And He said, "People and all nations shall be enlightened with the brightness of this light, and warmed by the intense heat of its rays."[209]

Sacred Heart of Jesus, shed Your light upon all nations, drawing them to Your Heart. Blessed Mary, pray for us!

July 26

William of Saint Thierry (c. 1080–1148) was a Cistercian abbot whose mystical writings mirror those of his close friend and fellow religious, St. Bernard of Clairvaux. In the following prayer, William considers the piercing of Christ's side and its manifestation of God's mercy. From this blessed source flows the sacraments, allowing man to partake of this life-giving Body. Comparing the Heart of Jesus to the saving Ark, William prays that all those who gather therein be granted salvation.

> Unsearchable are the riches of Your glory, Lord, that laid hidden secret with You in heaven, until the soldier's lance opened the side of Your Son and our Redeemer upon the cross, and the sacraments of our redemption poured forth. We cannot now place a finger or hand into His side, like Thomas; yet, through this open door, all may enter into Your Heart, Jesus, the sure seat of mercy, and into Your holy Soul, filled with all the fullness of God, and filled with grace and truth, our salvation and consolation. Open Lord, the side of Your Ark, wherein all who enter may be granted salvation from the flood that inundates the earth. Open unto us the side of Your Body so that those who desire to perceive the secrets of the Son may enter and receive the sacraments that flow from Him, the price of their redemption.[210]

Sacred Heart of Jesus, source of the celestial banquet, let flow the Blood that unites mankind to You. The feasts of this world can only weary our spirits, but Your graces are ever new! Sacred Heart of Jesus, unite us in the Eucharist!

July 27 | *St. Titus Brandsma*

St. Titus Brandsma (1881–1942) died at Dachau after publicly opposing the Nazi party. This poem, written by St. Teresa of Ávila, captures the sentiments of a dying saint.

O gentle Spouse! Aid with Thy grace,
And with the palm my soul invest
That's due to love's subservient quest,
That in its Bridegroom's fond embrace
My soul may find its perfect rest!

Since Thou dost thus Thine arms extend
I'll give my soul to be their prey,
And while Thou drawest it away,
Thine eyes, my Christ, upon me bend,
Whose soul dost from my body rend!

While I to Thee my soul confide,
Let Thy five wounds my comfort be
To which my soul finds passage free,
For they as heaven's portals bide
Which, for my sake, were opened wide.

I do not fear the anguish rife
In that last parting's bitter sting
If unto Thee, my Christ, I cling,
For in that hour of final strife
I hold within my clasped hands — Life.[211]

Sacred Heart of Jesus, let my soul pass through Your wounds as open gates, purifying my soul. Saint Titus, pray for us!

July 28

Fearful that preoccupation with academic matters would lead to an inflated spirit, Thomas à Kempis engaged himself with scribal work and devotional writings. This excerpt is from his *Meditations on the Life of Christ.*

> Enter, O my soul, enter boldly into the tender mercies of your God who is hanging upon the cross. Enter into the deep hollows of His wounds, safe from the face of the serpent who is everywhere, secretly and openly lying in wait for you. …
>
> [I beseech] You, O most gracious Jesus Christ, speak also to my soul Your saving word, which, as a mark of Your great love, You spoke to Your holy apostle Thomas, strengthening him in faith, and forgiving him all his sins: "Put your finger here, and see my hands" [Jn 20:27], which hard nails had lovingly fixed to the cross for you. Put out your hand and touch Me, considering it well. Put it into My side, which was in tender mercy opened for you: that side, so cruelly pierced by the soldier's spear, that Blood and water flowed freely from it for the perfect remission of all sins, in compassion for all believers. "Do not be faithless, but believing" [Jn 20:27]. Not doubting, but firm and steadfast; not overly curious, but honest and devout; not idle nor forgetful, but zealous and ever thankful to God for benefits so great.[212]

Sacred Heart of Jesus, let me draw living waters from Your Sacred Side, delivering its drink to those who faint along the way!

July 29

St. Justin de Jacobis (1800–1860; memorial, July 31) was a Vincentian missionary priest, known for his humility, whose travels brought him to Abyssinia, Africa. In 1849, he was named the titular bishop of Nilopolis by Ven. Guglielmo Massaia (1809–1889), who composed the following account of his episcopal ordination.

> Here, indeed, was the victim prepared for the sacrifice — not the bishop invested with dignity and honor! Thus did he offer himself, like Our Divine Lord, as a living sacrifice for the people of his adoption. He was bishop for twelve years, during which time he never wore the episcopal dress.
>
> At the moment of consecration, to inaugurate him in his new position, I was obliged to place my own mitre on his head, my own ring on his finger, and to give him my own crozier and pectoral cross. The ceremony over, he resumed his poor tattered clothes and his apostolic life of hardship and penury. Thus he lived, and thus he died, in the desert, under a little mimosa tree (a specimen, incidentally, of the spina-christi; a fitting emblem of the only crown he sought on earth); and thus did God send into Abyssinia this prodigy of humility, to be to them a living Gospel, a true image of Him who was meek and humble of Heart.[213]

Sacred Heart of Jesus, send forth a host of missionary priests configured to Your kindly love, seeking only the glory of the cross. Saint Justin, pray for us!

July 30 | *St. Peter Chrysologus*

A fifth-century bishop of Ravenna, St. Peter Chrysologus (c. 380–c. 450) delivered homilies so clever they earned him the appellation *golden-worded, (Chrysologus).* In *Sermon 137,* he expounds upon Luke 3:11: "He who has two coats, let him share with him who has none; and he who has food, let him do likewise."

> Do you consider it overmuch to ask him with two tunics to give one? It is not so; for he does not ask for a gem, but a tunic; not for gold, but bread. And if he who has two tunics does not give one, he is guilty. For what sort of man is he who has plenty and denies one; who locks up his clothes, who hides his bread, so that the poor perish of hunger and are consumed by cold? He buries those clothes … in the grave. What he denies to the poor, he gives up to the moth. … [But] the hunger of the poor has stricken Christ; the sorrow of man has broken the Heart of God; the laments of the prisoner have penetrated the Heart of Christ. Such a man's contempt for the needy has overflowed so as to offend his Creator, as Christ himself declared, "I was hungry and you gave Me no food, I was naked and you did not clothe Me" [see Mt 25:42–43].[214]

Sacred Heart of Jesus, help us to recognize You in the poor and to dedicate ourselves to Your service. Saint Peter, pray for us!

July 31 | *St. Ignatius of Loyola*

St. Ignatius of Loyola (1491–1556) was a solider whose grave battle injuries occasioned his conversion to Christ. He established the Society of Jesus (Jesuits), known for its advanced theological studies and missionary service.

> Of the Mysteries of the Cross: John 19:25–37
>
> First Point. First: He spoke seven words on the Cross: He prayed for those who were crucifying Him; He pardoned the thief; He recommended Saint John to His mother and His mother to Saint John; He said with a loud voice, "I thirst," and they gave Him gall and vinegar; He said that He was abandoned; He said, "It is consummated"; He said, "Father, into Thy hands I commend My Spirit!"
>
> Second Point. Second: The sun was darkened, the stones broken, the graves opened, the veil of the temple was rent in two from above to below.
>
> Third Point. Third: They blasphemed Him. … His garments were divided; His side, struck with the lance, sent forth water and Blood.[215]
>
> What I have so far said to awaken those that may be sleeping, and to spur on those who may be lagging or loitering along the road, must not be so understood as to constitute a plea for falling into the opposite extreme of indiscreet fervor. For spiritual sickness proceeds not only from chilling causes, such as tepidity, but also from heated causes, such as excessive fervor.[216]

Sacred Heart of Jesus, make of me a living offering to the Father, united to Your perfect sacrifice. Saint Ignatius, pray for us!

August

August 1 | *St. Alphonsus Liguori*

St. Alphonsus Liguori's devotional writings have never lost their popularity as they combine rich theology and piety. Here, Saint Alphonsus begs to be consumed by the love of the Sacred Heart.

> O most loving Heart of my Jesus, worthy to possess the hearts of all creatures — Heart all and ever full of flames of most pure love! O consuming fire, consume me entirely, and give me a new life of love and grace! Unite yourself to me in such a way that I may nevermore be separated from You! O Heart, opened to be the refuge of souls, receive me! O Heart, which on the cross was in such agony for the sins of the world, give me true sorrow for my sins! ...
>
> Ah, by Your merits, my beloved Jesus, be pleased yourself to wound me, to bind me, to force me, to unite me in all things to Your Heart. I am now determined, by Your grace, to give You all the pleasure that I possibly can, by trampling underfoot all human respect, inclinations, repugnance, all my tastes and conveniences, which may prevent me from entirely pleasing You.
>
> Do You, my Lord, so help me, that I may execute this determination in such a way that henceforth, all my works, opinions, and affections may be all in conformity with Your good pleasure.[217]

Sacred Heart of Jesus, heedless of the opinions of men, help me to transcend the world's judgments, seeking only Your good pleasure. Saint Alphonsus, pray for us!

August 2 | *St. Peter Julian Eymard*

In his book *On Holy Communion,* St. Peter Julian Eymard (1811–1868) styles the ecstatic tranquility found in Eucharistic adoration as a "sleep of the soul on the breast of Jesus." In silence, the adorer spiritually reclines upon the Sacred Heart.

> Having received Jesus into your heart at Holy Communion, spend some time in simple recollection, without vocal prayers. Adore Him in silence: Sit like Magdalene in humble and adoring love at His feet; gaze upon Him like Zacchaeus; love Him in voiceless worship like Mary, His mother. …
>
> While your soul remains recollected in the hushed calm of His holy Presence, do not seek to disturb it. It is the sleep of the soul upon the breast of Jesus, and this grace, which strengthens and unites it to Our Lord, will be more profitable than any other exercise. Adore Jesus upon the throne of your heart, and kiss His sacred feet and wounded hands. Rest upon that Heart which is burning with love for you. Offer Him the keys of your home, like St. Catherine of Genoa, "with full power to do all."
>
> Thank Jesus for having so honored and loved you as to give you this Communion; to you, so poor and miserable, so imperfect and unfaithful. Call upon Mary and all the saints and angels to thank and praise Jesus for His wonderful love and excessive goodness.[218]

Sacred Heart of Jesus, capture my senses beneath Your gaze, and grant me Your surpassing peace. St. Peter Eymard, pray for us!

August 3

In his spiritual autobiography, St. Peter Faber, the first Jesuit priest, considers Christ's tears shed at the Nativity, over Jerusalem, and upon the cross, and surveys the still greater effusions of His Precious Blood.

> O wretched and cruel soul of mine! ... Why have you held out until He shed Blood? See, even as a child eight days old, He shed tears and Blood in the circumcision, and yet you have not been moved. What do you wait for? See, unhappy soul, see that shedding of tears which came over Him regarding Jerusalem, weeping over the ingratitude and ultimate ruin of that nation — that shedding of tears was made for you and over you. See also those tears that, as He surrenders His Soul into the hands of His Father upon the cross, He sheds so plentifully for your salvation! ...
>
> See, moreover, the Blood that issues from every part of His Body, bound, smitten, torn, and crowned with thorns. And to end all, consider how, on the cross, all His veins were entirely emptied of that most Precious Blood, and how after death He opened His most sacred side, sending forth water and blood to heal and enlighten you, as well as Longinus. Do not seek, then, for any greater sign of His divine goodness in the sufferings of His sacred humanity, for now He can suffer no more.[219]

Sacred Heart of Jesus, let me be poured out as a libation to You, moved with compassion by Your wounded Heart. St. Peter Faber, pray for us!

August 4 | *St. Jean Vianney*

In his *Catechism,* St. Jean Vianney urges his parishioners to immerse themselves in the ocean of charity contained in the Sacred Heart of Jesus, where they will they receive a foretaste of heaven on earth.

> Believe what God has promised us: We believe that we shall one day see Him, that we shall possess Him, that we shall be eternally happy with Him in heaven. By hope, we expect the fulfilment of these promises: We hope that we shall be rewarded for all our good actions, for all our good thoughts, for all our good desires; for God takes into account even our good desires. What more do we want to make us happy?
>
> In heaven, faith and hope will exist no more, for the mists which obscure our reason will be dispelled; our mind will be able to understand the things that are hidden from us below. We shall no longer hope for anything, because we shall have everything. We do not hope to acquire a treasure that we already possess. … But love! Oh, we shall be inebriated with it! We shall be drowned, lost in that ocean of divine love, annihilated in that immense charity of the Heart of Jesus! So that charity is a foretaste of heaven. Oh! How happy should we be if we knew how to understand it, to feel it, to taste it! [220]

Sacred Heart of Jesus, grant us a foretaste of heaven, where we will be wholly possessed by You. St. Jean Vianney, pray for us!

August 5

Johannes Tauler's fervent pursuit of the vision of God inspired his life of prayer and fasting. His meditative work *On the Life of Christ* speaks of the Heart of Jesus as a school of love, which delivers man to the Heart of the Father. This "heart within a heart" is the very cell of heaven wherein man may find unending rest.

> Hence appears Christ's boundless love to us in that He gave himself wholly for us. What more could He do than He has done? He unlocked His Heart for us as His most secret chamber, to bring us therein as His elect spouse. For His delight is to be with us, and to rest with us in silent calm, in peaceful silence. He gave us His Heart, sorely wounded, that we might abide there, until, thoroughly purged, cleansed, and conformed to that Heart, we might be fit and worthy to be drawn, together with Him, into the Divine Heart of the Eternal Father.
>
> He gives us then His Heart, that it may be our dwelling, and asks for ours in turn, that it may be His abode. He bestows His Heart on us as a bed decked with the ruddy roses of His purple Blood, and requires in turn our heart — a bed adorned for himself with the white lilies of good works.[221]

Sacred Heart of Jesus, may I rest upon You in sacred silence, forever listening to Your canticle of love. Sacred Heart of Jesus, I adore You!

August 6 | *Feast of the Transfiguration*

Today we recall Christ's radiant appearance on Mount Tabor to Peter, James, and John. Like those holy apostles, St. Margaret Mary Alacoque sounded the depths of God's love for man, dedicating herself to His merciful Heart. In this letter to her novices, she urges them to center their lives on the Sacred Heart, the harbor of refuge.

> When you find yourself plunged in an abyss of sadness, go and lose yourself in the joy of the Sacred Heart. There, you will find a treasure that will cause all your sadness to disappear. If you are in trouble and anxiety, go and plunge yourself into the peace of His adorable Heart — no one can take this place from you. Often plunge yourself into the charity of this loving Heart so that you may never do anything to another that could wound this virtue. …
>
> [If suffering,] hide yourself in the Heart of Jesus, where you will find a treasure of joy that will make you submissive to His will. Remain in the abyss of His Heart silently and without complaint. Are you in an abyss of fear? Bury yourself in that of the confidence of the Sacred Heart and your fear will give place to love. If you feel overwhelmed with discontent and bitterness, bury yourself in the Sacred Heart so that you may find your joy in Him alone.[222]

Sacred Heart of Jesus, transfigure us in the brightness of Your glory, overwhelming all resistance to Your love. St. Margaret Mary, pray for us!

August 7 | *Saint Cajetan*

In the annals of Saint Cajetan's history (1480–1547) is the following vision of Christ, which took place one Easter Sunday. Christ reveals His Heart to Cajetan, identifying it as the wellspring of eternal life.

> "See, Cajetan, my pierced side, from whence My Church derives all her treasures and sacraments! This fountain of grace will ever be open to you; drink freely of this water of life, which I have shed on behalf of the whole world."

Though he burned with the love of God, Saint Cajetan understood that sanctity is not simply a matter of affection, but of freely willed correspondence with grace, and expressed his desire to be crucified with Christ.

> Certainly, I have no wish or desire but to stay where He wills and as He wills; for in this obedience and death to myself consists the glory of my Creator. It is not by the fervor of our affections, but by practical and effectual obedience that our souls are purified.
>
> We must be nailed with Jesus to His cross, and crucify all our own natural desires and wills, without allowing ourselves any choice of our own. And as he who is nailed to a cross cannot move of himself, so a Christian who is crucified with Jesus can no longer move or act according to his own will, but must receive the motive power from Christ himself.[223]

Sacred Heart of Jesus, give us to drink of the cup of life, granting us a share in Your victory. Saint Cajetan, pray for us!

August 8

A Jewish philosopher, St. Teresa Benedicta of the Cross (1891–1942; memorial, August 9) embraced Jesus as Messiah after a single reading of St. Teresa of Ávila's *Autobiography.* She joined the Carmelites, and was later arrested by the Gestapo and martyred at Auschwitz. In Teresa's meditation on the Epiphany, she ponders the angelic purity of St. John the Apostle.

> Neither will the Savior allow him who was particularly dear to Him during His life, the disciple whom Jesus loved, to be absent from the manger. He is entrusted to us as the example of *virginal purity.* Because he was pure, he pleased the Lord. He was allowed to rest on the Heart of Jesus to be initiated there into the secrets of the Divine Heart. As the heavenly Father witnessed to His Son when He cried out, "This is My beloved Son, listen to Him!", so the Divine Child also seems to point to the beloved disciple and to say, "No *frankincense* is more pleasing to me than the loving submission of a pure heart. Listen to him who was permitted to look at God because he was pure of heart." No one has looked more deeply into the hidden abyss of the divine life than he. Therefore, he proclaims the mystery of the eternal birth of the Divine Word in the liturgy each feast day during the days of Christmas and continues to do so at the end of daily Mass.[224]

Sacred Heart of Jesus, sanctify me completely, conforming my heart to Yours. St. Teresa Benedicta, pray for us!

August 9 | *Bl. John of La Verna*

The miraculous works of Bl. John of La Verna (1259–1322) are recorded in *The Little Flowers of St. Francis of Assisi,* a collection of Franciscan stories. This narrative describes the conclusion of Blessed John's three-year trial of spiritual darkness and a vision of the wounded side of Christ.

> No sooner had [John] come up to Him than did the blessed Christ turn and look upon him with a joyful and gracious countenance. Then, opening His most holy and merciful arms, He embraced him very sweetly. And as He opened His arms, John beheld rays of shining light coming from the Savior's most holy breast that illumined all the forest, and himself as well, in soul and body. Then, John knelt at Christ's feet and devoutly said, "I pray You, my Lord … make my soul live again in the grace of Your love. For this is Your Commandment: That we love You with all our hearts and affections, which none can keep without Your aid."
>
> [Then] Jesus stretched forth and offered him His most holy hands. And when John had kissed them, he drew nigh and leaned on Christ's bosom and embraced Him and kissed Him, and Christ likewise embraced and kissed him. And in these embraces and kisses John perceived such divine fragrance. … And thereby was Friar John ravished and consoled and illumined.[225]

Sacred Heart of Jesus, enliven us with Your grace, bestowing upon us the fire of devotion. Bl. John of La Verna, pray for us!

August 10

In this excerpt from *Christ in His Mysteries,* Bl. Columba Marmion describes the divine-human love of the Sacred Heart of Jesus, which overflowed with charity for both God and man.

> The Gospel one day shows us Christ's Heart, overflowing with enthusiasm for the Father's unfathomable perfections, burst forth in praise before His disciples. At the same hour He rejoiced in the Holy Spirit and said, "I thank you, Father, Lord of heaven and earth, that you have hidden these things from the wise and understanding and revealed them to infants; yes, Father, for such was your gracious will" [Mt 11:25–26].
>
> See again at the Last Supper how His Sacred Heart is full of affection for His Father and how this affection is expressed in an ineffable prayer.
>
> And so as to show the whole world the sincerity and intensity of this love, *Ut cognoscat mundus quia diligo Patrem,* Jesus immediately goes to the Garden of Olives where He is to enter into the long series of humiliations and sorrows of His passion.
>
> This double character is found likewise in His love towards mankind. … Above all, see Him at the tomb of Lazarus. Jesus weeps, He sheds tears, real human tears. Can there be a more touching, a more authentic manifestation of the feelings of His Heart? And at once He puts His power into the service of His love: "Lazarus, come forth."[226]

Sacred Heart of Jesus, may we adore the perfections of Your divine-human Heart and emulate Your perfect love. Blessed Columba, pray for us!

August 11

A Jesuit at age seventeen, St. John Berchmans (1599–1621; memorial, August 13) died at twenty-two, leaving behind an extraordinary witness of holiness and virtue. His personal notes reveal his resolve to imitate the humble Heart of Jesus.

> Motives for doing away with pride: (1) Christ on the cross, saying to me, "Learn of Me, you who pretend to be of My Society, because I am meek and humble of Heart." (2) If in your heart you foster pride, you are a liar, for your dress [proclaims you for Christ] when, nevertheless, within you are really a companion of the devil. (3) I must root out pride, if I wish to have Mary for my mother. …
>
> Remedies: (1) I will choose for myself a patron, who excelled marvelously in the opposite virtue; it shall be the most Blessed Virgin Mary. (2) I will [pursue] self-knowledge. What I was — nothing; what I am — the ulcer of the world; what I will be — a corrupted corpse.
>
> I resolve the whole of [1620], with God's grace, to go in for humility. (1) That I may proceed in an orderly way in building up the house of holiness, by beginning with the foundation; (2) because if I am not humble, I am no use to the Society; (3) because "nothing is difficult unto the humble, and nothing hard unto the meek."[227]

Sacred Heart of Jesus, grant me constant remembrance of my lowly station, and awe before Your glory. St. John Berchmans, pray for us!

August 12

Widowed at twenty-eight, St. Jane Frances de Chantal (1572–1641; memorial, August 21) subsequently cofounded the Congregation of the Visitation with her spiritual director, St. Francis de Sales. In this letter, Saint Jane explains that perseverance is an expression of submission to the divine will, and a means of ravishing the Heart of Jesus.

> Yes, my daughter, and I would have you accept your trouble and bear it with great patience and gentleness, awaiting the hour destined by divine providence for your relief. God still delays, but He will come, do not doubt it; tarry His time in profound submission. Meanwhile, keep your lamp burning, overcoming yourself as much as possible that you may give to this Divine Lord all He asks of you. . . .
>
> Often say a few words to Our Lord without reverting to the way in which you are acting and speaking to Him; for to find relish and satisfaction therein is not in your power, and thinking that actions done and words said thus, as it were by violence, could not be acceptable to God nor profitable to your soul would depress and sadden you. But herein you deceive yourself, for it is just this violence, my dearest daughter, that God at present requires of you. By it you will ravish His Divine Heart and attain to His blessed paradise.[228]

Sacred Heart of Jesus, solace amid storms, strengthen my faith in times of trial. Keep me vigilant in prayer, trusting in Your mercy. St. Jane de Chantal, pray for us!

August 13 | *St. Hippolytus of Rome*

St. Hippolytus of Rome (c. 170–c. 235) was a priest and theologian who fell into schism, but reconciled with the Church before his martyrdom. In this homily, he provides deep insight into the Blood and water that poured forth from the Heart of Jesus. Acknowledging that Christ's mortal Body had truly expired upon the cross, Saint Hippolytus further explains that only a life-giving Body — indeed, one united to the Godhead — could produce those twin founts of precious drink: "If anyone thirst, let him come to me and drink" (Jn 7:37).

> The Body of the Lord presented both these to the world: the sacred Blood and the holy water. And His Body, though dead after the manner of man, possesses in it great power of life. For streams which flow not from dead bodies flowed forth from Him, that is, Blood and water, in order that we might know what power for life is held by the virtue that dwelt in His Body, so as that it appears not to be dead like others, and is able to shed forth for us the springs of life. And not a bone of the Holy Lamb is broken, this figure showing us that suffering does not touch His strength. For the bones are the strength of the body.[229]

Sacred Heart of Jesus, flooding the earth with grace, pour yourself upon those tempted with despair. Enlighten them with those life-giving sacraments flowing from Your blessed side. St. Hippolytus of Rome, martyr of the Faith, pray for us!

August 14

Utterly devoted to the Sacred Heart of Jesus, St. Mechtilde of Hackeborn here reveals Jesus' instructions on the reception of Holy Communion and the fragrant gifts that flow from His Heart.

> The first perfume is the living water that divine love distilled from the noble rose of the Divine Heart in the furnace of charity. With this perfume, wash the face of your soul. If after a serious examination you find any stain of sin, beg that it may be cleansed in that fountain of mercy which bathed the thief on the cross.
>
> The second perfume is the generous wine of the Precious Blood of the crucified, which issued with water from the wound of His Sacred Heart. Beg that the face of your soul may be marked with it so as to be worthy of a place at so great a banquet.
>
> The third perfume is the marvelous meekness that overflows from the Divine Heart. This meekness, which the bitterness of death could not exhaust, is a perfume of balsam: It surpasses every aromatic perfume and is a remedy for every infirmity of soul. Beg that this perfume may be poured into your soul so that it may taste and see that the Lord is sweet [see Ps 34:8]. It will be nourished by this sweetness. It will expand and enter entirely into Him who has given himself to you in so much love.[230]

Sacred Heart of Jesus, adorn my soul with Your virtues, and graciously accept them as a gift! Saint Mechtilde, pray for us!

August 15 | *Solemnity of the Assumption of the Blessed Virgin Mary*

Today, the Church honors the upraising of the Virgin Mary to heaven in both body and soul. In Ven. Mary of Ágreda's monumental work, *The Mystical City of God,* Mary's assumption is described as an event of rapturous charity.

> Hence it happened once, that the ardors of love in the most Blessed Mother grew to such proportions, that she could truly be said to be languishing with love (Sg 2:5); for without being affected by the infirmities of our earthly passions, she languished on account of the impetus of her loving heart drawn toward the Lord, in order that just as He was the cause of her ailment, He might also be its glorious medicine and cure. …
>
> Then, her Divine Son came down from heaven. … Coming to the most Blessed Lady, He refreshed and comforted her in her pains, and said, "My mother, most beloved and chosen for our delight, the clamor and sighs of your loving soul have wounded My Heart. Come my dove, come to my celestial fatherland, where your sorrow shall be turned to delight, your tears into gladness, and where you shall rest from your sufferings." Immediately the holy angels, at His command, placed the Queen at the side of the Lord, her Divine Son, and with celestial music they all ascended to the empyrean heaven.[231]

Sacred Heart of Jesus, shattering the chasm between heaven and earth, summoning the Blessed Virgin, inspire us to greater love. Holy Mary, pray for us!

August 16

St. Anselm of Canterbury was the first of the great Scholastics who pursued a systematic treatment of theology. Here, he reveals his capacity for soaring poetry as he wonders at the ecstatic sweetness found in the Sacred Heart.

> Sweet Jesus! … sweet in His outstretched arms; sweet in His opened side; sweet in His feet fastened together with a nail!
>
> Sweet in the stretching of His arms. For stretching out His arms He lets us know that He, yes He, desires our embraces and seems to say, as it were, "O come to Me, you who labor and are burdened, and refresh yourself within My arms, within My embraces; you see that I am ready to fold you in My arms. Come then, come all of you; let none fear he will be turned away. …
>
> Sweet in the opening of His side; for indeed that opened side has revealed to us the treasures of His goodness, His Heart and His Heart's love for us.
>
> O good Jesus! O Lord all lowliness! O Lord all pity! O sweet in mouth, sweet in heart, sweet in ear; unsearchably and unutterably pleasant; all merciful and pitiful, almighty and all wise, all bountiful yet not prodigal; O altogether sweet and kind. You alone are sovereign good, "fairest of the sons of men" (Ps 45:2), fair and lovely, and chosen out of thousands, and altogether to be desired (see Sg 5:10, 16).[232]

Sacred Heart of Jesus, reveal to me Your mercy, manifest in Your cloven Heart! Saint Anselm, pray for us!

August 17 | *St. Jeanne Delanoue*

St. Jeanne Delanoue (1666–1736), foundress of the Congregation of the Sisters of Saint Ann of Providence, possessed a profound understanding of the Sacred Heart devotion, which she expresses in the following prayer of supplication for her sisters.

> I present them to You, O my Holy Spouse, and pray that You enkindle them, melting away their ice. … Annihilate them, these hearts, and put Your own Heart in their place; or take them and place them within Your Heart, that they would perceive the divine ardor with which You burn and would be protected against the enticements of the world, the flesh, and the temptations of the devil.
>
> Oh! Who will empower me to make known, my sisters, the divine kindnesses of your Spouse? And who will enable me to open your hearts, that the tenderness of His love would flow therein? There is none but You, O my Savior, who can make docile these hearts, which would remain deaf to my voice if You did not call them. You yourself call them — yes! You call them, and their hearts, nevertheless, remain closed! What would You, then, have me do? Do You desire that I be a victim? I consent with all my heart and demand no better than to shed all my blood — if only You make them receptive to Your love! [233]

Sacred Heart of Jesus, melt away all obstinacy and sin in Your furnace of charity, impressing Your image upon us. St. Jeanne Delanoue, pray for us!

August 18

St. Ezequiél Moreno y Diaz (1848–1906) was an Augustinian missionary priest and bishop. In this letter, Saint Ezequiél describes the Eucharist as the eternal memorial of Christ's love, instituted that the heart of man might ever be plunged into the recesses of the Sacred Heart.

> Jesus Christ, Our Savior, driven by His love for man, and not permitting this love to be removed from them, *"summoning heart within heart,"* according to the sublime words of Tertullian, took unleavened bread in His hands and looked to heaven, sounding that omnipotent voice that had once said, "Let there be," and all things were made, pronounced these solemn words: "Take and eat, this is My Body. Take and drink, this is My Blood." And in the Eucharist, He gave himself whole and entire to the apostles. This is how Jesus Christ instituted the eternal memorial of His love for men.
>
> If Jesus Christ had not established this prodigy of love by His own word, then who would have come to — I do not merely say *ask* for it — but *imagine* it? … However much in heaven that is great, majestic, adorable, beautiful, splendid, lovable, charming, sweet, and gracious, we can possess and enjoy; for here, Christ has given us His whole Being. And there can be nothing greater, nor richer, nor more excellent, nor more worthy of adoration and love, either in heaven or on earth.[234]

Sacred Heart of Jesus, embrace me in Your Sacrament of Love, immersing me in Your Blood Divine! Saint Ezequiél, pray for us!

August 19 | *St. John Eudes*

St. John Eudes zealously promoted devotion to the Sacred Heart of Jesus and composed its first liturgical celebration. In his "Salutations to the Sacred Heart," Eudes praises the Heart of the Savior, extolling its virtues and excellence.

Hail, Heart most holy!
Hail, Heart most meek!
Hail, Heart most humble!
Hail, Heart most pure!
Hail, Heart most devoted!
Hail, Heart most wise!
Hail, Heart most patient!
Hail, Heart most obedient!
Hail, Heart most watchful!
Hail, Heart most faithful!
Hail, Heart most blessed!
Hail, Heart most merciful!
Hail, Heart most loving, of
  Jesus, Son of Mary.
We adore You,
We praise You,
We glorify You,
We give You thanks.
We love You:
  with all our heart,
  with all our soul,
  with all our strength.
To You, our heart:
  we offer,
  we give,
  we consecrate,
  we immolate;
accept and take possession of
  it entirely,
and purify it,
and enlighten it,
and sanctify it,
and live and reign in it,
now and ever, forever and
  ever. Amen.[235]

Sacred Heart of Jesus, divine craftsman, let all creation give You praise. All were made through You, and all were made for You. Sacred Heart of Jesus, may my soul ever give You glory!

August 20 | *St. Bernard of Clairvaux*

St. Bernard of Clairvaux is popularly honored as "the last of the Church Fathers" for his impressive intellect and eloquence of speech. *Jesu dulcis amor meus* is a medieval hymn, traditionally attributed to Saint Bernard, which movingly surveys the wounds of the crucified. In five verses, Bernard recounts the agonies and humiliations that Christ endured for love of man.

Loving Jesus, sweet and tender,
Be my bosom's fond defender,
Love for love my soul shall render,
Prostrate at thy holy feet.

Lo, I see thee naked, wounded,
By thy trembling friends surrounded,
Staring on thee, sore astounded,
Folded in thy winding-sheet.

Hail, dear head so torn and gory;
Face, whose roses blanched and hoary,
So have lost their wondrous glory
That the angels quake to see.

Hail, O heart of man's salvation,
Prone I bow in adoration;
Hail, meek wound, thou dark carnation
Bringing healing unto me.

Holy hands, all perforated
By the men yourselves created;
Let me ne'er with love be sated,
Kneeling near the sacred feet.[236]

Sacred Heart of Jesus, oblation of love, thank You for the gift of yourself in the Blessed Sacrament. Wipe away every trace of sin in me, transforming death most bitter into everlasting life. Sacred Heart of Jesus, make me live unto You!

August 21 | *Pope St. Pius X*

In his encyclical on St. Gregory the Great, *Iucunda Sane,* Pope St. Pius X reassures the faithful of the Church's immunity to doctrinal error, underscoring her supernatural source in the Heart of Jesus.

> Kingdoms and empires have passed away; peoples once renowned for their history and civilization have disappeared; time and again the nations, as though overwhelmed by the weight of years, have fallen asunder; while the Church, indefectible in her essence, united by ties indissoluble with her heavenly Spouse, is here today radiant with eternal youth, strong with the same primitive vigor with which she came from the Heart of Christ dead upon the cross. Men powerful in the world have risen up against her. They have disappeared, and she remains. Philosophical systems without number, of every form and every kind, rose up against her, arrogantly vaunting themselves her masters, as though they had at last destroyed the doctrine of the Church, refuted the dogmas of her Faith, proved the absurdity of her teachings. But those systems, one after another, have passed into books of history, forgotten, bankrupt; while from the rock of Peter the light of Truth shines forth as brilliantly as on the day when Jesus first kindled it on His appearance in the world, and fed it with His divine words: "Heaven and earth will pass away, but my words will not pass away" (Mt 24:35).[237]

Sacred Heart of Jesus, protect us from the false teachings of this world, grounding us in the Truth. St. Pius X, pray for us!

August 22 | *Feast of the Queenship of the Blessed Virgin Mary*

A scholar and strong administrator, Pope Benedict XIV (1675–1758) sought to reconcile Catholic, Eastern Orthodox, and Protestant Christians. In this papal decree, he quotes Aquinas at length, proposing Christ's humility as the remedy for man's pride.

> Among the potential parts of temperance, we have enumerated humility; and among its subjective parts, chastity, purity, and virginity; so that it would seem necessary to say a few words on each of them. Regarding humility, [remember] "Learn from me; for I am gentle and lowly in heart" (Mt 11:29), with reference to which Saint Thomas says, "Christ is thought to have recommended to us humility above all things, because by this the chief impediment to the salvation of man is removed. For in this way it is, that when a man tries to rise to heavenly and spiritual things, he is kept back from them by the desire of exalting himself. And so Our Lord, in order to remove this obstacle to our salvation, showed us by the example of His humility, that external greatness ought to be despised. Thus humility is a certain disposition in a man towards readily embracing divine and spiritual goods. Inasmuch, then, as perfection in a thing is better than a disposition towards it, so also charity and other virtues, which lead a man directly to God, are better than humility." [238]

Sacred Heart of Jesus, may humility be upon me as a breastplate and meekness as a shield; grant that I may glory in You alone!

August 23

The extraordinary spiritual gifts of Bl. Mary of the Divine Heart were complemented by her affective humanity. Here she shares her fears concerning physical pain, which were tempered by the consolation she found in Christ. Alluding to Scripture, Christ lovingly assures her of His abiding Presence amid the sufferings of the world.

> The violent headache from which I suffered some days ago made me fear I should lose my reason. I resigned myself to the will of God, but I begged Our Lord to preserve me from this misfortune and not allow me to be reduced to a state in which I could no longer love Him nor communicate. He granted my petition and told me I should communicate till the very end. He added: My spouse, you will always love Me, because I have written you in My Heart. He promised me that I should never lose my reason. Then a great fear came over me lest I myself should wish to lose consciousness if my sufferings became more than I could bear. This was a temptation, and Our Lord consoled me: I will be with you in the midst of your greatest sufferings. I forgot to say that Our Lord gave me to understand that I should suffer much.[239]

Sacred Heart of Jesus, be with me in my greatest sufferings, that I may accept each trial as a gift. Bring faith out of darkness, hope from despair, and victory out of defeat. Bl. Mary of the Divine Heart, pray for us!

August 24

St. Teresa of Ávila was a Carmelite religious and mystic who famously received the gift of transverberation, wherein God mystically pierces the heart. Once penetrated by divine love, the soul is made capable of practicing charity to an eminent degree. Her famous poem — here felicitously titled "The Pact" — meditates upon this transformative event through the words of Solomon: "I am my beloved's and my beloved is mine" (Sg 6:3).

Now am I wholly yielded up,
foregone,
And this the pact I made,
That my beloved is my own,
And I am His alone!

Struck by the gentle hunter
And overthrown,
Within the arms of love
My soul lay prone.

Raised to new life at last
This contract between us
passed,
That my beloved is my own,
And I am His alone!

With lance embarbed with
love,
He took His aim —
One with its maker hence
My soul became.

No love but His I crave
Since self to Him I gave
For the beloved is my own,
And I am His alone! [240]

Sacred Heart of Jesus, Beloved Heart, may I be wholly penetrated with Your love. Take possession of me entirely, and let me perfectly possess You. St. Teresa of Ávila, transpierced with love, pray for us!

August 25

Deeply committed to the restoration of Catholicism in England, Bl. Dominic Barberi (1792–1849; memorial, August 26), in his *Lamentation of England,* mourns the country's spiritual state, offering the Precious Blood of Jesus to the Father.

> We have sinned against You, we have forsaken You, the fountain of living waters, and we have abandoned Your holy spouse the Catholic Church; we have hewn out for ourselves cisterns, broken cisterns, which cannot afford us one drop of true consolation. We have erred, O Lord, we have forfeited the title of Your children. We have no right to call You by the sweet name of Father, we who have refused to own for our mother, Your holy spouse, the Church: Alas we confess it. …
>
> I do not deserve to be heard, I know it, I confess it. But at least Your Divine Son, Our Lord Jesus Christ, well deserves to be heard: Those wounds, which He endured for our sakes, and that divine Blood that was shed for us, and that cries better than the blood of Abel, cannot fail to move Your pity. I know that Jesus stands at Your right hand, ever living to make intercession for us … can You deny an entrance to His prayers, O Lord? No, my God, no, this is not possible: You yourself protest that You will grant all that He asks of You. [241]

Sacred Heart of Jesus, may the lamps of Your Church burn brightly in every land, spreading Your saving power. Bl. Dominic Barberi, pray for us!

August 26 | *Bl. Pope John Paul I*

Bl. Pope John Paul I (1912–1978) was elevated to the papacy thirty-three days before his death, constituting one of the shortest pontificates in Church history. His *Urbi et Orbi* address established the dominant themes of his papacy, which would ultimately be taken up by his successor, Pope St. John Paul II. Pope John Paul I here voices the desire of Christ's Heart that all may be one (see Jn 17:21). This sublime unity can only be realized in and through the divine-human Heart of Jesus.

> We wish to continue the ecumenical thrust, which we consider a final directive from our immediate predecessors. We watch with an unchanging faith, with a dauntless hope, and with endless love for the realization of that great command of Christ: "That they may all be one" (Jn 17:21). His Heart anxiously beats for this on the eve of His sacrifice on Calvary. The mutual relationships among the churches of the various denominations have made constant and extraordinary advances as anyone can see; yet division remains a cause for concern, and indeed a contradiction and scandal in the eyes of non-Christians and nonbelievers. We intend to dedicate our prayerful attention to everything that would favour union. We will do so without diluting doctrine but, at the same time, without hesitance.[242]

Sacred Heart of Jesus, for whom nothing is impossible, bring about the reconciliation of Christians. May all come to dwell in the household of God, drinking of the cup of unity. Bl. Pope John Paul I, pray for us!

August 27 | *Saint Monica*

Saint Monica (331–387) tirelessly prayed for the conversion of her son, Augustine, pleading and trusting for over thirty years. The fruit of her efforts is evident in Augustine's *Commentary on John,* wherein he contemplates Jesus' words: "Peace I leave with you; my peace I give to you; not as the world gives do I give to you" (Jn 14:27).

> When the Lord proceeded to say, "Not as the world gives do I give to you" (Jn 14:27), what else does He mean except, "not as those who love the world give, do I give to you?" For their aim in seeking peace is that — free from the annoyance of lawsuits and wars — they may find enjoyment, not in God, but in the friendship of the world. And although they give the righteous peace in ceasing to persecute them, there can be no true peace where there is no real harmony, because their hearts are at variance. … Let us, therefore, beloved, with whom Christ has left His peace, and to whom He gives His own peace, not in the manner of the world, but in a way worthy of Him by whom the world was made, that we should be of one heart with himself, having our hearts run into one; that this one heart, set on that which is above, may escape the corruption of the earth.[243]

Sacred Heart of Jesus, let our hearts flow into Yours, surrendering themselves to Your will. Saint Monica, tireless intercessor, pray for us!

August 28 | *St. Augustine of Hippo*

St. Augustine of Hippo famously converted from a life of philosophical wanderings and sin to the fullness of grace and Truth found in Christ, becoming one of the greatest theologians in Church history. In this sermon, he considers that uniquely Christian doctrine that "God is love" (1 Jn 4:16) and shocks his hearers by reversing the terms of this verse.

> Understand that to act against love is to act against God. Let no man say, "When I do not love my brother, I sin against man; but, sin against man is only a light matter — only, let me not sin against God." How do you not sin against God when you sin against love? Love is God. Do we say this [of our own accord]? If we said, "Love is God," one of you might be offended and say: "What did he say? What did he mean by saying 'Love is God'? God gave love; as a gift God bestowed love." Love is of God: Love IS God.
>
> Look, brothers, here you have the Scriptures of God: This epistle is canonical. Throughout all nations it is recited. It is held by the authority of the whole earth. It has edified the whole earth. You are here told by the Spirit of God: Love is God. Now if you dare, go against God, and refuse to love your brother![244]

Sacred Heart of Jesus, grant me Your Heart that I may participate in the exchange of divine love. Make my heart like Yours!

August 29

St. Gertrude the Great was a Benedictine mystic who put aside her scientific studies to pursue Christ and His Sacred Heart. Here, she shares the prayer that led to her union with the crucified Lord, and the affliction of the invisible stigmata, those wounds that marked Christ's hands, feet, and side.

> "O Lord Jesus Christ, Son of the living God, grant that I may aspire toward You with my whole heart, with full desire, and with a thirsting soul, seeking only Your sweetness and delights, so that my whole mind and all that is within me may ardently sigh to You, our true beatitude. O most merciful Lord, engrave Your wounds upon my heart with Your most Precious Blood, that I may read in them Your grief and Your love; and that the memory of Your wounds may ever remain in my inmost heart to excite my compassion for Your sufferings and to increase in me Your love. Grant me also to despise all creatures and that my heart may delight in You alone. Amen."
>
> Having learned this prayer with great satisfaction, I repeated it frequently, and You, who despises not the prayer of the humble, heard my petitions. ... I perceived in my spirit that You had imprinted in the depths of my heart the adorable marks of Your sacred wounds. ... You had given [my soul] the precious drink of Your love.[245]

Sacred Heart of Jesus, may all my powers be wholly turned toward You. Saint Gertrude, pray for us!

August 30

St. Margaret of Cortona spent ten years living in open scandal as mistress to an unmarried man before experiencing radical conversion to Christ. Her mystical writings overflow with tender expressions of God's mercies. Here Christ details His zealous pursuit of her friendship.

> Know then, that as I went in search of you through such suffering and anguish, so shall you also come to Me by much sorrow and affliction. Prepare yourself for greater trials. The cry of your worldly life formerly rose against Me from the tongue of murmurers, who detailed your scandal in the village, the forest, the field, the meadow. … Hence, you shall never cease to preach the history of My passion and to remind the world how, for love of mankind, I lived incessantly amid travails and trials. …
>
> Remind them … with tears how, on the bed of the cross, My head, rent with thorns and wounded with blows, had not whereon to lie. Remind them how, having recommended My Spirit to My Father, I bowed down My head upon My breast in the presence of My sorrowing mother, and left My lifeless Body upon the cross. Remind them how My pitiless enemies pierced My side after My death; and how Blood and water, the price of your redemption, flowed therefrom. … I wish you to say that My love for souls alone induced Me to do these things.[246]

Sacred Heart of Jesus, restore us to Your grace, and console us with Your love. Saint Margaret, pray for us!

August 31

John Justus Lanspergius helped spread devotion to the Sacred Heart through his work as a translator and author. His writings reveal a substantive spirituality of the Sacred Heart, which he rightly reveres as Love Incarnate. In the following exhortation, Lanspergius recommends a singular devotion to the Sacred Heart of Jesus, as this Heart alone is wholly trustworthy and ever faithful.

> From this loving Heart, appropriate to yourself all the graces imaginable; you will never exhaust it. It is useful; nay, it is necessary to honor the Sacred Heart of Our Lord Jesus Christ with singular devotion. It is your refuge; you must fly to it in all your necessities to draw from it the consolation and all the help that you need. Even though all men should abandon and forget you, Jesus will be your one faithful friend. He will always keep you in His Heart. Trust in Him: Rest upon Him. Others may and will deceive you. The Sacred Heart of Jesus is the only one that loves you sincerely. He alone will never deceive you.[247]

Sacred Heart of Jesus, friend of the friendless, Your arms alone provide the serenity I long for. Beneath Your holy gaze, I need only to drink in Your love. Sacred Heart of Jesus, be my strength!

September

September 1 | *St. Teresa Margaret of the Sacred Heart*

St. Teresa Margaret of the Sacred Heart (1747–1770) was a Florentine Carmelite nun who served as the monastery infirmarian. In the following poem, she writes of a despondent shepherdess who believes herself lacking in charity and is comforted by an angel, who enlightens her on the true nature of love.

Elpina the shepherdess
burning with a great desire
to know how God
could be loved upon earth.

Eh! Who can teach me
to love God who loves me
and who, before the existence
of the world He created
with this same love
of His Heart Divine,
loved me …

While thus grieved
she wept to herself
not being able to console
the pain of her heart;
the virgin now a hermit,
swooned and fell
a prey to languor …

Behold, there before
her, ornate with gilded wings,
brimming with celestial
    delight,
stood suddenly a gracious
    spirit,
and his loving lips
like lilies and roses
opened into these beautiful
    accents:

Elpina, how can you say
you do not love God,
when your very desire
of loving is love itself?
It is the sweet flame
which escapes from
the secret furnace of your
    heart.[248]

Sacred Heart of Jesus, may I never stand upon my own strength, but only on Your sure mercy. Saint Teresa Margaret, pray for us!

September 2

The fourteenth-century Middle English work on contemplative prayer, *The Cloud of Unknowing*, emphasizes the process whereby the soul is purged of earthly concepts in its pursuit of God. In this excerpt, Christians are encouraged to carry out all their duties for the love of Jesus. By ordering all actions toward God, the soul is united with God, and no time is ever ill spent.

> Love Jesus, therefore, and all that is His is made common to thee with Him. He, by His Godhead, is the maker and giver of times. He, by His manhood, is the true keeper of time. And He, by His Godhead and manhood together, is the true judge and asker of account for the spending of time. Knit thyself therefore to Him by love and faith; and then by virtue of that knot, thou shalt be made partner with Him, and with all those that are by love so knit to Him — to wit — with our Blessed Lady, who being replenished with the grace of God was a diligent and faithful keeper of time; with all the angels and blessed spirits in heaven who, being perfectly established in grace, never lose any time; and with all the saints that are both in heaven and earth who, by the grace of Jesus, do justly keep all time, in the virtue of His holy love.[249]

Sacred Heart of Jesus, let all my works be done in love and each be pleasing to You! Sacred Heart of Jesus, I consecrate my life to You!

September 3 | *St. Gregory the Great*

St. Gregory the Great (540–604) was an influential pope who reformed the Roman Liturgy. In *Moralia in Job*, he takes up Job 3:16 — "Why was I not as a hidden untimely birth, as infants that never see the light?" Saint Gregory understands this cry to be of those born before Christ, the Light of the World, and thus recommends the rest and consolation found in the humble heart of Jesus.

> We have already said that the hearts of sinners are possessed with a tumult of desires and are grievously oppressed by a host of goading thoughts; but in this light, which the "infants conceived" never saw, the wicked are said to "cease from their disquiet" for this reason. ... In this light then, the wicked "cease from disquietude," inasmuch as the minds of the untoward, when they have come to the knowledge of the Truth, eschew the wearisome desires of the world, and find rest in the quiet haven of interior love. Does not the light itself call us to this rest when it says, "Come unto Me, all ye that labor and are heavy laden and I will give you rest. Take My yoke upon you and learn from Me, for I am meek and lowly in heart: And you shall find rest for your souls. For My yoke is easy and My burden light."[250]

Sacred Heart of Jesus, guard my heart from vain imaginings, that I might find peace in You. Saint Gregory, pray for us!

September 4

Ven. Mary Potter was the English foundress of the Little Company of Mary. In *The Brides of Christ,* she warns that Christians cannot recline upon the breast of Jesus unless they are first espoused to Him in Holy Communion.

> A true spouse of Jesus must be united with Him in His sacramental life. … For union with Jesus in the Blessed Sacrament makes easy what would otherwise be so difficult to our unaided human nature. [Thus] we are raised above ourselves. …
>
> You have drawn us, Dear Jesus, and we have come to live with You upon the cross; to be molded into a work of Your Holy Spirit; to be known as spouses of Jesus crucified, but, oh, sweet Jesus, we must first be spouses of Yours in Your Sacrament of Love ere we lean upon Your breast with Your beloved disciple and hear the pulsations of Your Sacred Heart! Oh, dear Jesus, we need to be thus drawn closely to You, if we would live with You upon the cross, and feel those other beatings of Your crushed Heart as they come and go with intermittent throbs in Your death agony!
>
> Cultivate this union of thought with Jesus in the Blessed Sacrament by frequent visits, by receiving Holy Communion daily, or often as allowed, and by constantly making spiritual communions, which, we are told, merit grace more precious than pearls of great price.[251]

Sacred Heart of Jesus, when You rest within my heart, I want for nothing. Ven. Mary Potter, pray for us!

September 5 | *St. Teresa of Calcutta*

St. Teresa of Calcutta (1910–1997) became a living image of the meek and lowly Jesus through her life of charitable service and solidarity with the poor. In the following remarks, Saint Teresa reflects on the heavenly air of humility that surrounded Jesus, Mary, and Joseph. They never sought vengeance but endured personal injuries with patience, forbearance, and mercy. Saint Teresa exhorts Christians to walk in the way of loving kindness, imitating the Heart of Jesus.

> I believe when Jesus passed by, the children cried, "Sweetness is passing." In the community, love as Mary loved Jesus and Jesus, Mary. Joseph, when he learned that Our Lady was with child, he could have made it public — [but] see his meekness. He did nothing special. He could have been harsh with Mary, but he was ready to risk his own life. … See Jesus in His passion. He never blamed; He did not shout. "Why did you strike?" — only that one question. See the delicate meekness of Jesus. He knew the whole time what Judas would do. Let us ask for this meekness. Keep that meekness, kindness, thoughtfulness. Jesus wanted to teach humility: He washed their feet; He did not explain. "Learn of Me; I am meek and humble of heart." Jesus taught simply. We need meekness, thoughtfulness. Let us pay attention to our words. One word — so much hurt.[252]

Sacred Heart of Jesus, create in me a kindly heart that echoes Your own. St. Teresa of Calcutta, model of humility, pray for us!

September 6

St. Clement of Alexandria (c. 150–c. 215) was an early theologian who applied Platonic philosophy to Christian theology. Here, he speaks of the Greek philosophers' belief in the final judgment, but also the striking hope of finding an embrace in God's love.

> And this agrees with the tragedy in the following lines:
>
> "For there shall come, shall come that point of time
> When Ether, golden-eyed, shall ope its store
> Of treasured fire; and the devouring flame,
> Raging, shall burn all things on earth below,
> And all above."
>
> And after a little while he adds:
>
> "And when the whole world fades
> And vanished all the abyss of ocean's waves,
> And earth of trees is bare; and wrapt in flames,
> The air no more begets the winged tribes;
> Then He who destroyed, shall all restore."
>
> We shall find expressions similar to these also in the Orphic Hymns, written as follows:
>
> "For having hidden all, brought them again
> To gladsome light, forth from his sacred heart,
> Solicitous."[253]

Sacred Heart of Jesus, reveal Your Heart to all nations, manifesting the fullness of Your mercy. Saint Clement, pray for us!

September 7

St. Margaret Mary Alacoque led a life of austerity, carrying out extreme forms of penance — inadvisable to all others — in reparation to the Sacred Heart. Knowing that the source of her sanctification was not human action as such, but divine grace, she here speaks of the atoning power of the Sacred Heart, which alone satisfies for the sins of the world.

> When we fall into any fault, we must ask this Divine Heart to satisfy His justice for us and to give us His grace and mercy; although we are not worthy. Have recourse to Him always and everywhere: He delights in doing us good. Let us unite ourselves to Him in all our actions, for thus alone shall we merit. Above all, let us try to please Him by a loving confidence.
>
> Remember if I die before you, that you are to take my place before the Blessed Sacrament and ask pardon for all the irreverence and outrage He has received from me. And if God has mercy on me, I promise not to forget you, but to do everything in my power for you. Let us love each other in the Sacred Heart. Let us love Him for each other; love Him under all circumstances and take for a motto: "Thy will be done." Love and do what you will, for whoever possesses love has all.[254]

Sacred Heart of Jesus, in whom the Father is well pleased, teach us that perfect submission which ever prays, "Thy will be done!" Saint Margaret Mary, pray for us!

September 8 | *Feast of the Nativity of the Blessed Virgin Mary*

The Nativity of the Blessed Virgin commemorates the birth of that most favored of women, who became mother to the Sacred Heart. Here, Bl. Columba Marmion argues that the Sacred Heart devotion ought to claim pride of place in Christian life as it embraces Christ's entire character of self-giving love.

> Devotion to the Sacred Heart of Jesus is one of those which should be especially dear to us. And why? Because it honors Christ Jesus not only in one of His states or particular mysteries, but in the generality and totality of His love, wherein all His mysteries find their deepest meaning. Although being a clearly defined devotion, devotion to the Heart of Jesus bears something that is universal. In honoring the Heart of Christ, it is no longer to Jesus as infant, youth, or victim, that our homage is especially addressed. It is on the Person of Jesus in the plenitude of His love that we especially linger.
>
> Moreover, the general practice of this devotion tends, at the last analysis, to render to Our Lord love for love; *Movet nos ad amandum mutuo;* to penetrate all our activity with love in order to please Christ Jesus. The special exercises of the devotion to the Sacred Heart of Jesus are but so many means of expressing to Our Divine Master this reciprocity of love.[255]

Sacred Heart of Jesus, set all hearts ablaze with love, following after Your revered mother, Mary. Immaculate Heart of Mary, pray for us!

September 9

Theophylact of Ohrid (c. 1050–c. 1107) was a Byzantine archbishop and biblical commentator who lived shortly after the Great Schism. Despite tensions between the East and West, his works found favor with Catholic theologians and never lost their currency. The following text reflects upon that climactic moment recorded in the Gospel of John: "But one of the soldiers pierced his side with a spear, and at once there came out blood and water" (Jn 19:34). For Theophylact, the dual streams of Blood and water provide evidence of Christ's humanity and divinity — a symbolism represented in the use of water and wine in the Liturgy of the Eucharist.

> The contumely is changed into a miracle, and wonderful it was that Blood flowed forth from a dead Body. But a disputant might say that some vital force might probably remain in the Body. But the water which flowed forth puts the matter beyond all dispute.
>
> Confounded be the Armenians who in the Mysteries do not mix water with the wine. For, as it seems, they do not believe that water flowed forth from the side (which would be more wonderful), but Blood only. And in this passage, they do away with a mighty miracle. The Blood then is the symbol of a crucified man, but the water of one who is above man, that is, of God.[256]

Sacred Heart of Jesus, You let flow a spring of Blood and water, manifesting Your unfathomable mercy. Descend within my soul in Holy Communion and embrace this heart of mine. Amen!

September 10

Theodoret of Cyrus (c. 398–c. 466) was an Antiochene bishop who vocally opposed St. Cyril of Alexandria in the Christological controversies of the fifth century. Despite his theological disputes, the following passage remains a beautiful meditation on the sufferings of Christ.

> The Word associated with himself and brought upon himself what the humanity of the Word suffered, that we might be able to share in the Godhead of the Word. And marvelous it was that the sufferer and He who did not suffer were the same; sufferer in that His own Body suffered, and He was in it while suffering, but not suffering because the Word, being by nature God, was impassible. And He himself, the incorporeal, was in the passible Body, and the Body contained in itself the impassible Word. …
>
> For being God and Lord of glory, He was in the Body ingloriously crucified; but the Body suffered when smitten on the tree, and water and Blood flowed from its side; but being temple of the Word, it was full of the Godhead. Wherefore, when the sun saw its Creator suffering in His outraged Body, it drew in its rays, and darkened the earth. And that very Body with a mortal nature rose superior to its own nature on account of the Word within it, and was no longer touched by its natural corruption, but clothed with the superhuman Word, became incorruptible.[257]

Sacred Heart of Jesus, by partaking in Your humanity, may we participate in Your divinity. Your kingdom come!

September 11

Battista Vernazza (1497–1587) was an Augustinian canoness regular whose mystical writings boldly treat the soul's union with God. Here, she reflects on Luke 12:49: "I came to cast fire upon the earth; and would that it were already kindled!" Battista identifies this fire as God's burning love, poured into souls.

> By these divine words, we can partly understand the importance of this most happy fire, since the Eternal Word came down from heaven to enkindle it in His dearly-loved rational earth. And this great effect could not but follow, since the paternal goodness willed to communicate the order which He possesses eternally in His Heart to our misery.
>
> In His infinite courtesy, His majesty delights in abiding with the children of men. But He desires that these delights should proceed from both sides, so that, as He takes delight in us by His own intrinsic natural goodness, He similarly wills that we, by means of that same goodness which is poured into us by that fire that Christ casts upon our earth — as Paul shows when he says, "God's love is poured forth in our hearts by the Holy Spirit who is given to us" — He wills that, set in motion by the immense potency of this infused fire, we should, in return, place all our delights in His majesty. Then His unmeasured love attains its intent, so to speak.[258]

Sacred Heart of Jesus, embrace me in an exchange of heavenly conversation, and fill me with Your Spirit. I consecrate myself to You!

September 12

St. Catherine of Genoa (1447–1510; memorial, September 15) was an Italian laywoman and mystic who composed the *Spiritual Dialogue.* Here, Christ reveals to Catherine how He wounds the heart of man, drawing it to himself.

> I let down into the heart of man the slender golden thread of My hidden love, to which is attached a hook that enters the heart, and man feels himself wounded, but knows not by whom he is bound and taken. …
>
> As the feet of one who has been hanged do not touch the earth, but his body remains attached to the cord by which he received his death, so the spirit remains suspended by the slender thread of love whereby all the subtle and hidden imperfections of man receive their death: All that he now loves, he loves by virtue of the tie by which he is bound. All his actions are done by means of that love [because] it is now God who works alone … without man's assistance. And God, having thus taken man into His own keeping, and drawn him entirely to himself, so enriches him with His favors that when he comes to die, he finds himself drawn unconsciously by that thread of love into the divine abyss. And although man, in this state, appears a lifeless, lost, and abject thing, yet his life is hidden in God amid the treasures of eternal life.[259]

Sacred Heart of Jesus, rend this separational veil, that I might rest in You. Saint Catherine, pray for us!

September 13 | *St. John Chrysostom*

St. John was the great patriarch of Constantinople whose eloquent sermons earned him the moniker "Golden Mouth," *Chrysostom.* In his *Commentary on the Gospel of Saint John,* he reflects on the alternating reverence and confidence with which the disciples approached Christ.

> "Just then his disciples came," — most timely, as the teaching was finished — "They marveled that he was talking with a woman, but none said, 'What do you wish?' or, 'Why are you talking with her?'" [Jn 4:27]
>
> At what did they marvel? At His lack of pride and exceeding humility. That esteemed as He was, He bore such lowliness of heart to talk with a poor woman and a Samaritan. Yet in their amazement, they did not ask Him the reason — so well were they taught to keep their station as disciples; so much did they fear and reverence Him. Though they did not yet hold the right view of Him, they heeded Him as one marvelous and paid Him much respect.
>
> Nevertheless, the disciples are frequently seen acting with boldness — such as when John lay upon His bosom, and ... when the sons of Zebedee entreated Him to set one of them on His right hand and on His left. Why, then, did they not question Him here? Because those other instances related to themselves, whereas this was of no great importance to them.[260]

Sacred Heart of Jesus, grant me an increase of reverential love, that I might confidently respond to Your charity. St. John Chrysostom, pray for us!

September 14 | *Feast of the Exaltation of the Holy Cross*

Today the Church celebrates the finding of the cross of Christ and the salvation wrought upon that holy rood. In this soliloquy, St. John of Ávila inquires of Jesus if He ever rested from His sufferings. Answering for Him, he concludes that Christ so wrapped himself in suffering that pain struck Him unto the Heart.

> Tell us, O beloved Jesus, by Your sweetest cross, was there a single day that You put off Your robe of suffering to wrap yourself in rest? Or did You ever put off that white garment, which so wore its way to Your very Heart, that You said: "My soul is sorrowful even unto death" (Mt 26:38).
>
> Ah no! You never rested; for You never ceased to love us, and therefore never ceased to suffer for us! … Your Blood flowed from Your head with the thorns, from Your face with the blows, from Your hands with the nails, from Your feet with another nail. …
>
> Looking upon You, He who loves himself and not You does You great wrong. If, when the soul sees You in such a plight, it flies from the sufferings that would make it resemble You, its love for You is imperfect; for it does not wish to be made like You, and therefore has but little desire to suffer for You.[261]

Sacred Heart of Jesus, break down my defenses and reign over me as king. St. John of Ávila, help us to embrace the cross!

September 15 | *Feast of Our Lady of Sorrows*

On this feast, the Church commemorates the incomparable sufferings and inestimable moral strength of the Blessed Virgin Mary. The visionary St. Bridget of Sweden vividly describes Mary's tremendous grief at the foot of the cross.

> Then His mother, seeing this, trembled all over, and would have fallen to the ground in her bitter anguish had she not been supported by the other women. …
>
> Finally, all standing around mockingly cried against His mother. Some said: "Mary, your Son is dead." … One running up with great fury, plunged a lance into His right side so powerfully that the lance seemed about to come forth in the opposite side of the Body. And when it was drawn out, a very river of Blood gushed impetuously from that wound, and the lance-head and part of the handle came forth blood-stained. Seeing this, His mother trembled so violently and with bitter groans that her countenance and manner showed that her soul was then pierced with a keen sword of grief.
>
> When the crowd had departed, His friends took down Our Lord, whom His pious mother received in her holy arms, and inclined Him, sitting on her knee, all wounded, torn, and livid. And then His dolorous mother wiped His whole Body and wounds with her veil, and closed His eyes, kissing them.[262]

Sacred Heart of Jesus, entrust Your mother to us once more. O Mary, Mother of Sorrows, come to our assistance when our hearts are heavy and laden with grief. Amen!

September 16 | *St. Cyprian of Carthage*

St. Cyprian of Carthage (c. 210–258), a North African bishop who advocated for the readmission of lapsed Catholics after a period of penance, here reflects on the Old Testament prophecies of water flowing from the desert rock, which he identifies as Christ.

> Moreover, it is again predicted and foretold that the Jews, if they should thirst and seek after Christ, should drink with us, that is, should attain the grace of baptism. "If they shall thirst," he says, "he shall lead them through the deserts, shall bring forth water for them out of the rock; the rock shall be cloven, and the water shall flow, and my people shall drink" [see Is 48:21].
>
> And this is fulfilled in the Gospel, when Christ, who is the rock, is cloven by a stroke of the spear in His passion, and who also, counselling what was before announced by the prophet, cries and says, "If any one thirst, let him come to me and drink. He who believes in me, as the Scripture has said, 'Out of his heart shall flow rivers of living water'" [Jn 7:37]. And that it might be more evident that the Lord is speaking there [of baptism] Scripture adds, "Now this he said about the Spirit, which those who believed in him were to receive" [Jn 7:39]. For by baptism, the Holy Spirit is received.[263]

Sacred Heart of Jesus, admit us to Your saving cup, which flows from Your cloven Heart. St. Cyprian, pray for us!

September 17 | *St. Hildegard von Bingen*

A Doctor of the Church, St. Hildegard von Bingen (1098–1179) was a Benedictine abbess, mystic and polymath. Her foremost work, *Scivias,* considers the synagogue personified, bringing the Messiah to birth. The synagogue prefigures the Blessed Virgin and the Church, all of whom, like beloved John, recline upon the Heart of the Lord.

> Concerning the synagogue as Mother of the Son of God in the flesh.
>
> This figure, which you see as a woman, pale from head to lap, is the synagogue, the very mother of the Incarnate Son of God. And from the first, when her sons arose with such strength as was in them, she saw the secrets of God, but darkly and not in their fullness. Yet is she not that rosy dawn which was clearly prophesied, but she perceives it from afar. With great wonder, she speaks thus of herself in the Song of Songs: "Who is that coming up from the wilderness, leaning on her beloved?" [8:5]. It is this new bride who raises herself by the multitude of her good works in the desert of unbelief, where men desiring laws rather than God's wisdom do but worship idols. But, rising to noble desire … she leans on her Spouse, the Son of God. For she is His portion, and she is joined to Him in shining virtues, and she overflows with the rich springs of the Word.[264]

Sacred Heart of Jesus, let all Christians lean upon Your Heart, multiplying works of mercy. Saint Hildegard, pray for us!

September 18

In *Steps of Ascension to God,* St. Robert Bellarmine (memorial, September 17), a Jesuit cardinal, contemplates the unimaginable rewards that await the just in heaven and resolves to walk in the way of virtue, patterned on the humble Heart of Jesus.

> The honor and glory of saints surpasses all eloquence, for upon the stage of the universe, every saint shall have the honor of divine applause and be presented with a victorious crown; [they shall be] seated on Christ's throne as copartners of His kingdom: For we read in Revelation, "He who conquers, I will grant him to sit with me on my throne, as I myself conquered and sat down with my Father on his throne" (Rv 3:21).
>
> What, my soul, have you to say to all this? Have you a mind to pursue childish diversions in building little houses of clay, and to disqualify yourself from the inheritance of that kingdom that shall never have an end? Will you be content [to delight] in brutish pleasures, you who are invited to angelic entertainments, and joys that cannot be expressed? Let Your mercy, blessed Lord, avert this from the soul of Your servant, but rather strike terror into my flesh, and let obedience to Thy laws become sweeter to me than honey, that by crucifying the flesh with the affections and lusts, I may boldly aspire to those spiritual and everlasting delights of Your paradise.[265]

Sacred Heart of Jesus, pour into my wounds Your mercy, and unite my heart to Yours! St. Robert Bellarmine, pray for us!

September 19 | *St. Émilie de Rodat*

St. Émilie de Rodat (1787–1852) founded the Sisters of the Holy Family of Villefranche in the wake of the French Revolution. In the following letter, she recommends the Sacred Heart of Jesus to her religious sisters as the remedy for human frailty.

> Gazing upon our Divine Spouse, it is impossible to lose heart. Frequently return to Him in your thoughts; in Him is the remedy for all our ills. It is, above all, in His Divine Heart that your confidence must be reanimated. This Heart so affectionate, which burns with such intense love for us, is our support and help in all times and circumstances. All of your actions ought to be carried out with the intense desire to respond to His love.

In another letter, Saint Émilie teaches that the pursuit of Truth leads to the Heart of God.

> I am very satisfied, my dearest sister, that you love the Truth; this is the way of finding the Heart of God. Seek it well then, this Heart, where we ought to find our peace and our only rest. Mother has told me that you have prepared the children for First Communion; I congratulate you. What is there more blessed than making known and loved the most tender of fathers? Let us be fervent ourselves so as to ignite in hearts the fire of divine love.[266]

Sacred Heart of Jesus, our confidence and love, sustain us in prayer, inspiring in us new devotion. St. Émilie de Rodat, ardent in love, pray for us!

September 20

Auctor beate sæculi is an eighteenth-century hymn of unknown authorship, which was included in the Roman Missal for the feast of the Sacred Heart. This sweeping hymn surveys the mystery of creation, the fall of man, and the restoration of all things in Christ. In this grand scheme, love is shown to be the motivating reason for each mystery. Love alone brought the Son of God down from heaven, and love permitted His Heart to be opened upon the cross.

Blessed Creator of the world,
Christ, the Redeemer of all,
light from the Father's light,
true God from God most true.

Love compelled You
to assume a mortal Body,
that the New Adam restore
what the man of old had lost.

That kindly love of the Creator,
who formed earth, sea, and stars,
pitying the sins of our fathers,
set free our bonds and fetters.

Let not Your Heart restrain
the power of its love prodigious!
Let flow that fount for the nations,
granting gracious pardon!

Transpierced by the lance,
suffering wound most cruel,
that corruption be cleansed
by streams of Blood and water.

Glory to the Father and the Son
and to the Holy Spirit,
who gloriously rule
and reign without end.[267]

Sacred Heart of Jesus, You join yourself to man to deify his mortal flesh. Restore Your blessed creation, O Lord, with Your abundant grace. Sacred Heart of Jesus, make us one in Holy Communion!

September 21

The writings of Thomas à Kempis gained worldwide popularity for their simple, yet profound, reflections on the spiritual life. In his *Meditations on the Life of Christ*, Thomas contemplates the fearful death of Christ and finds light in that hour of darkness. For upon Mount Calvary, the Holy Heart of Jesus was torn open, letting flow a fount of redemption.

> Lord Jesus Christ, unfailing fountain of love and grace, I bless and give You thanks for the cruel piercing of Your most sacred side, which You received after Your life had departed. For then, O Holiest of the Holy, You were so violently smitten and pierced in the right side by one of the soldiers that the iron point, penetrating inwardly, reached Your tender Heart. From the wide wound came forth a most saving fountain of water and Blood, which by its sprinkling, the whole world might be saved. O sacred and wondrous flow of the Precious Blood of Christ, pouring forth from His right side as He slept upon the cross for the redemption of man! O bright and grateful flow of blessed water, issuing from the inmost place of the Savior to cleanse us from all our sins![268]

Sacred Heart of Jesus, let the floodwaters of salvation that flow from Your side reach every corner of the earth. Sacred Heart of Jesus, I trust in You!

September 22 | *St. Thomas of Villanova*

St. Thomas of Villanova (1488–1555), a Spanish Augustinian bishop, here reflects on God's prodigious mercy in condescending to dwell within the human soul. Delighting in His creatures, He lays his Heart near them.

> O immensity of the soul, where God not only finds ample space to rest, but to walk about! What are, in effect, the powers of the soul if not the place where the Lord goes to walk? Every time that you sense those good desires and movements of holy affection within yourself, or the sting of repentance or fervent devotion, recognize within yourself the footsteps of God, the stirrings of the Holy Spirit who walks in His temple. …
>
> You do not disdain, O my Lord, to enter into the poor and abject dwellings of our souls! You do not disdain to live in us! Oh! What might we return to You, Lord, for so great a benefit! "What is man that You should magnify him? Or why do You lay Your Heart so near to his heart" [see Jb 7:17], when You are served by so many thousands of powers and principalities; when You are enthroned upon the cherubim? Not only do You not scorn our dwelling, but there You find Your glory, saying, "My delight is to be with the sons of men" (see Prv 8:31).[269]

Sacred Heart of Jesus, walk in the garden of my soul. Bring forth the flowers of virtue, and accept their harvest as a gift. Saint Thomas, pray for us!

September 23

In his *Commentary on Saint John's Gospel,* Cornelius à Lapide ponders the moment when Saint Thomas beholds the opened side of Christ, crying out in astonishment, "My Lord and my God!" (Jn 20:28).

> *Thomas answered and said unto Him, "My Lord and My God!"* Note the words, "My Lord." For though Christ is the Lord and God of all, yet He is especially mine, having as the Good Shepherd sought me as a sheep that was lost, and I love and venerate Him in return from my inmost soul, as specially my Lord and my God. You, Oh Jesus, are my God and my Lord, because by these Your wounds, which I have now touched and know to be most real, You have procured and obtained for me that faith with which I believe that You have really risen, and this hope of obtaining grace and glory through the merit of Your wounds, and such fervent charity as to love You most ardently as my God and Lord, and to offer and devote myself entirely to You as Your servant forever, so as henceforth to wish to do nothing, but that which pleases, lauds, and glorifies You. Would that I could lay open and breathe forth this my heartfelt feeling to the whole world! Would that I could proclaim and set forth to all the world this my faith, hope, and love towards You![270]

Sacred Heart of Jesus, by Your holy wound, impart to us an unshakable faith, unwavering hope, and abundant charity. Saint Thomas, pray for us!

September 24

In this "Consecration to the Sacred Heart of Jesus," Bl. Mary of the Sacred Heart expresses her desire to become a victim, utterly consumed by the flames of Christ's love.

> My most loving Jesus, I consecrate myself today anew, without reserve, to Thy Divine Heart. To Thee I consecrate my body with all its senses, my soul with all its faculties, and my whole being. To Thee I consecrate all my thoughts, words, and works; all my sufferings and labors; all my hopes, consolations, and joys; and chiefly my poor heart that I may love but Thee, and be consumed as a victim in the flames of Thy love.
>
> Accept, O Jesus, the desire that I have to console Thy Divine Heart, and to belong to Thee forever. … In Thy hands I lay all my cares, and principally that of my eternal salvation. I promise to love Thee and to honor Thee until the last moment of my life, and to propagate as far as I am able, with the help of Thy divine grace, the devotion to Thy Most Sacred Heart. …
>
> Grant me the grace to find in Thy Most Sacred Heart my dwelling place; there, I desire to pass each day of my life; there I wish to breathe forth my last sigh. Make also my heart Thy abode, the place of Thy repose. Amen.[271]

Sacred Heart of Jesus, I give You all. Claim everything for yourself, granting me only a place in Your Heart. Blessed Mary, pray for us!

September 25 | *St. Vincent Strambi*

In his meditations on the Precious Blood of Christ, Saint Vincent Strambi, a Passionist bishop, contemplates the depths of God's love for man. Inexhaustible, this Precious Blood has its source in the unfathomable depths of the Sacred Heart, which is rich in mercy.

> To further ignite our hearts with this blessed flame of love, consider who shed Jesus of His Precious Blood. Ah! Learn it well: He poured it out for us sinners, offering it all for our salvation. The most loving Heart of Jesus is, according to the prophet Joel, a perpetual fount, from which ever flows this Blood of charity unto the consummation of the ages. On the judgment seat of the cross, the debt contracted by all the offspring of Adam against the sovereign justice was paid by Jesus Christ, of which was never closed nor will ever be closed, but at every moment remains opened in the wounded side of the Savior. Nor is this fount exhausted by the multitude of its reception, because it comes from that Heart, which is *dives in misericordia.* And however much it dispenses, the more abundantly it remains. …
>
> Ah! Ignite our hearts once more with love! And love this Jesus, who so greatly loved us with a passionate love, uniting us to His sweetest Heart by means of this adorable Blood. Let us again say: *Quis nos separabit a caritate Christi?*[272]

Sacred Heart of Jesus, wholly possess us, making us to partake in Your exchange of love. St. Vincent Strambi, pray for us!

September 26

In the following commentary, Fr. Juan Eusebio Nieremberg (1595–1658) provides an allegorical interpretation, in the tradition of the Church Fathers, of the piercing of Christ's side. Identifying the heart of man as the seat of unruly passions, he concludes that the piercing of Christ's Heart symbolizes the purification of the human heart from sin.

> The Heart and Side of Jesus Pierced
>
> That part of man which is most ill-regulated is the heart: For this reason, it was fitting that, in order to purify it, the breast of Jesus should be wounded with a spear — the point of which pierced His very Heart, burning with love for God and for man. O my Savior, Your Heart was already wounded with the darts of love. What need was there that it should receive this second wound? O infinite charity of Jesus Christ, for which life was not enough! But which He desired to manifest to us even after His death by opening to us His Heart. … Ah, my soul! Since the door is open, enter into this hidden chamber of love. The beloved disciple has told us that Jesus loved us even to the end [see Jn 13:1]. He has done so, even beyond the end by giving us His Heart after death itself. … See, the breast of Jesus is laid open, His Heart is torn asunder, and yet we would keep our will unbroken![273]

Sacred Heart of Jesus, wound me with Your tender words, capturing my affections and my will. Have mercy on us!

September 27 | *St. Vincent de Paul*

On a voyage, St. Vincent de Paul was captured by Turkish pirates and sold into slavery. Having converted his captors, the priest returned to France to care for the incarcerated and impoverished. Here Saint Vincent ponders the loving condescension of God.

> O my Jesus, tell us what induced You to descend from heaven to share in the malediction of earth? What excess of love forced You to lower yourself to our level and to suffer the infamous death of the cross? What excess of charity made You expose yourself to all our miseries: to take upon the form of a sinner, to lead a life of suffering, and to undergo so shameful a death? Where else can charity so admirable, so excessive, be found? None but the Son of God is capable of it, and none but Him has had such a love for His creatures as to leave His throne of glory to come and assume a Body subject to the infirmities and miseries of this life. …
>
> O had we but a spark of the sacred fire that consumed the Heart of Jesus Christ, would we remain with our arms crossed and abandon those whom we could assist? … Those who have true charity within show it externally. It is the property of fire to give heat and light, and it is characteristic of love to be communicative.[274]

Sacred Heart of Jesus, form me in Your humility, making me meek of heart. Saint Vincent, obtain for us love of neighbor!

September 28

Jesuit priest St. Francis Borgia (1510–1572; memorial, September 30) here instructs those who find themselves distant from God to meditate on the love of the Sacred Heart.

> When your soul feels separated from God, and sighs [for deliverance] from the dangers of this state, consider what the Heart of Jesus suffered when, in His infinite charity, He asked of His Eternal Father that we might be united to Him, using these wonderful words: "That they may all be one; even as you, Father, are in me, and I in you, that they also may be in us" [Jn 17:21]. Who, then, is so negligent and so little desirous for his own good as to refuse the precious manna and inestimable treasures of grace that are offered to him? Who will be so ungrateful toward Jesus Christ not to testify his love for Him by the practice of at least a part of these exercises that we have proposed; exercises which are excellent, so full of love, and so necessary to salvation? O, devout soul, deprive not yourself of so great a blessing: Consider that what God asks of you is little in comparison to what He himself promises in return. He asks only those things that you are obliged to do every day and which are common to everyone. And He asks them from you only that they may not be lost to yourself.[275]

Sacred Heart of Jesus, wash me in Your Blood divine, renewing me in grace. St. Francis Borgia, pray for us!

September 29

St. Gregory the Illuminator (c. 257 – 331) is credited with converting Armenia to Christ. The ancient Armenian liturgy contains seven different hymns, particular to each day of the week, which are to be sung after the elevation of the Eucharist and before Holy Communion. The hymn for Friday fittingly sings of the blood and water that flowed from the side of the Savior.

> O Lord Jesus Christ, true and head cornerstone, Thou, who art glorified by the song of the heavenly host; Thou, who on the cross didst come to pour out from Thy sacred side the immortal stream which taketh away the sin of the world: Grant that we who thirst for Thee may drink from this sacred fount, and have mercy upon us.

Sacred Heart of Jesus, in a heart-to-heart embrace, cleanse me of all sin, and fill me with Your Spirit. St. Gregory the Illuminator, pray for us!

September 30 | *Saint Jerome*

Saint Jerome produced a trustworthy Latin translation of the Bible and promoted monasticism in the West. Here, he provides a gloss on the Song of Songs, praising virginity as that which charms God's Heart.

> On hearing this, the bride disclosed the mysteries of chastity: "My beloved is mine and I am his, he pastures his flock among the lilies" [Sg 2:16]; that is, among the pure virgin bands. Flee, He says, from the lion's den, flee from the pride of devils, that when you have been consecrated to Me, I may be able to say to you, "Thou hast wounded my heart, my sister, my spouse, thou hast wounded my heart with one of thy eyes, and with one hair of thy neck" [Sg 4:9, Douay-Rheims Bible]. What He says is something like this — I do not reject marriage: You have a second eye, the left, which I have given to you on account of the weakness of those who cannot see the right. But I am pleased with the right eye of virginity, and if it be blinded, the whole body is in darkness. And that we might not think He had in view carnal love and bodily marriage, He at once excludes this meaning by saying, "You have ravished My Heart, My bride, My sister." The name *sister* excludes all suspicion of unhallowed love.[276]

Sacred Heart of Jesus, make of me a sealed fountain, a garden enclosed, that I may be wholly dedicated to You. Saint Jerome, pray for us!

October

October 1 | *St. Thérèse of Lisieux*

Doctor of the Church St. Thérèse of Lisieux was a French Carmelite nun whose hidden life of prayer culminated in her Little Way — a spirituality in which "little souls" would exchange their sins and weakness for the mercy and strength of God. In her encouraging letter to a missionary religious, Saint Thérèse enunciates the key themes of her spirituality.

> You may well sing of the mercies of God! They shine forth in you with splendor. You love Saint Augustine and St. Mary Magdalene, those souls to whom many sins were forgiven because they loved much. I love them too. When I see Mary Magdalene come forth before all Simon's guests to wash with her tears her Master's feet — those feet that for the first time she touches — I feel her heart has fathomed that abyss of love and mercy, the Heart of Jesus; and I feel, too, that not only was He willing to forgive, but even liberally to dispense the favors of a divine and intimate friendship, and to raise her to the loftiest heights of prayer.
>
> My brother, since I also have been given to understand the love of the Heart of Jesus, I confess that all fear has been driven from mine. … When a soul with childlike trust casts her faults into love's all-devouring furnace, how shall they escape being utterly consumed?[277]

Sacred Heart of Jesus, may Your tender compassion, made visible in Your wounds, drive out all my fear. St. Thérèse, obtain for us unfailing love!

October 2

Bl. Raymond of Capua was a Dominican minister general and spiritual director to St. Catherine of Siena. In his biography of Saint Catherine, he recounts the following vision in which Christ clothed her with a garment, drawn from the depths of His Heart.

> The following night, while Catherine was praying, [Our Lord] appeared to her under the figure of the destitute man, holding in His hand the garment that she had given Him, richly embroidered with pearls and glittering with precious stones. "Beloved daughter," the Lord said to her, "do you recognize this garment? … Yesterday, you gave Me this article with great love; your charity clothed Me and preserved Me from ignominy. Now, I will bestow on you, from My own Body, a garment that shall be invisible to men, but perceptible to you, because it will preserve from cold — both your soul and your body, until the day in which I will clothe you with honor and glory before the saints and angels."
>
> And immediately, He drew from the wound of His adorable Heart a vestment tinged with the purple hue of His Precious Blood and beaming with light. He put it on her with His own sacred hands, saying to her, "I give you on earth this vestment with its exclusive right, as a symbol and pledge of the hope of glory that shall be yours in heaven!"[278]

Sacred Heart of Jesus, surround us with light, driving out the darkness of deception and evil. Bl. Raymond of Capua, pray for us!

October 3 | *Bl. Columba Marmion*

Benedictine abbot Bl. Columba Marmion integrated patristic, systematic, and spiritual theology into his writings. In this passage from *Christ the Life of the Soul,* Marmion speaks of the Eucharist as the last testament of the Sacred Heart, which manifests Christ's tender love for man.

> This is an ineffable subject. Even the priest, who makes the Eucharistic Sacrifice the center and sun of his life, is powerless to put into words the marvels that the love of Christ Jesus has there gathered up. All that man, a mere creature, can say of this mystery that has come forth from the Heart of God, remains so far beneath the reality that … it is as if we had said nothing. There is no subject the priest loves more and at the same time dreads more, to speak of; so high and holy is this mystery.
>
> Let us ask Faith to enlighten us. … And above all let us believe, as Saint John says, in love. *Et nos credidimus caritati.* Our Lord willed to institute this Sacrament at the moment when, by His passion, He was about to give us the greatest testimony of His love for us, and He has willed that it should be perpetuated among us "in commemoration of Him." It is like His last thought for us and the testament of His Sacred Heart: *Hoc facite in meam commemorationem.*[279]

Sacred Heart of Jesus, come to my heart, rest in me, and speak Your words of everlasting life. Bl. Columba Marmion, pray for us!

October 4 | *St. Francis of Assisi*

St. Francis of Assisi (c. 1181–1226) adapted the religious life of prayer and service by bringing it outside of monastery walls. A stigmatic, mystic, and radical ascetic, Saint Francis here begs to be consumed by the fire of God's love, that he might be detached from all created things.

> I beseech You, O Lord, that the fiery and sweet strength of Your love may absorb my soul from all things that are under heaven, that I may die for love of Your love as You did deign to die for love of my love.
>
> You are holy, Lord God, who alone works wonders. You are strong. You are great. You are most high. You are the Almighty King, You, Holy Father, King of heaven and earth. You are the Lord God, triune and one; all good. You are good, all good, highest good, Lord God living and true. You are charity, love. You are wisdom. You are humility. You are patience. You are security. You are quietude. You are joy and gladness. You are justice and temperance. You are all riches to suffice. You are beauty. You are meekness. You are protector. You are guardian and defender. You are strength. You are refreshment. You are our hope. You are our faith. You are our great sweetness. You are our eternal life, great and admirable Lord, God Almighty, merciful Savior.[280]

Sacred Heart of Jesus, Holy God, unite us in Your Heart, granting us everlasting life. St. Francis of Assisi, pray for us!

October 5 | *St. Faustina Kowalska*

St. Faustina Kowalska (1905–1938) was a Polish nun whose visions of Divine Mercy complement the Sacred Heart devotion as they emphasize its streams of Blood and Water. In this excerpt from her spiritual diary, Jesus speaks of the infinite compassion that flows from His Heart.

> My daughter, know that My Heart is mercy itself. From this sea of mercy, graces flow out upon the whole world. No soul that has approached Me has ever gone away unconsoled. All misery gets buried in the depths of My mercy, and every saving and sanctifying grace flows from this fountain. My daughter, I desire that your heart be an abiding place of My mercy. I desire that this mercy flow out upon the whole world through your heart. Let no one who approaches you go away without that trust in My mercy which I so ardently desire for souls. Pray as much as you can for the dying. By your entreaties, obtain for them trust in My mercy, because they have most need of trust, and have it the least. Be assured that the grace of eternal salvation for certain souls in their final moments depends on your prayer. You know the whole abyss of My mercy, so draw upon it for yourself and especially for poor sinners. Sooner would heaven and earth turn into nothingness than would My mercy not embrace a trusting soul.[281]

Sacred Heart of Jesus, inundate my heart with the waves of Your compassion, consuming me in love. Saint Faustina, pray for us!

October 6 | *St. Bruno of Cologne*

St. Bruno of Cologne (c. 1030–1101) established the Carthusians with a group of like-minded companions. In the following reflection, Saint Bruno describes the benefits of the contemplative life and its transformative effect on the heart. Purity of heart, he explains, captivates the Divine Heart.

> As to the blessing and sweetness of solitude and silence, let those who have chosen them tell their charm, for only those who have experienced these joys can speak of them worthily. It is there that generous men can enter into themselves, can dwell with God alone in the very center of their souls, can cultivate the germs of every virtue, and enjoy a foretaste of paradise. It is there that we can acquire that purity of heart and serenity of expression which wounds the Heart of the Divine Spouse, and unites us to Him in the pure love which contemplates God alone. It is there that perfect rest accompanies labor, and action hurts not the peace of the soul. It is there that in return for their brave conflicts, God gives to His stout warriors the reward they have desired — a peace which the world knows not, and the joy of the Holy Spirit. …
>
> O my brother, fear not then to fly from the turmoil and misery of the world. Leave the storms that rage without, to shelter yourself in this safe haven.[282]

Sacred Heart of Jesus, let me behold Your silent gaze in perfect contemplation, which contains an ocean of delights. St. Bruno of Cologne, pray for us!

October 7 | *Feast of Our Lady of the Rosary*

Today, the Church honors the intercessory power of the Blessed Virgin Mary through the recitation of the Rosary. Here, John Paul II teaches that the Incarnation afforded Christ a divine and human Heart with which to love man.

> Meditation on the mysteries of Christ is proposed in the Rosary by means of a method designed to assist in their assimilation. … If this repetition is considered superficially, there could be a temptation to see the Rosary as a dry and boring exercise. It is quite another thing, however, when the Rosary is thought of as an outpouring of that love. …
>
> In Christ, God has truly assumed a "heart of flesh." Not only does God have a Divine Heart, rich in mercy and in forgiveness, but also a human Heart, capable of all the stirrings of affection. If we needed evidence for this from the Gospel, we could easily find it in the touching dialogue between Christ and Peter after the Resurrection: "Simon, son of John, do you love me?" Three times this question is put to Peter, and three times he gives the reply: "Lord, you know that I love you" (see Jn 21:15–17). Over and above the specific meaning of this passage, so important for Peter's mission, none can fail to recognize the beauty of this triple repetition. … To understand the Rosary, one has to enter into the psychological dynamic proper to love.[283]

Sacred Heart of Jesus, grant me the protection of Your Mother and her guidance to Your Heart.

October 8

During his youth, Bl. Bartolo Longo (1841–1926; memorial, October 5) loathed the Church and experimented in the dark arts. Even after his conversion to Christ, the sins of his former life nearly drove him to despair. Working out his salvation by promoting the Holy Rosary, Blessed Bartolo wrote "An Act of Reparation to the Expiring Heart of Jesus," proposing reparation to the Heart of Jesus.

> O rent and meek Heart of my Lord, accept I beseech You, in compensation for the three hours when You were plunged into the tempest of the deep sea of desolation, this hour of prayer, and this day dedicated to Your exceedingly afflicted Heart. Accept this Holy Sacrifice and this Holy Communion as a reparation for all the bitterness You felt in the garden, when You foresaw all my sins. Accept all the sorrows, vexations, and even the indifferent acts, not only of this day, but of my whole life. … When shall I obey You without inconstancy? When shall I sincerely say to You in every circumstance: "Thy will be done and not mine"? Place me more inwardly in this Divine Heart, that I may better understand and love You. O Heart inflamed with the greatest charity, kindle in my frigid heart the fire of Your love; that I may worthily receive You, and abide with You. … So be it.[284]

Sacred Heart of Jesus, may I never abandon Your side, but ever keep watch, making reparation for the coldness of mankind. Bl. Bartolo Longo, pray for us!

October 9 | *St. John Henry Newman*

St. John Henry Newman was an Anglican priest who entered the Catholic Church in 1845, astonishing his English contemporaries. His spirit of piety is apparent in the following meditation on the Sacred Heart, which he praises for its divine-human perfections.

> My God, my Savior, I adore Thy Sacred Heart, for that Heart is the seat and source of all Thy tenderest human affections for us sinners. It is the instrument and organ of Thy love. It did beat for us. It yearned over us. It ached for us, and for our salvation. … O most sacred symbol and Sacrament of Love, divine and human, in its fullness, Thou did save me by Thy divine strength and Thy human affection, and then at length by that wonder-working Blood wherewith Thou did overflow. … O my God, when Thou do condescend to suffer me to receive Thee, to eat and drink Thee, and Thou for a while take up Thy abode within me, O make my heart beat with Thy Heart. Purify it of all that is earthly, all that is proud and sensual, all that is hard and cruel, of all perversity, of all disorder, of all deadness. So fill it with Thee, that neither the events of the day, nor the circumstances of the time may have power to ruffle it; but that in Thy love and Thy fear it may have peace.[285]

Sacred Heart of Jesus, reveal to me the mystery of Your mercy in the Eucharist. Saint John Henry, pray for us!

October 10

Fr. Franciscus Lucas Brugensis (c. 1548–1619) was a Dutch priest and theologian. His meditations on the Gospel of John consider the twofold significance of the piercing of Christ's side: it confirms Christ's death, while mystically revealing the life-giving gift of His Heart.

> One of the soldiers, thrusting his spear first into the side, then into the lung, and then the pericardium, at last pierced the Heart. . . . He did this partly through impulse, partly as a precaution — a precaution because, as Saint Cyprian says, doubting that He was dead, he wished to make sure of it. And in case He was not dead, he meant to put Him to death by this thrust, which went to the Heart. . . . In this we must admire the divine providence which wished, on the one hand, to make certain and evident that Jesus was dead, and on the other, to make strikingly manifest the immense love of Jesus Christ for us, in that He spared no part of himself, but sacrificed everything for us. Until then, the Heart of Jesus, so far as its substance was concerned, had not been touched. In order, then, to show that for our redemption He had not spared the principal part of His Body, He allowed His Heart to be wounded, so as to convince us that He had given himself wholly to us.[286]

Sacred Heart of Jesus, accept my living and my dying as a sacrificial gift, offered in thanksgiving for Your paschal mystery. I love You!

October 11 | *Pope St. John XXIII*

In *Princips Pastorum,* Pope John XXIII (1881–1963) voices his solidarity with Christian missionaries undergoing persecution and assures them that they are dearly beloved of the Sacred Heart.

> Many dioceses and Christian communities in mission territories are being harassed by difficulties and sometimes even by active persecution. We therefore exhort everyone to persevere courageously in the battle which he is fighting for God's cause: the pastors who are giving their children in God the example of a faith which does not falter even in mortal danger; and the faithful who are being so grievously tried by adversity and are therefore so dear to the Sacred Heart of Jesus, who promised beatitude and abundant rewards to those who suffer persecution for justice's sake. God, in His inscrutable but always merciful designs, will sustain them with heavenly favors, consolations, and joy. The whole Church is united with the persecuted in a communion of prayer and sorrow, with the certainty that final victory will be hers.
>
> From the bottom of our heart, we call down upon the missions the worthy protection of their patrons and martyrs, and, first and foremost, the intercession of Mary, Mother and Queen of the Missions. With the greatest affection we impart to each one of you, venerable brethren, and to all those who in any way contribute to the propagation of God's kingdom, our apostolic blessing.[287]

Sacred Heart of Jesus, enlighten me with the light of faith, and drive out every fear. Pope St. John XXIII, obtain for us missionary hearts!

October 12

In the following exhortation, St. Claude de la Colombiére recommends that Christians lock themselves within the Heart of Jesus and there be molded after it; for it is a school of love.

> How happy it would be if we could save our enemies by our prayers! What joy and triumph would there be in heaven! How great would be their gratitude! It will be great in those who are saved by their friends, but to what a height will it not reach in those who owe their salvation to the persons they have persecuted!
>
> "Learn of Me, not how to make the world and all visible things, but something far more divine." The Heart of Jesus must be our school if we would learn this lesson; let us make our abode in it during this Lent; let us study its movements, and try to conform our own hearts to it.
>
> Yes, O divine Jesus! I will dwell in Your Heart, and there pour out all my bitterness; it will soon be consumed. I have no fear that impatience should come to assail me in that retreat. There I will study to practice silence, resignation to Your will, an invincible constancy. I will thank You daily for my crosses and ask pardon for those who persecute me. I will strive to acquire patience ... for the love of You. Amen.[288]

Sacred Heart of Jesus, constant in love, remove all obstacles to Your grace that I might imitate Your mercy. Saint Claude, pray for us!

October 13

In *A Little Book of Eternal Wisdom,* Bl. Henry Suso enumerates the sorrows of Jesus and Mary, whose hearts were pierced on Mount Calvary. Marveling at such sacrificial love, Blessed Henry prays that he might be bathed in the Blood and water flowing from the Sacred Heart.

> Ah, my Lord! Remember: (1) How the sharp spear was thrust into Your divine side; (2) how the purple Blood ran out; (3) how the living water gushed forth; (4) and with what bitter toil You did garner me up; (5) and how generously You ransomed me; loving Lord! May Your deep wounds shelter me from all my enemies; Your living water cleanse me from all my sins; Your rose-colored Blood adorn me with all graces and virtues. Tender Lord! May the prize You so bitterly won bind me to You; the ransom You so freely paid unite me eternally with You!
>
> Oh, you chosen consolation of all sinners! Oh, sweet queen! Remember today: (1) How you did stand under the cross, and how, as your Son hung dead above you, you cast on Him many a look of misery; (2) how affectionately His arms were received by you; (3) with what fidelity pressed to your Blood-stained face; (4) his bleeding wounds, His dead and ghastly features, were by you kissed again and again; (5) how many a death-wound your heart then received.[289]

Sacred Heart of Jesus, let those twin streams of love that flowed from Your Heart fall upon us. Bl. Henry Suso, pray for us!

October 14

St. Gerard Majella (1726–1755; memorial, October 16) was a Redemptorist brother known for his childlike simplicity and obedience. In the following letter, Saint Gerard commends his religious sisters to the Heart of Jesus, beseeching them to ever dwell therein. In his view, consecrated life is a perpetual abiding in the Heart of Jesus, wherein one is molded according to the divine will.

> O my divine love! Be always in the hearts of these Your beloved spouses! … Oh, how greatly I desire that You and Your very good sisters should dwell in the pierced and open side of Jesus Christ and in the sorrowful heart of the Blessed Virgin! It is there we can find all sweetness and rest.
>
> My sister, let us conform to the divine will. The true love of God consists in entire submission to God and His holy will. Let us take care never voluntarily to commit a fault; such faults afford God the greatest displeasure.
>
> Believe me dear sister, in Jesus Christ, I do not cease to pray to the Lord for you and your whole community, that it be His holy will to make you His true spouses. I say it in all truth, I think of you at every visit to the Sacred Heart. I find you all enrolled in His most holy side.[290]

Sacred Heart of Jesus, You watch over us at every step, providing for our needs. Guide us on our pilgrimage to heaven, for we surrender ourselves to You! St. Gerard Majella, pray for us!

October 15 | *St. Teresa of Ávila*

A mystic and Doctor of the Church, St. Teresa of Ávila returned the Carmelite Order to its ascetic roots. In this letter to Bishop Alona Valasquez, Teresa offers a guided meditation on the passion of Christ, styling the pierced Heart of Jesus as Noah's ark.

> Behold His head crowned with thorns, and then consider the dullness and blindness of our understanding. Beg of Our Lord that He would be pleased to open the eyes of the soul, and enlighten our understanding with the light of faith, that so we may with humility learn who God is, and what *we* are. …
>
> View His feet nailed, considering the diligence with which He seeks us, and the sloth with which we endeavor to seek Him. Cast your eyes on that side opened with a lance, which shows us His Heart, and the intense love wherewith He has loved us, when He was pleased to become our harbor and refuge, that so by this gate we might enter the ark, when the deluge of our temptations and tribulations shall come. Beg of Him, that as He was pleased to have His side opened in testimony of the love He bore us, so He would command *ours* also to be opened, that we might make our necessities known, and obtain a remedy for them.[291]

Sacred Heart of Jesus, as You impressed Your sacred image upon the shroud, imprint Your wounds upon my soul, conforming it to Your selfless love. St. Teresa of Ávila, pray for us!

October 16 | *St. Margaret Mary Alacoque*

St. Margaret Mary Alacoque's extraordinary visions of the Sacred Heart of Jesus inspired its contemporary devotion, and in 1675 Jesus requested the establishment of the feast of the Sacred Heart so mankind might return love for love.

> I received from God the most special graces of His love. I felt moved with the desire of making Him some return, and giving Him love for love, and He said to me, "You cannot make Me a more acceptable return of love than by doing what I have so often asked of you." Then, showing me His Divine Heart, He said, "Behold this Heart which has so loved men, that it has spared nothing, even to exhausting and consuming itself to prove to them its love. In return, I receive from the greater number nothing but ingratitude, contempt, irreverence, sacrilege, and coldness in this Sacrament of My love. But what I feel still more is that there are hearts consecrated to Me who use Me thus. Therefore, I ask of you that the first Friday after the Octave of the Blessed Sacrament shall be kept as a special feast in honor of My Heart. … My Heart shall shed in abundance the influence of its divine love on all those who shall thus honor it or cause it to be so honored."[292]

Sacred Heart of Jesus, grant us a spirit of devotion, that we may worthily approach the mystery of the altar with reverence and love. Saint Margaret Mary pray for us!

October 17 | *St. Ignatius of Antioch*

St. Ignatius of Antioch (c. 35–c. 107) is believed to have succeeded St. Peter the Apostle as the bishop of Antioch, an office he carried out until his martyrdom in 107. His seven letters, composed shortly before his execution, burn with an ardent love of the Incarnate Lord and proclaim His Eucharistic Body to be "love incorruptible." Rejecting all material pleasures, Saint Ignatius contents himself with that living water, of which Christ had prophesied: "He who believes in me, as the Scripture has said, 'Out of his heart shall flow rivers of living water'" (Jn 7:38).

> Use not the words "Jesus Christ" and yet desire the world. Let not envy make its dwelling within you. Even though I should come and entreat you, harken not even unto me, but rather trust these words which I write to you. For I write unto you in the midst of life, enamored of death. My Love has been crucified, and there is not within me any fire of earthly desire, but only water that lives in me and speaks in me, saying from within: "Come to the Father." I have no pleasure in the food of corruption nor in the pleasures of this material life. I desire God's bread, which is the Flesh of Christ, who is the seed of David, and for drink I desire His Blood, which is love incorruptible.[293]

Sacred Heart of Jesus, crucify my desire for this world, that I may thirst for You alone. St. Ignatius of Antioch, pray for us!

October 18

St. Peter of Alcántara (1499–1562; memorial, October 19) was a Franciscan priest whose heroic practices of abstinence and penance surprised even St. Teresa of Ávila. In this excerpt from his *Rule of Life,* Saint Peter asks Christians to keep watch with Christ.

> In all times and places, secretly have recourse to the Blessed Jesus lodged in your heart, and never let His Incarnation and passion depart from your memory; for however much you exercise yourself in this holy contemplation, that much more sweetness you will find therein, and more consolations and favors shall you receive from God, which human prudence can neither relish nor attain to. And you shall experience in your heart a continual burning of the fire of charity and vehement desire to be freed from this world and enjoy God who lives and reigns, world without end. Amen.

In *Pax Animæ,* Saint Peter says peace of soul is found in God alone.

> When all other things grow bitter and distasteful, and God alone is your delight, then shall you possess true comfort. Address all your miseries to Our dear Lord, who is the mediator between God and man. Love Him, open to Him your heart, and communicate to Him all its secrets without the least fear or reserve. He will satisfy all your doubts. [294]

Sacred Heart of Jesus, grant that we may grow in dependence on You, who alone can bring us peace. St. Peter of Alcántara, pray for us!

October 19 | *Feast of the North American Martyrs*

Today the Church honors those early North American missionaries — Sts. Jean de Brèbeuf, Isaac Jogues, and other Jesuit martyrs. Here, an anonymous missionary describes the glories of his vocation and the conformation of his heart to that of God.

> One of the thoughts that weighs most upon those who are so fortunate as to serve God among these forests is their unworthiness of their apostolic and so-exalted calling, and that they have so few of the virtues worthy of a noble work. He who sees New France only through the eyes of the flesh and of nature, sees only forests and crosses; but he who looks upon these with the eyes of grace and of a noble vocation, sees only God, the virtues, and the graces. My God! How good it is to be in the place where God has placed us by His grace; truly I have found here what I had hoped for, a heart in harmony with God's Heart, which seeks God alone. …
>
> [Yet I] cannot forbid one thought which presses upon my heart. *Cupio impendi, et superimpendi pro vobis*: Poor New France, I desire to sacrifice myself for your welfare; and though it should cost me a thousand lives, if thus I can aid in saving a single soul, I shall be too happy, and my life will be well spent.[295]

Sacred Heart of Jesus, grant me faith and perseverance in every trial, seeking only the glory of Your Kingdom. North American Martyrs, pray for us!

October 20

Founder of the Passionists St. Paul of the Cross (1694–1775; memorial, October 19) sought to combine the contemplative life with apostolic service. Here, he offers what might be called a theology of the Sacred Heart, teaching that the Christian heart must be offered and sacrificed in and through Christ's own Heart.

> I wish your heart to be more and more consumed as a holocaust to the Supreme Good, in that *sancta sanctorum,* the Sacred Heart of Jesus, plunging the ashes of the holocaust into the boundless ocean of divine charity. Now more than ever, it is the time to die to everything that is not good, to converse with greater love alone with the Supreme Good. What do you want with creatures? Remain alone as much as possible, hidden, shut up, buried, in the great cabinet of the Sacred Heart, where the Divine Spouse gives us to drink of that new wine which inebriates, comforts, strengthens, inflames, exalts, and raises us on high to the contemplation of the sovereign Monarch, where is learned the true science of the saints, which is taught to the truly humble.
>
> I beg of you to be truly detached, hidden, and annihilated. In the Heart of Jesus, we feel compassion for His sufferings. And the soul purifies herself in that bath of His Blood, which inflames her with love.[296]

Sacred Heart of Jesus, burn away all that is false in me, that I may adore You in spirit and truth. St. Paul of the Cross, pray for us!

October 21

The Italian noblewoman St. Camilla Battista da Varano became a Poor Clare nun, despite great pressure to marry. Here, Saint Camilla recommends entering into Jesus' Heart in order to contemplate the sufferings of His Soul.

> When Jesus prayed in the Garden of Olives, His mental sorrows became more intense than they had previously been throughout His life, because He had then arrived at the most elevated point of His suffering love.
>
> It was shown to me in the revelation of which I speak, that there is the same difference between a soul that meditates on the mental sorrows of Jesus, and a soul that stops at the crucifixion of His sacred humanity, as between honey (or balsam) enclosed in a vessel, and that which exudes from it exteriorly. He, then, who wishes to nourish himself on the passion of the Savior, should not confine himself to simply tasting the edge of the vessel, by which I mean His admirable wounds and the Blood that flowed from His most holy Body; for in this way he will never appease the hunger that devours him. Let him enter into the vessel itself, that is to say, into the Sacred Heart, and he will find there more than enough to satisfy him.[297]

Sacred Heart of Jesus, honeycomb and balsam, let me contemplate the depths of Your sufferings. Look upon me with love, wounding me sweetly with compassion. St. Camilla Battista, bride of Christ, pray for us!

October 22 | *Pope St. John Paul II*

In his encyclical *Redemptor hominis*, Pope John Paul II recalls the key teaching of *Gaudium et spes* — that the Incarnation not only manifested God to man, but revealed man to himself.

> Christ, the Redeemer of the world, is the one who penetrated in a unique unrepeatable way into the mystery of man and entered his "heart." Rightly therefore does the Second Vatican Council teach: "The truth is that only in the mystery of the Incarnate Word does the mystery of man take on light. For Adam, the first man, was a type of Him who was to come (Rom 5:14), Christ the Lord. Christ the new Adam, in the very revelation of the mystery of the Father and of His love, *fully reveals man to himself* and brings to light his most high calling." And the Council continues: "He who is the 'image of the invisible God' (Col 1:15), is himself the perfect man who has restored in the children of Adam that likeness to God which had been disfigured ever since the first sin. ... For, by His Incarnation, He, the Son of God, *in a certain way united himself with each man.* He worked with human hands, He thought with a human mind. He acted with a human will, and with a human Heart He loved."[298]

Sacred Heart of Jesus, generous in love, let me lose myself in Your love, that I may find myself in You. Pope St. John Paul II, pray for us!

October 23

Ven. Mother Anne-Marguerite Clément (c. 1590–1661) was a Visitandine abbess. This letter, composed by her spiritual director and biographer, Fr. Giovanni Agostino Gallicio, testifies to the extraordinary graces afforded this holy soul.

> On the night between the 21st and 22nd of October, as she was making the Sign of the Cross when retiring … her heart was suddenly seized with a sense of the presence of Jesus Christ. … "Ah, Lord! what do You desire of me? What do You wish to do?"
>
> "I wish to practice you," said Jesus Christ, "in a new kind of conflict. It is against Me you must fight, and with My own weapons; for love will begin the combat, love will carry it on, and love will end it in your heart. I mean to make it die of love." At the same time, He shot into her heart three arrows all burning with the fire of His love, and she felt herself wounded so deeply that she thought she would lose her life. Jesus Christ, however, took pleasure in her pain and at seeing her languish with it, and then showing her His Divine Heart, He said, "Here is the mark at which you must shoot your arrows in your turn; these arrows are nothing more than the movements of your heart; love Me and you will wound My Heart."[299]

Sacred Heart of Jesus, divine archer, strike the inmost center of my heart, making it die to itself and live in You. Venerable Anne-Marguerite, pray for us!

October 24

Ludolph of Saxony (c. 1295–1378) spent thirty years in the Dominican Order before transferring to the more austere life of the Carthusians at Strasburg. Among his celebrated works is his *Vita Christi,* which helped popularize the medieval practice of pious meditation on Christ's life. This imaginative spirit is present in the following prayer, wherein Ludolph ponders Christ's solemn resignation of His Spirit. That he might be made a gift of love, Ludolph prays his heart will be pierced by a sword of charity.

> O Lord Jesus, when You were hanging on the tree of the cross at the ninth hour of the day, crying with a loud voice, You commended Your Spirit to Your Father and bowing Your head, yielded it up to Him. Then, after Your death, You permitted Your side to be pierced by a soldier's spear. Suffer me in like manner to commend to You my spirit now and forever, and vouchsafe to pierce my heart with the sword of love. Imprint the wounds of Your Body in the depths of my soul, that sinful thoughts may be banished, and when my earthly course is run, vouchsafe to receive among the spirits of the blessed the spirit I have confided to Your paternal care. Amen.[300]

Sacred Heart of Jesus, You endured the insults and violence of men to rescue us from death. Pierce my heart, removing the venom of sin and healing me with Your Blood divine. Sacred Heart of Jesus, have mercy on us!

October 25

St. Cyprian of Carthage was an African bishop who guided the Church through successive waves of Roman persecutions and who ultimately gave his life in witness to the Faith. In his treatise *On Works and Alms,* Saint Cyprian speaks of the charity and unity of those early Christians who were of "one heart and soul" (Acts 4:32).

> Let us consider, beloved brethren, what the congregation of believers did in the time of the apostles, when in the beginnings the mind flourished with greater virtues, when the faith of believers warmly burned with new faith. Then they sold houses and farms, and gladly and liberally presented the proceeds to the apostles to be dispensed to the poor. Selling and alienating their earthly estates, they transferred their lands to where they might receive the fruits of an eternal possession, and there prepared homes where they might begin an eternal habitation. Such, then, was the abundance in labors, as was the agreement in love, as we read in the Acts of the Apostles: "Now the company of those who believed were of one heart and soul, and no one said that any of the things which he possessed was his own, but they had everything in common" [Acts 4:32]. This is truly to become sons of God by spiritual birth; this is to imitate by the heavenly law the equity of God the Father.[301]

Sacred Heart of Jesus, stir up a spirit of charity among Christians who live as a single people in You. Saint Cyprian, pray for us!

October 26

A noblewoman who renounced her privileges to become a religious, Bl. Mary of the Divine Heart here recommends practical acts of self-sacrifice to overcome human frailty and self-interest. She counsels hastening to the Sacred Heart of Jesus to find strength.

> We wound charity, because we will not put up with a little injurious word. We fail in watchfulness with the children, punctuality in the little observances, because all this demands sacrifice. Let us, therefore, love mortification, self-abnegation, and if you feel that nature rebels, then have recourse to prayer; go to the Heart of Jesus and draw from this source a generous spirit, and be courageous in conquering your repugnance. Fight unceasingly, overcome self bravely, and you will thus acquire great mastery over yourselves and your bad inclinations; you will make progress in virtue and render yourselves pleasing to the Heart of Jesus. Our Lord himself promised that He would shed the unction of His grace upon communities consecrated to Him. Let us recall His words to Blessed Margaret Mary: Behold the Heart which has loved man so much! This is the object of our devotion, the Sacred Heart of Jesus, filled with love for us. Our sweet Savior took a human Heart when He united himself to our humanity. The human nature united to the divine is the object of our adoration.[302]

Sacred Heart of Jesus, You extended Your arms in blessing upon the cross, letting fall every kind of grace: may we never fail in charity. Blessed Mary, pray for us!

October 27

The English anchoress Julian of Norwich identifies four types of fear in her *Revelations of Divine Love*: fear born of a scare, fear of death and judgment, despairing fear, and filial fear. Only one form is wholly true and pleasing to God.

> Love and dread are brethren, and they are rooted in us by the goodness of our Maker, and they shall never be taken from us without end. We have of nature to love and we have of grace to love: And we have of nature to dread and we have of grace to dread. It belongs to the Lordship and to the Fatherhood to be dreaded, as it belongs to the goodness to be loved. …
>
> All dreads other than reverent dread, though they come under the color of holiness, yet are not so true. That dread that makes us hastily to flee from all that is not good and fall into Our Lord's breast, as the child into the mother's, knowing our feebleness and our great need, knowing His everlasting goodness and His blissful love, only seeking Him for salvation, cleaving to [Him] with sure trust: That dread that brings us into this working, it is natural, gracious, good, and true. And all that is contrary to this, either it is wrong, or it is mingled with wrong. Then is this the remedy, to know them both and refuse the wrong.[303]

Sacred Heart of Jesus, guard us against presumption and despair, and establish us in hope. I trust in You!

October 28

As recounted in her *Dialogues,* Christ instructed St. Catherine of Siena on three stages of the spiritual life. In the second stage, symbolized by His Sacred Heart, the soul gazes into the wounded side of Christ, drinking deeply of His love.

> The feet of the soul … carry the body as the affections carry the soul. Wherefore, these pierced feet are steps by which you can arrive at His side, which manifests the secret of His Heart, because the soul, rising on the steps of her affection, commences to taste the love of His Heart, gazing into that open Heart of My Son with the eye of the intellect, finding it consumed with ineffable love. I say consumed, because He does not love you for His own profit, because you can be of no profit to Him; He being one and the same thing with Me. Then, the soul is filled with love, seeing herself so much loved. Having passed the second step, the soul reaches out to the third — that is — to the mouth, where she finds peace from the terrible war she has been waging with her sin. On the first step, then, lifting her feet from the affections of the earth, the soul strips herself of vice; on the second, she fills herself with love and virtue; and on the third, she tastes peace.[304]

Sacred Heart of Jesus, may we ascend from glory to glory, contemplating Your beauty. Reveal to us the profundity of Your love. St. Catherine of Siena, pray for us!

October 29

Though no longer in communion with the Catholic Church, the Syrian Orthodox Church's liturgical prayers reflect agreement with the sacramental theology of Catholicism. During its Eucharistic prayers, the saving fountain that flowed from Christ's side is proclaimed as a propitiation for the world.

> The Fraction and Consignation
>
> *The priest breaks and signs saying:*
>
> Thus truly did the Word of God suffer in the Flesh and was sacrificed and broken on the cross: And His Soul was severed from His Body, albeit His Godhead was in no wise severed either from His Soul or from His Body + and He was pierced in His side with a spear + and there flowed thereout Blood and water a propitiation for the whole world + and His Body was stained therewith + and for the sins of the circle of the world + the Son died upon the cross + and His Soul came and was united to His Body and He turned us from an evil conversation to the good and by the Blood of His cross He reconciled and united and knit heavenly things with the things of earth and the people with the peoples and the souls with the body. And the third day He rose again from the sepulcher and He is one Emmanuel.[305]

Sacred Heart of Jesus, assume Your rightful throne upon my heart, making of me a tabernacle. Your kingdom come!

October 30

Carmelite priest St. John of the Cross is renowned for his masterpiece "Dark Night of the Soul." His "Spiritual Canticle" is another classic of spiritual theology, expressing the soul's anxious longing for Christ and ultimate union with Him. The following selections of the canticle outline this mystical exchange.

Where have You hidden yourself?
Why have You forsaken me in my groaning, O my beloved?
You did fly like the hart, away,
When You wounded me.
I ran after You, crying; but You were gone.

In search of my love
I will traverse mountains and strands;
I will gather no flowers,
I will fear no wild beasts;
And I will overpass the mighty and the frontiers.

In the inmost cellar
Of my beloved have I drunk; and when I went forth
Over all the plain
I knew nothing,
And lost the flock I followed before.

There He gave me His breasts,
There He taught me the science full of sweetness,
And there I gave to Him
Myself without reserve;
There I promised to be His bride.

My soul is henceforth occupied,
And all my substance in His service;
Now I guard no flock,
Nor have I any other employment:
My sole occupation being love.

If, then, on the common
I am no longer seen or found,
Say that I am lost;
That, being enamored,
I lost myself; and yet I gained.[306]

Sacred Heart of Jesus, gaze of peace, bind my faculties in You, setting them about the work of charity. St. John of the Cross, pray for us!

October 31 | *St. Alphonsus Rodriguez*

The lay Jesuit St. Alphonsus Rodriguez (1532–1617) led a life of extraordinary holiness. In his autobiography, the *Memoriale,* He speaks of the "second manner" of prayer, which is infused contemplation.

> This mode of communicating himself to the soul is a pure favor of God; nor does this feeling come through the imagination, but it is a spiritual certainty by which the soul feels that God is within the soul and everywhere. The pleasure which God takes in seeing us walking with Him is so great, that, should it chance that the soul, for good reasons, should be engrossed in some necessary occupation, it is wonderful to see how, without any trouble on its part, it feels God present within it, and how this makes up for a want of attention. …
>
> In the same way, when Our Lord places the soul within His Heart, all is on fire with charity. It inflames it with its love; and by the immense love which is given to it, through the communication of Christ and of His grace, the soul is made like, united to, and transformed into Him. And this Presence of Christ Our Lord within him is so real that he went about the streets so absorbed in Christ crucified that the people who passed by seemed to him like shadows.[307]

Sacred Heart of Jesus, draw my heart to Yours, plunging it in endless adoration. St. Alphonsus Rodriguez, pray for us!

November

November 1 | *Solemnity of All Saints*

Today, we honor all those saints who overcame the world and now partake of the delights of heaven. In her *Spiritual Dialogue*, St. Catherine of Genoa recalls the centrality of charity in the lives of saints and martyrs who imitated the sacrificial love of Christ.

> O sweet Jesus, my love, what has brought You from heaven to earth? Love. What has caused You to suffer such great and terrible torments, even unto death? Love. What has induced You to give yourself as food to Your beloved soul? Love. What moved You to send us, what still continually moves You to send us, the Holy Spirit for our support and guide? Love.
>
> Many other things can be said of You. Through love You appeared in this world so poor, so abject, and so humiliated in the eyes of men that You were not esteemed as God, but scarcely as a man. …
>
> But You, Lord, have brought from heaven the sweet manna, this delicious food, which has in itself such vigor that it gives strength for every trial — as we have witnessed first in You, our most sweet Master, and afterwards in Your saints. Oh, how much they have done and suffered in the strength of the love infused by You into their hearts, and by which they were so inflamed and united to You, that no torture could separate them from You![308]

Sacred Heart of Jesus, inspiring multitudes of saints and myriads of martyrs, enkindle in us the fire of love!

November 2 | *Commemoration of All the Faithful Departed*

Today, we remember those holy souls who have departed from this world yet remain in need of intercessory prayer. Here, Bl. Columba Marmion recalls Christ's sorrow over death as He wept over Lazarus and Jerusalem, and manifested His solidarity with suffering mankind upon the cross.

> He wept over Jerusalem, His own city which He loved despite its ingratitude; the thought of the disaster that would fall upon it after His death drew tears from His eyes.
>
> He wept at the death of Lazarus as we weep over those we cherish, [shedding] tears because His Heart was touched; He wept for him who was His friend: The tears sprang from the depth of His Heart. Several times too it is said of Him in the Gospel that His Heart was touched with compassion. …
>
> All the mockeries, all the outrages with which He was saturated in His passion, being buffeted and spit upon; all these insults, far from leaving Him insensible, caused Him intense suffering. His nature being more perfect, His sensibility was the greater and more delicate. He was plunged in an abyss of suffering. Lastly, after having shown himself to be truly man, He willed to endure death like all the sons of Adam: *Et inclinato capite tradidit spiritum.*[309]

Sacred Heart of Jesus, tender and kind, grant rest unto those holy souls who have departed this world in Your friendship. All saints, pray for us!

November 3

The Shepherd of Hermas (c. 89–150) is an ancient work of Christian piety which enjoyed great popularity in the early Church. In the following passage, Christians are instructed to live in union with God, allowing His works to flow through them. Enthroned upon the heart of man, God may bring forth blessing to him who gives and to him who receives. In this way, Christians may participate in the economy of grace, showing themselves to be members of the Body of Christ.

> Take care then, you who serve the Lord and have Him in your heart, that you work the works of God, remembering His Commandments and promises, believing that He will bring them to pass if His Commandments are observed. Instead of lands, therefore, buy afflicted souls, according as each is able, and visit widows and orphans, not overlooking them; and spend your wealth and all your preparations — which you received from the Lord — upon such lands and houses. For this end did the Master make you rich, that you might perform these services unto Him. And it is much better to purchase such lands and possessions and houses, as you will find in your own city, when you come to reside in it. This is a noble and sacred expenditure, accompanied neither with sorrow nor fear, but with joy.[310]

Sacred Heart of Jesus, source of all riches, inspire in me true Christian charity and grant me Your own detachment from worldly goods. Make my heart like Yours!

November 4 | *St. Charles Borromeo*

Though St. Charles Borromeo (1538–1584) is primarily remembered as a theologian and administrator, the following text evidences his mastery of the interior life. Saint Charles here offers a prescient expression of the Little Way of spiritual childhood — a spirituality that would be popularized by St. Thérèse of Lisieux centuries later. Contemplating the manner in which Christ was little in all things, Saint Charles assures all such little souls of their safe harbor in Jesus.

> There surely ought to be a way for little ones to Christ the Little One; for the humble to Christ the Meek and Humble of Heart. For Christ was little in His Nativity; born very lowly in a little city by the wayside, between poor brute animals, in the little manger at Bethlehem. Nazareth, His own home, was little; He was little because of His reputed father: "Is not this the Son of the carpenter; is not His mother called Mary?" Little because of His disciples — He chose fishermen; little because of the doctrine of humility, which He preached; little as long as He lived. "Foxes have holes, the birds of the air have nests; but the Son of Man has not where to lay his head." Little in His death. Let us then allow the little ones to come to Him who was in every way little, for the like will mingle easily with the like.[311]

Sacred Heart of Jesus, renew me in meekness and humility, lovingly submitting me to Your will. St. Charles Borromeo, pray for us!

November 5

The anonymous author of the *Ancren Riwle* contends that acts of meekness tricked the pride of the devil into defeat. Accounting ourselves as nothing before God, we safeguard ourselves from the perilous sin of pride.

> "O!" thought Our Lord when He beheld all this, "I shall practice upon thee a sleight of humility, which is the falling stratagem." And He fell from heaven to earth, and stretched himself in such a manner on the earth that the fiend thought that He was all earthly; and he was outwitted by that stratagem, and is still every day, by humble men and women who are well skilled in it. The wild boar cannot stoop to smite him who falls down, and through meek humility stretches himself on the ground: He is quite secure from his tusks. …
>
> Humility can never be sufficiently commended, for it was the lesson which Our Lord most earnestly taught all His elect, both by word and works: "Learn of Me, for I am meek and lowly in heart." In this, He pours not merely drop by drop, but He pours in a flowing stream the fountains of His grace, as the psalmist says, "In the dales, You make fountains to well up." But a heart inflated, and swollen, and lifted up as a hill — such a heart retains none of the dew of God's grace.[312]

Sacred Heart of Jesus, grant that we never stand upon our own strength, but humbly cast ourselves upon You. Have mercy on us!

November 6

St. Eugène de Mazenod fled France before the French Revolution, but eventually returned to serve his homeland as a priest. Here, Eugène details his resolution to walk in humility with confidence in God's mercy, trusting in the loving Heart of Jesus.

> I must make it a constant practice to ever keep before my mind the remembrance of my many transgressions, that I may fully understand that I am the last in the house in the eyes of that just God, who pays no attention to birth, or rank, or education, but puts everyone in the place he merits by his virtues. …
>
> But these sentiments alone should not occupy my heart. The dread of the terrible judgments of God should not so possess me as to exceed, in any way, the fullest confidence in His mercy. Ah! Lord, what would become of me if anything held me back from approaching Your Sacred Heart, there to consume, in the fire of its love, those sins of mine that otherwise would become matter for the eternal fire of Your anger? No, Lord, my grief for sin will not be like that of the traitor Judas; I will not flee from Your Presence as he did, but I will run to You and cast myself at Your feet, and crave Your pardon, which You will not refuse me.[313]

Sacred Heart of Jesus, inspire me with confidence in Your love that I may never shrink from seeking Your pardon. St. Eugène de Mazenod, pray for us!

November 7

In the following passage, the great Benedictine Bl. Columba Marmion — a spiritual master who personally knew the divine subject he sought — describes the vivifying power of the Sacred Heart of Jesus. Once the love of this divine-human Heart is impressed upon man, he will no longer walk, but run in the way of the spiritual life.

> This fundamental attitude responding to the reality of our heavenly adoption is particularly furthered by devotion to the Heart of Jesus. In causing us to contemplate the human love of Christ for us, this devotion admits us into the secret of divine love; in inclining our souls to answer to it by a life whereof love is the motive power; it stirs within us those sentiments of filial piety that we ought to have toward the Father.
>
> When we receive Our Lord in Holy Communion, we possess within us that divine Heart which is a furnace of love. Let us ask Him earnestly that He will himself grant us to understand this love, for, in this, one ray from on high is more efficacious than all human reasoning; let us ask Him to enkindle within us the love of His Person. "If, by Our Lord's grace," says Saint Teresa, "His love is imprinted one day in our heart, all will become easy to us; very rapidly and without trouble we shall come by this means to works of love."[314]

Sacred Heart of Jesus, reveal to me Your unmeasured mercy, increasing in me Your grace. Bl. Columba Marmion, pray for us!

November 8 | *St. Elizabeth of the Trinity*

Though a tempestuous child, St. Elizabeth of the Trinity engaged in soaring contemplations that often invite comparison with her Carmelite predecessor, St. Thérèse. Inspired by Saint Paul's epistles, Saint Elizabeth sought to live as the "praise of his glory" (Eph 1:12), considering this her vocation. Here, she marvels at Christ's sufferings, resolving to return sacrifice for sacrifice and love for love.

> O Christ … while You endured a thousand torments on the cross; my countless faults and infidelities were before Your eyes. Ah! How dearly they cost You! Yet, You also foresaw the love that I should bear You, and how, in return for Your love for me, I should be ready to yield You my life a thousand times. O my Jesus! Forgive me all the anguish I have caused Your Divine Heart! Grant me pardon, and look solely on my love. …
>
> Who can describe how sweet it is when heart speaks to heart; when one no longer seems to belong to this world, but sees and listens to nothing but God? God, who speaks tenderly to the heart, asking it to suffer for Him, and to console Jesus, who longs for a little love. … I strive by my love, my interest, my sacrifices, and my prayers, to make Him forget His sorrows! I desire to love Him for those who love Him not.[315]

Sacred Heart of Jesus, untold love, help us to imitate Your forbearance as we commend our brothers and sisters to You. Saint Elizabeth, pray for us!

November 9 | *Feast of the Dedication of the Lateran Basilica*

St. Stephen the Sabaite (c. 725–c. 807), the nephew of St. John Damascene, was an early hymnographer. In the following Greek *idiomelon,* he tenderly speaks of the consolation found in Jesus' glorified wounds.

Art thou weary, art thou languid,
Art thou sore distrest?
"Come to me" — saith One — "and coming,
Be at rest!"

Hath He marks to lead me to Him,
If He be my guide?
"In His feet and hands and wound-prints,
And His side."

Is there Diadem, as Monarch,
That His brow adorns?
"Yea, a crown, in very surety,
But of thorns!"

If I find Him, if I follow,
What His guerdon here?
"Many a sorrow, many a labor,
Many a tear."

If I still hold closely to Him,
What hath He at last?
"Sorrow vanquish'd, labor ended,
Jordan past!"

If I ask Him to receive me,
Will He say no nay?
"Not till earth, and not till heaven
Pass away!"

Finding, following, keeping, struggling,
Is He sure to bless?
"Angels, martyrs, prophets, virgins,
Answer, yes!"[316]

Sacred Heart of Jesus, touched by human sorrows, sustain us on the rough road of our pilgrimage Stephen, pray for us!

November 10 | *Pope St. Leo the Great*

In his "Letter to Flavian (Number Twenty-Four)," Pope St. Leo the Great enunciates his Christological views: that in the stable of Bethlehem, the tiny beating of a child's heart upended all of creation, shattering divisions between heaven and earth.

> The humiliation by which the Master and Creator of immortals was willing to become a man, subject to death, is not a defect of power, but an effort of mercy all-powerful, such that in taking all the properties of our nature, He did not lose anything of His own. The divine nature was not altered by the grace which it bestowed upon us; the human nature was not absorbed by the dignity which it received. He became as truly man as He remains immutably God. …
>
> Since the Son begotten before all time has received a new birth, there exists a new order of things. He who in His own nature is invisible has made himself visible to ours; the incomprehensible has put himself within reach of our conception; the source of all beings has begun to be; the Master of things which are, and of things which yet are not, has taken the form of a servant; the infinite has enclosed himself in the heart of a babe; the impassible has clothed himself with members which suffer; and the author of life has made himself subject to death.[317]

Sacred Heart of Jesus, complete Your saving work of reconciliation in us, filling us with Your grace. Pope St. Leo the Great, pray for us!

November 11 | *St. Martin of Tours*

Over a thousand years after St. Martin of Tours (316–397) lived, St. Teresa of Ávila wrote of her mysterious kinship with this early bishop. This account by Bl. Anne of Saint Bartholomew relates Teresa's vision of Saint Martin resting upon the Heart of Jesus.

> At the sight of Martin causing the Trinity to be adored and Christ known ... Teresa was filled with joy and fell into an ecstasy. ... The soul of the seraphic virgin, identifying itself with the sentiments of the Church, exclaimed with her, "O blessed apostle of Christ, at your passing from earth to heaven, the saints welcomed you with songs of joy, the choirs of angels saluted you with transport, the army of all the celestial virtues went before you singing hymns of triumph: The Church is strengthened by your sanctity in heaven, bishops are glorified by this revelation from God."
>
> It is Saint Michael who finally takes him under his care, and with his angels leads him to the throne of God, and when the Holy Trinity crowns him, when Christ takes him in His arms and presses him to His Heart and conducts him to His throne; when, in a word, this soul has taken possession of paradise, Teresa's soul is carried away by the triumph of the Blessed Martin; she rejoices with the angels."[318]

Sacred Heart of Jesus, surround us with the angels and saints, who may conduct us toward eternal life. St. Martin of Tours, pray for us!

November 12

In his *Book of Mutual Love*, Adam of Perseigne (c. 1145–1221) extols the excellence of celibacy as he contemplates the mystical verse, "You have ravished my heart with a glance of your eyes" (Sg 4:9). He promises that those who call upon the Lord in love will not be left unanswered.

> The eyes of the Spouse are said to have the look of love; for to Him — to Him whom she sighs in complete love — they are raised tenderly, opened and turned, as she says with a murmur, "My eyes are ever toward the Lord" [Ps 25:15]. … And at other times: "Let my beloved come to his garden … I sought him, but found him not; I called him, but he gave no answer" [Sg 4:16; 3:1]. And with good reason! "His cheeks are like beds of spices … his body is ivory work" [Sg 5:13–14]. By such wonderful expressions, the Bridegroom is called, desired by the virginal soul. Soon, she will hear one so blessedly wounded with love, responding, "Come from Lebanon, My spouse, come from Lebanon, come! You have wounded My Heart with one of your eyes, because of your simplicity, and My conversation is with the simple, and My eyes upon the faithful of the earth" [see Sg 4:8–9]. Certainly, where there is love, there is the eye; and where love is not, neither is the eye.[319]

Sacred Heart of Jesus, grant me heavenly entrance to Your Holy Heart, binding mine to Yours, for I completely adore You!

November 13

In 1899, at the request of Bl. Mary of the Divine Heart and in response to his own miraculous recovery from illness, Pope Leo XIII consecrated the entire world to the Sacred Heart of Jesus. In this excerpt from his promulgation, he exhorts all Christians to join in this filial act of love.

> And since there is in the Sacred Heart a symbol and a sensible image of the infinite love of Jesus Christ which moves us to love one another, therefore is it fit and proper that we should consecrate ourselves to His Most Sacred Heart — an act which is nothing else than an offering and a binding of oneself to Jesus Christ, seeing that whatever honor, veneration, and love is given to this Divine Heart is really and truly given to Christ himself.
>
> For these reasons we urge and exhort all who know and love this Divine Heart willingly to undertake this act of piety; and it is our earnest desire that all should make it on the same day, that so the aspirations of so many thousands who are performing this act of consecration may be borne to the temple of heaven on the same day. … As we have already sent messengers of Christ over the earth to instruct [so now do we commend and] consecrate them to the Sacred Heart of Jesus.[320]

Sacred Heart of Jesus, font of wisdom, renew all cultures, institutions, and nations in Your love. O Divine Heart of Christ, reign over us as King!

November 14

The following letter, dated July 21, 1672, evidences St. John Eudes' early advocacy of the Sacred Heart. He assures his correspondents a new outpouring of grace for those who honor both the Sacred Heart and the Immaculate Heart of Mary.

> What more worthy, more holy, or greater could there be than that which is the principle of all that is great, holy, and venerable in all other solemnities? What heart is more adorable, more loving, more admirable than the Heart of the man-God, JESUS?
>
> What honor does this Heart deserve, which has ever rendered more glory and love to God each moment than the hearts of all men and angels could render throughout eternity! What great zeal we ought to have, promoting the veneration of this Holy Heart, which is the source of our salvation and of all happiness and graces to the earth. It is a living furnace of love for us, which day and night only thinks of doing us good, and which died upon the cross.
>
> I beg of you, my very dear brothers, to celebrate this feast with all possible solemnity and devotion. … So will you cause me great joy, who ardently desires for you the greatest blessing from Our good Savior and His sweet mother, and who in the sacred love of their Divine Hearts is entirely yours.[321]

Sacred Heart of Jesus, enthroned above the earth, lead all to right worship, teaching us to adore You in spirit and truth. St. John Eudes, pray for us!

November 15 | *St. Albert the Great*

Called the Universal Doctor for the breadth of his studies, St. Albert the Great (c. 1200–1280) here provides spiritual insights into mystical union, and its tendency to draw the lover out from himself so as to rest in the heart of the beloved.

> There is nothing keener than love, nothing more subtle, nothing more penetrating. Love cannot rest till it has sounded all the depths and learned the perfections of its beloved. It desires to be one with Him. …
>
> Love has the power of uniting and transforming; it transforms the one who loves into Him who is loved, and Him who is loved into him who loves. Each passes into the other, as far as it is possible.
>
> First consider the intelligence. How completely love transports the loved one into him who loves! … Think next of the will, by which also the loved one lives in him who loves. Does He not dwell in him by that tender affection, that sweet and deeply-rooted joy, which he feels? On the other hand, the lover lives in the beloved by the sympathy of his desires, by sharing His likes and dislikes, His joys and sorrows, until the two seem to form but one. Since "love is strong as death" [Sg 8:6], it carries the lover out of himself into the heart of the beloved, and holds him prisoner there.[322]

Sacred Heart of Jesus, make my heart docile, that it may freely flow into You. Saint Albert, pray for us!

November 16 | *St. Gertrude the Great*

St. Gertrude the Great's dedication to the Sacred Heart helped lay the foundation for its modern devotion. In this revelation, Christ instructs Gertrude not to rely on her own strength to advance in virtue, but to call upon His Heart, which will stand in her place.

> Behold, I present to the eyes of your soul My loving Heart, which is the organ of the Most Holy Trinity. Present it to God with confidence, that it may supply all that you cannot do perfectly yourself, and thus all that you do will seem quite perfect in My sight. … My Heart will ever be at your disposal to repair your faults and negligence.
>
> If you have a beautiful and melodious voice and take much pleasure in chanting, will you not feel displeased if another person, whose voice is harsh and unpleasant and who can hardly utter a correct sound, wishes to sing instead of you, and insists on so doing? Thus My Divine Heart, understanding the frailty and inconstancy of human nature, desires with incredible ardor to be invited … to take your place and perform for you what you are quite incapable of doing for yourself. And as My omnipotence can do all things, and My inscrutable wisdom knows all things, so [does] My Divine Heart have but one desire, to do this work for you with loving ardor.[323]

Sacred Heart of Jesus, be our advocate and Redeemer, obtaining for us pardon and everlasting peace. St. Gertrude, pray for us!

November 17

In her ministry to the publicly fallen, Bl. Mary of the Divine Heart formulated a spirituality of the Sacred Heart in which she meekly trusted in Christ's mercy. Here she affirms the Sacred Heart's unrestricted power to convert any sinner, no matter how desperate the case.

> The first grace that the Divine Heart of Jesus granted to me after clothing was that of being among the penitents ... I looked upon it as a special attention of the part of my Divine Spouse who willed that I should have, from the very first, a share in the work so dear to His Heart — that of the conversion of sinners. ...
>
> To the Heart of Jesus alone do I attribute the success I have always met with in my dealings with the penitents. Often when things seemed hopeless, He removed every difficulty. Although He may require on occasion much prayer, sacrifice, and suffering, the Sacred Heart of Our Lord never refuses us when we entreat for a soul. The more impossible the conversion of a sinner may seem, the more entire should be your confidence in the Sacred Heart of Jesus. You must expect much suffering and weariness, but you must never lose courage. ... The Heart of Jesus in the end will triumph over the hardened heart and will strengthen its weakness. But you must by your trust offer holy violence to Our Lord.[324]

Sacred Heart of Jesus, let all creation revere Your mercy and rejoice in Your unfading love. Blessed Mary, pray for us!

November 18 | *St. Rose Philippine Duchesne*

A religious of the Society of the Sacred Heart, St. Rose Philippine Duchesne (1769–1852) zealously established missions in Missouri and Kansas. In this lyrical letter, she describes the spirit of thanksgiving that imbued her arrival in America.

> At nine o'clock in the evening, we got into the carriages, blessing the Heart of Jesus and devoting to Him our hearts anew. The night was beautiful, the sky clear and starry. We drove alongside the river in which thousands of stars were reflected in the still and peaceful waters.

If her arrival was described in idealistic terms, Saint Rose confronted the hardships of missionary life with holy indifference, caring only for the glory of the Sacred Heart.

> Our field of labor is still very small, but without us, the few persons to whom we devote ourselves here would never have known their religion and the adorable Heart of Jesus … I only wish to live in order to spend my life in greater labors. I feel that rest is not for this world. We must suffer in body and in mind. If I can be of the smallest possible use for the glory of the Sacred Heart, I am willing to live on without success, without recompense, for the sole glory of that Heart, in which I remain your unworthy daughter.[325]

Sacred Heart of Jesus, send forth missionaries in all directions, spreading the Good News of salvation, answering love for love. Saint Rose, pray for us!

November 19 | *St. Mechtilde of Hackeborn*

St. Mechtilde of Hackeborn was inspired by her sister to enter the Benedictine monastery at Helfta, where she served as headmistress of the convent school. In time, Mechtilde was entrusted with the formation of St. Gertrude the Great, in whom she instilled a deep love of the Sacred Heart. In the following passage, Saint Mechtilde instructs those souls afflicted with dryness to call upon the Heart of Jesus, asking for the grace of true piety. United to this Heart, and inflamed with its love, man may not only advance in holiness, but rejoice "as a giant to run the way" (Ps 19:5, Douay-Rheims Bible).

> The love of the Sacred Heart watches with great care over souls that have consecrated themselves to its service. Therefore, whenever a man feels his devotion diminished, his heart becoming cold, and perceives that he has strayed from God, he ought to call on this love; entrusting to it all his desires, praying it to obtain the grace or zeal of true devotion. He should also beg love to guard all the good he does, and love will carefully preserve it in the jewel case of the Divine Heart, returning it faithfully to the soul increased and ennobled. In all his sorrows and trials, let him call love to his help. With love, man does not feel weakness nor faints in adversity.[326]

Sacred Heart of Jesus, let the light of Your Resurrection reach the depths of my heart, imbuing it with Your life-giving Blood. St. Mechtilde of Hackeborn, pray for us!

November 20

Despite his personal defects, which included a pridefulness that led to formal schism, Tertullian (c. 155–c. 220) provided lasting insights into Western theology and the Faith. Contemplating God's creation, Tertullian here observes creation's ultimate root in the eternal procession of the Word.

> In this good work, God employs a most excellent minister, even His own Word. "My heart," He says, "has uttered my most excellent Word" (Ps 44:2). Look at the total result: How fruitful was the Word! God issued His *fiat*, and it was done: ... because it was good, He therefore saw it, honored it, set His seal upon it, and consummated the goodness of His works by His vouchsafing to them that contemplation. ...
>
> That image was wrought by a goodness even more operative than previously shown. For not by an imperious word was man wrought, but with a friendly hand preceded by an almost affable utterance: "Let us make man in our image, after our likeness" (Gn 1:26). Goodness spoke the word. Goodness formed man of the dust of the ground into so great a substance of the flesh, built up out of one material with so many qualities. Goodness breathed into him a soul, not dead but living. Goodness gave him dominion over all things, which he was to enjoy and rule over, and even give names to.[327]

Sacred Heart of Jesus, You reveal man to himself, manifesting the glory of his nature. Breathe Your Spirit into us, renewing us in Your grace. Make our hearts like Yours!

November 21

In *Visits to the Blessed Sacrament*, St. Alphonsus Liguori contemplates the Sacred Heart of Jesus and offers it to the Father. Knowing that Christians share in the grace and merits of Christ's Heart, he raises it, asking for pardon, perseverance, and paradise.

> Eternal Father, I now offer You all the virtues, the actions, and the affections of the Heart of Your dear Jesus. Accept them, and by His merits, which are all mine — for He has given them to me — grant me those graces that Jesus asks of You, for my sake. With these merits, I thank You for the many mercies that You have shown me; with these, I satisfy for the debt I owe You because of my sins; through these, I hope for every grace from You — pardon, perseverance, paradise, and above all, the crowning gift of Your pure love. I well see that I myself place impediments to all these gifts; but do You also remedy this. I ask it of You in the Name of Jesus Christ, who has promised: "Whatever you ask in my name, I will do it" (Jn 14:13–14). Then, You cannot refuse me.
>
> Lord, my only desire is to love You, to give myself to You without reserve, and no longer be ungrateful to You as I have thus far been. … I love You, my God! I love You, infinite goodness![328]

Sacred Heart of Jesus, let me be poured out as a libation, spending myself for love of You. Saint Alphonsus, pray for us!

November 22

Lanspergius was a Carthusian monk who came to be associated with the name of his hometown, Landsberg, rather than his given name, John Justus. His Bavarian heritage put him in contact with the writings of St. Gertrude the Great and her revelations of the Sacred Heart. The following text manifests Lanspergius's own devotion to the Sacred Heart, which is remarkably developed in its expressions. Prefiguring those formal consecrations known in later centuries, Lanspergius here recommends a life of dedication to the Sacred Heart of Jesus.

> The Sacred Heart of Jesus is not only the seat of all virtues, but the fountain of graces by which these virtues are acquired and preserved. Have a tender devotion to this loving Heart, which is so full of love and mercy. Through it, ask for all that you wish to obtain and offer all your actions. For this Sacred Heart is the treasury of all supernatural gifts. It is, so to speak, the way by which we unite ourselves more closely with God and by which God communicates himself more lovingly to us. You have in this Sacred Heart all the graces and all the virtues of which you stand in need, and you need not fear to exhaust this infinite treasure. Have recourse to it in all your necessities. Be faithful in the holy practices of a devotion so reasonable and useful, and you will soon perceive its effects.[329]

Sacred Heart of Jesus, magnify Your mercy in me, making me a missionary of Your love. I trust in You!

November 23 | *St. Clement of Rome*

In the following excerpt of his "Epistle to the Corinthians" (c. 96), Pope St. Clement of Rome (c. 35–99) urges dissenting Christians to humility and peace, citing the example of King David, the man after God's own Heart.

> But what shall we say of David, to whom such testimony was borne, and of whom God said, "I have found a man after My own Heart, David the son of Jesse, and in everlasting mercy have I anointed him"? Yet, this very man said to God: "Have mercy on me, O Lord, according to Your great mercy, according to the multitude of Your compassion, blot out my transgression. Wash me from my iniquity, and cleanse me from my sin. For, I acknowledge my iniquity and my sin is ever before me. Against You only have I sinned and done what is evil in Your sight." …
>
> The humility and heavenly submission of so great and illustrious men have rendered us, and all generations before us, better; even as many have received His oracles in fear and truth. Having so many great and glorious examples before us, let us turn again to the practice of that peace which from the beginning was the aim set before us; and look steadfastly to the Father and Creator of the universe, cleaving to His mighty and surpassingly great gifts and benefits of peace.[330]

Sacred Heart of Jesus, there is none beside You, none above You — You alone are the Most High. St. Clement of Rome, pray for us!

November 24

The Englishwoman Catharine Burton (1668–1714) became Carmelite Mother Mary Xavieria of the Angels (1668–1714), in Antwerp. Here, she recalls a mystical vision and reminder that all vows are preciously kept within the Sacred Heart of Jesus.

> During the three years that I was sub-prioress, God gave me great consolation in prayer. I no sooner put myself on my knees that I could say, "I have found Him whom my soul loves. I will hold Him, and neither will I let Him go." Thus I seemed to be united to God by a straight union.
>
> It is our custom to renew our vows and to prostrate in the choir on the Twelfth Day of Christmas. … I begged earnest of Almighty God that I might keep these vows perfectly, and after Communion, Our Lord showed me in an interior and intellectual way that He would keep them in His own Heart. I seemed to see my vows engravened there, *obedience* and *chastity*, in gold and silver letters, very bright, but I was troubled for a considerable time because I did not see anything of my vow of *poverty*. I was afraid this was a sign that I should not be exact in this vow, until I had light in prayer that if I kept those two in perfection, the other was included in them.[331]

Sacred Heart of Jesus, dearest friend and confidant, hold me close to Your Heart, making me to forget all suffering and strife. May my heart ever rest in Yours.

November 25

The well-known prayer Anima Christi has been attributed to Pope John XXII (1249–1334), though the text itself appeared in many forms throughout the Middle Ages. Fittingly associated with Eucharistic piety, it may serve as a prayer of spiritual communion to be made throughout the day. Its successive meditations on the Body, Blood, and wounded side of Christ invite one to take refuge in the glorified humanity of Christ. There, the Christian may be spiritually renewed and brought to participate in His life of redemption.

Soul of Christ, sanctify me.
Body of Christ, save me.
Blood of Christ, inebriate me.
Water from the side of Christ, wash me.

Passion of Christ, strengthen me.
O good Jesus, hear me.
In Your wounds, hide me.
Permit me not to be separated from Thee.

Against the malevolent host, defend me.
In the hour of my death, call me;
And bid me to come unto Thee.
That with Thy saints, I may praise Thee
Forever and ever. Amen.[332]

Sacred Heart of Jesus, radiant in love, You alone can satisfy my soul, setting it at peace. Immerse me in Your glorious wounds, which change death into life. Sacred Heart of Jesus, I give myself to You!

November 26

St. John Fisher's resolute witness to the Faith resulted in his execution under King Henry VIII. In his *Commentary on Psalm 130,* Saint John enumerates the seven times that Jesus shed Blood during His earthly life, culminating with the piercing of His Heart.

> When, after all this, His side was opened with a sharp spear, so great a wound was then made that no Blood was left in any part of His most Precious Body; in witness thereof water issued out with Blood. These be the riches; this is the treasure wherewith the ransom of our redemption was paid — for sinners that have passed and gone out of this world, for us who are now alive, and also for them who are to come; and for all who will ask for mercy and forgiveness with true penance. This most Precious Blood was shed without measure [to] redress our sins, be they ever so great and many. For they shall in every hour, every moment, by virtue of this Precious Blood be cleansed and done away with, that we may partake of this redemption once done; if at any time in this life we come to Almighty God with true penance, asking mercy for our offenses. One drop of His Blood, as Saints Bernard and Anselm bear witness, was sufficient for the redemption of all the world — also of many worlds.[333]

Sacred Heart of Jesus, let no soul lose hope of pardon at the sight of Your copious mercy. St. John Fisher, pray for us!

November 27 | *St. Leonard of Port Maurice*

In his profound love for the Sacred Heart, the Franciscan missionary priest St. Leonard (1676–1751) left us this "Act of Adoration."

> O God, I profoundly humble myself and adore You. I adore You, beloved Jesus, in the Sacrament. Most Holy Virgin, you angels, saints, and souls who love God, adore with me my Jesus: Make up for the defects of my worship and ask for me living faith and profound veneration, now that I approach and receive Jesus Christ.
>
> What can be wanting to you, O my soul, now that the Almighty comes to visit you? He comes to illuminate you, to unite himself Heart to heart with you, in order to give you a lively pledge of that glory which He has prepared in heaven. Up! Arise! Enlarge your heart and increase your confidence. Know that as much as you hope for, you shall obtain. Your Jesus is omnipotent and can give you every good thing. It costs Him no more than the opening of His hand. Your Jesus is as a Father to you: Much does He love you and wish to bestow every sort of benefit. Your Jesus, who is faithful, has promised to hear you. Bound by His word, He will do you great favors. Well then, to grow rich in soul, you need only to seek His graces and to ardently hope.[334]

Sacred Heart of Jesus, fill us with confidence in Your love that we may dare to approach Your glory. Saint Leonard, pray for us!

November 28

Thomas à Kempis initially published *The Imitation of Christ* anonymously until misattribution led him to sign a codex of his works. In his lesser-known work, *Meditations on the Life of Christ,* Thomas depicts the Sacred Heart of Jesus as a sanctuary from the tempestuous world.

> Enter, O my soul, enter into the right side of your crucified Lord. Through this renowned wound, enter into the most loving Heart of Jesus, transpierced for love, that you may find a resting place from the tempests of the world.
>
> Draw near, O man, to this Heart — so deep, hidden, and secret — to the Heart of God, who opens His door unto you. Come in, you blessed of the Lord. Why do you remain outside? The vein of life is open to you; the way of salvation, the heavenly Ark from which sweet spices abundantly flow. Behold, a place of refuge from the tempter. . . .
>
> This is the ever-flowing fountain of unction and grace, which never ceases to provide pardon for sinners who seek to draw near with heartful repentance.
>
> This is the source of the sacred river that goes forth from the midst of paradise, watering the face of the earth, to quench the thirst of the parched mind, to cleanse sins, to quell carnal desires, and to stay the turmoil of anger. Take, therefore, the cup of love from this fountain of the Savior.[335]

Sacred Heart of Jesus, hallowed sanctuary, cradle us in Your tender love. Wholly subdue my will, for I trust in You!

November 29

St. Margaret Mary Alacoque's life was marked by two great loves — the Sacred Heart and the Holy Eucharist. Alluding to Saint Paul's exclamation, "It is no longer I who live, but Christ who lives in me" (Gal 2:20), Jesus here instructs Saint Margaret Mary that she must no longer live in herself, but in His Heart.

> After having received my Beloved in Holy Communion, He said to me, "Behold the Wound in My Side wherein you are to dwell now and forever; it is there you will be able to preserve the robe of innocence with which I have clothed your soul, so that you may live henceforth the life of the Man-God. Live as no longer living, in order that I may live perfectly in you. Think of your body and all that may happen to it no more than if it no longer existed. Act as if you no longer acted, but I alone in you. For this, all your powers and senses must be buried in Me, that you may be deaf, blind, and dumb to all the things of earth. You must will as though you had no longer any will of your own, without desire, private judgment, affection, or any wish, save that of My good pleasure which must be all your delight."[336]

Sacred Heart of Jesus, let me fall upon You as a grain of wheat, that I might bear much fruit. Act in and through me, so I might be an instrument of Your blessing. Saint Margaret Mary, pray for us!

November 30

St. Edmund Campion (1540–1581; memorial, December 1) initially consented to King Henry VIII's Oath of Supremacy, before renouncing it. Following this, he sent an impassioned letter to his friend, the Anglican Bishop Cheyney, earnestly begging Cheyney to listen, invoking the Heart of Jesus.

> We have already been too long subservient to popular report, to the times, to reputation. … I beg you, by your own natural goodness, by my tears, even by the pierced side of Christ and the wounds of the crucified, to listen to me. …
>
> There is but one plain known road, not enclosed by your palings or mine, not by private judgment, but by the severe laws of humility and obedience; when you wander from this you are lost. You must be altogether within the house of God, within the walls of salvation, to be sound and safe from injury; if you wander and walk abroad ever so little, if you carelessly thrust hand or foot out of the ship, if you stir up ever so small a mutiny in the crew, you shall be thrust forth; — the door is shut, the ocean roars, you are undone.
>
> Pardon, my venerated old friend, for these just reproaches and for the heat of my love … let me avert the perilous crisis of so noble a man and so dear a friend, with any dose however bitter.[337]

Sacred Heart of Jesus, sovereign over every soul, gather all people into Your saving ark, the Holy Catholic Church. St. Edmund Campion, pray for us!

December

December 1 | *St. Charles de Foucauld*

St. Charles de Foucauld (1858–1916) squandered his youth on worldly pleasures before a powerful encounter with Christ inspired him to become a priest, religious, and hermit. In this letter, Saint Charles consoles Monsignor Guérin, on the death of his mother, observing that she has come into the full possession of her hopes.

> [My Mass] was offered for this soul so dear. And if she is dear to you, she is dearer to the Heart of Jesus. We love with the poor heart of sinful man, but He loves with a Heart Divine. She is in good hands and in a good place; in the place that we yearn to be, where one day we will be with her and the one whom she taught you to love.
>
> She is at rest. She no longer has need of refreshment. She has entered that place inundated with peace where there is no longer wind nor winter, because these former things have passed. When will we be there? … For my part, I hardly dare to say; I am so unworthy of that journey. Would one dare to hope if the good God had not commanded it? Hope is faith in His Heart. Our conversation is more and more in heaven. There, you will not only meet the one adored, but also your dear mother.[338]

Sacred Heart of Jesus, let Your perpetual light shine upon the faithfully departed, and grant them everlasting peace. St. Charles de Foucauld, pray for us!

December 2 | *Bl. Jan van Ruysbroeck*

Augustinian canon Bl. Jan van Ruysbroeck (1293–1381) speaks of man's communion with God the Father in and through the Son, sacramentally present in the Eucharist. Overwhelmed at the thought of receiving so reverend a Lord, Ruysbroeck voices his desire to be crucified with Christ and united to His Heart of love.

> In the Sacrament of the Altar, He further bestows upon us His sublime personality and His incomprehensible light. …
>
> If a man has diligently considered these things, he will meet Christ in the same way that Christ comes to him. He will rise to receive Christ with eager joy in his heart; with his desires, his love, and all his powers. And it is thus that Christ himself receives. … In this union and joy, great delights often come to men, and many mysterious and secret marvels of divine treasures are manifested and revealed. When in so receiving, a man meditates on the torment and the sufferings of the Precious Body of Christ of which he is partaking, there sometimes enters into him a devotion so loving, and a compassion so keen, that he desires to be nailed with Christ to the wood of the cross, and to shed his heart's blood in honor of Christ. And he presses into the wounds and into the open Heart of Christ his Savior.[339]

Sacred Heart of Jesus, come to me in Communion, filling my heart with supernal delights and healing every wound. Bl. Jan van Ruysbroeck, pray for us!

December 3 | *St. Francis Xavier*

St. Francis Xavier (1506–1552) was one of the seven founding members of the Society of Jesus; his extensive missionary travels led him to Africa, India, and Japan. His remarkable accomplishments were founded upon his ardent love of God, which he admirably expressed in his "Act of Love." Here, Saint Francis declares that his worship of God is not motivated by any potential profit, but by God's goodness, manifested in the crucifixion. This translation of the poetic text is rendered by the celebrated English poet and convert, John Dryden (1631–1700).

O God, Thou art the object of my love,
Not for the hopes of endless joys above,
Nor for the fear of endless pains below,
Which those who love Thee not must undergo:
For me, and such as me, Thou once didst bear
The ignominious cross, the nails, the spear,
A thorny crown transpierced Thy sacred brow,
What bloody sweats from every member flow!
For me in torture Thou resign'st Thy breath,
Nailed to the cross, and sav'dst me by Thy death:
Say, can these sufferings fail my heart to move?
What but Thyself can now deserve my love?
Such as then was and is Thy love to me,
Such is, and shall be still, my love to Thee.
Thy love, O Jesus, may I ever sing,
O God of love, kind Parent, dearest King! Amen.[340]

Sacred Heart of Jesus, You spared no sacrifice to win my devotion; may I be wholly given to You. St. Francis Xavier, tireless missionary, pray for us!

December 4 | *St. John Damascene*

St. John Damascene (c. 675–c. 749) was a Greek Father who synthesized the collected wisdom of previous centuries, anticipating the Scholastic movement of the West. The following hymn was composed for the Sunday after Easter, known in the Eastern Church as Thomas Sunday, on which the whole Church, East and West, reads the gospel passage of Saint Thomas's confession.

"Christ, we turn our eyes to Thee
And this mighty mystery!"
Habakkuk exclaimed of old,
In the Holy Spirit bold,
"Thou shalt come in time appointed,
For the help of Thine anointed!"

Taste of myrrh He deign'd to know,
Who redeemed the source of woe:
Now He bids all sickness cease
Through the honeycomb of peace:
And to this world deigns to give
That sweet food by which we live.

Patient Lord! With loving eye
Thou invitest Thomas nigh,
Show him that wounded side:
While the world is certified,
How the third day, from the grave,
Jesus Christ arose to save.

Blest, O Didymus, the tongue
Where that first confession hung:
First the Savior to proclaim
First the Lord of life to name:
Such the graces it supplied,
— That dear touch of Jesus' side![341]

Sacred Heart of Jesus, draw all mankind to Your glorified Heart, so they might have life in You. St. John Damascene, pray for us!

December 5

In his *Little Book of Eternal Wisdom*, Bl. Henry Suso considers the tender compassion that Christ had for His mother and which wounded His Sacred Heart. For upon the hill of Calvary, two Hearts beat and broke together — Christ's, which was pierced by a lance, and Mary's, which was riven by a sword of sorrow.

> Tender Lord! (1) At that hour You were forsaken by all men for my sake. (2) Your friends had renounced You. (3) You stood naked and robbed of all honor and raiment. (4) Your power then seemed overcome. (5) They treated You without mercy, and You bore it all in meekness and silence. (6) Alas, for Your gentle Heart, You who alone knew the depth of Your mother's sorrow of heart at that time. (7) And You did see her deplorable state. (8) And You did hear her lamentable words. (9) And at Your mortal separation, You commended her to the filial piety of Your disciples. (10) And the disciple [You gave] to her maternal love.
>
> Oh, therefore, You pattern of all virtues, take from me all pernicious love of men, and all inordinate affection of friends. Strip me of all impatience. Give me steadfastness against all evil spirits, and meekness against all violent men. Give me, gentle Lord, Your bitter death in the bottom of my heart, in my prayers, and in the practice of good works.[342]

Sacred Heart of Jesus, forsaken by the apostles so that all might find You, reconcile us to yourself. Bl. Henry Suso, pray for us!

December 6

The great Syrian monk St. John Climacus pursued a life of solitary prayer upon the barren heights of Mount Sinai. His ascetic writings, such as the *Ladder of Paradise*, provide ordered accounts of the spiritual life and growth in virtue. This passage distinguishes meekness from humility, drawing upon Matthew 11:29: "Learn from me; for I am gentle and lowly in heart."

> The light of dawn goes before the sun; meekness precedes humility. Therefore, let us first hear Christ the light, who disposes those things, as it were, by steps. Learn of Me, He says, for I am meek and lowly in heart. Meekness is the immutable state of the mind, which preserves an equable frame in good fortune and in disgrace. Meekness is to sincerely and *ex animo* pray for those who trouble you, without being troubled yourself. Meekness is a jutting rock against the fury of the sea, which breaks all its waves, while remaining itself unmoved and unbroken. Meekness is the prop of patience, the gate of charity, yea its very parent, the proof of prudence. For He will teach, says the Lord, the meek His ways. It is the procurer of pardon, the confidence of sinners in prayer, the habitation of the Holy Spirit. "For upon whom shall I look, save upon the meek and quiet person?" (Ps 66, Vulgate)[343]

Sacred Heart of Jesus, the same yesterday and today, place us high upon a rock where we will be untouched by the floods of the world. St. John Climacus, pray for us!

December 7 | *St. Ambrose of Milan*

In the following tract, Saint Ambrose boldly defends the consubstantial nature of the Trinity, citing Psalm 44: "My Heart has brought forth out of its depths the good Word" (see Ps 44:2, Douay-Rheims Bible). In this way, he teaches that the Son of God shares in the essential goodness of the Father, as they possess the same divine nature.

> Hear, then, the Father saying, "My Heart has brought forth out of its depths the good Word" [see Ps 44:2]. The Word, then, is good — the Word of whom it is written, "And the Word was with God, and the Word was God" [Jn 1:1]. If, therefore, the Word is good, and the Son is the Word of God, surely, the Son of God is God — though it displeases the Arians. Let them then at least blush in shame.
>
> He is good who forgives the sin of one man; then, is He not good who has taken away the sins of the world? For, it was of Him that it was said, "Behold, the Lamb of God, who takes away the sin of the world" [Jn 1:29]. Then, why do we doubt? The Church has believed in His goodness all these ages and confessed its Faith in the saying: "O that you would kiss me with the kisses of your mouth! For your love is better than wine" [Sg 1:1].[344]

Sacred Heart of Jesus, increase my trust in You, so I might not concern myself with tomorrow. St. Ambrose of Milan, pray for us!

December 8 | *Solemnity of the Immaculate Conception*

Today the Church rejoices in the wondrous mystery that the Creator should create His mother, preserving her from original sin. Here, St. Marguerite Bourgeoys (1620–1700) reflects on the Immaculate Conception and how Mary's heart sweetly echoes the Sacred Heart of Jesus, ever distributing His graces.

> The charity of the Holy Virgin is like a crystalline water. … It is through Mary that we must go to God, because it is through her that the Eternal Father has given us His Son. We go to Mary, observing the great precept of charity that she herself had observed, insofar as our weakness will permit. Conceived without sin, in the state of original justice of the first man, but more faithful than he, she began loving her God from her own conception and became porter to him by an act of the most perfect love; love in spirit and truth. She recognized His greatness and gave thanks for His graces; yet at the same time, she recognized her frailty as one drawn from nothingness and was utterly annihilated in the presence of her God. Because of His love of humility, God cast a favorable glance on the lowliness of His handmaid, choosing her to be the mother of Him who burns with love for mankind, the Redeemer of all.[345]

Sacred Heart of Jesus, by the intercession of Your mother, purify our souls of every sin. O Mary, mother of mercy, my mother: Be with us at the hour of death!

December 9

In his *Life of Christ,* St. Bonaventure, a Franciscan and bishop, reflects on Christ's sublime example of humility. He urges his readers to contemplate the lowliness of Christ, so as to imitate His humility of heart.

> You observe, then, how the Lord Jesus "first began to do, then to teach"; for He was soon to say: "Learn of Me, for I am meek and lowly in heart." It was this that He would first unfeignedly practice, doing it from the heart; for He was truly and from the heart lowly and meek. There could be no disharmony in Him; but rather, He abased himself more and more profoundly in lowliness, vileness, and abjection; yea, He made himself of no account in the sight of all men, so that even after He began to preach and to reveal high and divine truths, and also to do actual miracles and mighty works, they still held Him in no reputation, but vilified and derided Him, saying, "Who is this? Is not this the carpenter's son?" and used similar derisive and reproachful expressions. In this sense were indeed verified the words of the apostle, when he said of Our Lord, "He emptied himself, and took upon Him the form of a servant"; not only of a servant, by His Incarnation, but of a seemingly unprofitable servant by His lowly and abject mode of life.[346]

Sacred Heart of Jesus, deign to stoop to my soul, binding its wounds and tending to its needs. Saint Bonaventure, pray for us!

December 10

In *Christ in His Mysteries*, Bl. Columba Marmion teaches that every aspect of life — adoration, work, recreation — ought to be ordered toward the Sacred Heart of Jesus and offered as a token of love.

> Let us accustom ourselves to do all things, even the smallest, in order to please Christ Jesus. To work, to accept our pains and sufferings, to fulfill our duties of state out of love, so as to be agreeable to Our Lord, in union with the dispositions of His Heart when He lived here below like us, constitutes an excellent practice of devotion towards the Sacred Heart. All our life is thus referred to Him. …
>
> As you know, every act of virtue, of humility, of obedience, of religion, done in a state of grace, possesses its own merit, its special perfection, its particular splendor: But when this act is dominated by love, it gains a new efficacy and beauty, without losing anything of its own value. … The psalmist sings to God, "The queen stands at Your right hand in gilded clothing; surrounded with variety": *Adstetit regina a dextris tuis in vestitu deaurato circumdata varietate.* The queen is the faithful soul in whom Christ reigns by His grace. She stands at the King's right hand, clad in a robe woven of gold, which signifies love … which is the deep source of these virtues, enhances their splendor.[347]

Sacred Heart of Jesus, I offer my prayers, sufferings, and deeds, asking that You make them bear fruit. Blessed Columba, pray for us!

December 11

An English laywoman and mother, Margery Kempe (c. 1373–c. 1438) undertook great pilgrimages to the Holy Land and to Santiago de Compostela. In the following excerpt from her autobiography, she recounts a vision of Christ, who reassures Margery of His forgiveness, concerning himself only with her repentance and present holiness.

> "Ah! Daughter," said Our Lord, "fear thee nothing. I take no heed what a man hath been, but I take heed what he will be. Daughter, thou hast despised thyself; therefore thou shalt never be despised of God. Have mind, daughter, what Mary Magdalene was, Mary of Egypt, Saint Paul, and many other saints that are now in heaven, for of unworthy, I make worthy, and of sinful, I make rightful. And so have I made thee worthy. To Me, once loved, and ever more loved by Me. There is no saint in heaven that thou wilt speak with, but He shall come to thee. Whom God loveth, they love. When thou pleasest God, thou pleasest His mother, and all the saints in heaven. Daughter, I take witness of My mother, of all the angels in heaven, and of all the saints in heaven, that I love thee with all My Heart, and I may not forget thy love."
>
> Our Lord said then to His blissful mother: — "Blessed Mother, tell ye My daughter of the greatness of the love I have unto her."[348]

Sacred Heart of Jesus, whose glance is as fire, convert me unto You, driving away the darkness of sin, for I adore you!

December 12 | *Feast of Our Lady of Guadalupe*

Today we recall the history-altering apparitions of the Blessed Virgin Mary to St. Juan Diego, who transcended his attachments to the world, becoming obedient to the voice of his heavenly mother. In the following text from *Devotion to the Sacred Heart of Jesus,* Fr. Secondo Franco argues that the daily experience of suffering should inspire Christians to similarly transcend worldliness in order to rest in the cross, thereby uniting themselves to the heavenly Heart of Jesus.

> What is the end in view concerning our sufferings? Our Lord does not take pleasure in our troubles, but He permits them, that we may detach ourselves from creatures — and especially from ourselves — and draw more closely to Him, uniting ourselves to Him more and more. But if this is the end proposed by our sweet Jesus in the afflictions that He sends us and permits to be heaped upon us, if these are His loving designs in regard to our tribulations, it is evident that nothing can be more agreeable to Him than to see us have recourse to His Divine Heart, while at the same time, we practice eminent acts of virtue. A soul that turns from the depths of its misery to the Heart of Jesus tends to elevate itself above the trifles of the world to rise superior to the troubles of life, to break the bonds that hold it captive to the earth.[349]

Sacred Heart of Jesus, sustain us in our tribulations, crowning our efforts with Your blessing. I trust in You!

December 13

The work of Fr. Cornelius à Lapide exemplifies a spirit of faith seeking understanding. Here, he emphasizes that the piercing of Christ's side (see Jn 19:34) was foreseen and intended by Christ that His Heart be given to mankind.

> Instead of His legs being broken, His side was pierced with the spear. This was after He was dead, not while He was alive as some have thought. This error was condemned in the Council of Vienne. For as Christ gave up His whole Body for us while alive, so did He wish to give us His Heart in death. For this it was pierced by the spear, and Blood and water flowed forth from it, so that He gave himself entirely to us.
>
> You will say that Christ was already dead, and that therefore He merited nothing by this piercing of His Heart. But I reply that He knew, when alive, this wound would be inflicted, and that He offered it to the Father for us, and thus merited and effected our salvation. You will say next, we see that blood flows from the body of a slain person if the murderer is present. This, then, is a natural effect. I say that it is not natural, but very nearly miraculous; to point out and confound the murderer. And much more was it miraculous in the case of Christ.[350]

Sacred Heart of Jesus, inflame our hearts with that holy fire that You came to cast upon the earth. Sacred Heart of Jesus, I love You!

December 14 | *St. John of the Cross*

A reformer of the Carmelite order, St. John of the Cross described the *via negativa,* in which the soul is stripped and led to rely on God alone. In this excerpt from his "Dark Night of the Soul," he speaks on the virtue of hope, which guides souls through the travails of the dark night and captivates the Heart of the Beloved (see Sg 4:9).

> In the green vesture of hope, the soul is then ever looking upwards unto God, disregarding all else and delighting only in Him. This is so pleasing to the beloved that the soul obtains from Him all it hopes for. This is why He tells the soul in the Canticle, "You have ravished my heart with a glance of your eyes" [Sg 4:9]. It would not have been expedient for the soul to claim such love if it had not put on the green robe of hope; for it would not have succeeded, because that which influences the beloved, and prevails, is persevering hope. It is in the vesture of hope that the soul goes forth disguised, secure in the secret and obscure night; for it goes forth so detached from all possessions and consolations that it regards nothing, and its sole anxiety is about God, putting its "mouth in the dust [so] there may yet be hope" [Lam 3:29].[351]

Sacred Heart of Jesus, raise us from desolation to the heights of confident love, leading us to Your heavenly embrace. St. John of the Cross, pray for us!

December 15

In this sermon, St. John Chrysostom relates the opening of Christ's side to the mystery of God's providence, observing that the soldiers, by piercing Jesus, accomplished God's designs when Christ's wounded Heart poured forth life-giving Blood and water.

> See how powerful a thing is Truth? By means of the very objects of their zeal, prophecy is fulfilled; for by occasion of those things, this plain prediction, unconnected with them, receives its accomplishment. For when the soldiers came, they broke the legs of the others, but not those of Christ. [They] pierced His side with a spear, insulting the dead Body. O abominable and accursed purpose! Yet, beloved, do not be confounded nor despondent; for the things that these men did with a wicked will fought on the side of the Truth, since there was a prophecy saying, "They [shall] look on him whom they have pierced" (Zec 12:10). ... With this too an ineffable mystery was accomplished. For "there came out blood and water" [Jn 19:34]. Not without a purpose, or by chance did those founts come forth, but because by means of these two together the Church consists. And the initiated know it, being by water indeed regenerate, and nourished by the Blood and the Flesh. Hence the mysteries take their beginning; that when you approach that awful cup, you may approach as drinking from the very side.[352]

Sacred Heart of Jesus, let fall a shower of grace from Your opened side, granting us a share in Your redemption. St. John Chrysostom, pray for us!

December 16

In this narrative, Bl. Mary of the Divine Heart recalls entering her community and discovering that another religious sister was already called "Mary of the Sacred Heart of Jesus." Concerned, but meekly silent, she found Jesus' promise nevertheless fulfilled when she was named "Mary of the Divine Heart."

> Before ringing the doorbell, we paid a visit to the church. What was my joy to find the Blessed Sacrament exposed. My Spouse — my Jesus — was awaiting me with His Heart open to receive me. I was overwhelmed with confusion and gratitude, and I felt my heart burning with love and with a desire to be all His own and to possess Him entirely. … My Divine Spouse was thus the first to receive me into the monastery. …
>
> I lost no time in making inquiries if anyone in the community bore the name of Sister Mary of the Sacred Heart of Jesus. When I found that such was the case, I felt sorry, as I thought it belonged to me in some degree. Our Lord did not, after all, want me as the spouse of His Heart. The words I had heard in 1884, and all His favors, were delusions. I resigned myself to God's will, though with difficulty. But He who had never deceived me, though I had several times been wanting in confidence in Him, had settled everything.[353]

Sacred Heart of Jesus, bring all things to their perfect end. Guide me on right paths, leading me to Your heavenly Heart. Blessed Mary, pray for us!

December 17

Julian of Norwich's *Revelations of Divine Love* vividly portrays the passion, death, and Resurrection of Christ. Here Julian famously compares the love of Jesus to that of a tender mother, considering how Christ nourishes Christians from His opened side.

> He sustaineth us within himself in love; and travailed, unto the full time that He would suffer the sharpest throes and the most grievous pains that ever were or ever shall be; and died at the last. And when He had finished, and so borne us to bliss, yet might not all this make full content to His marvelous love; and that sheweth He in these high overpassing words of love: *If I might suffer more, I would suffer more.*
>
> He might no more die, but He would not stint of working: Wherefore then it behoveth Him to feed us; for the dear-worthy love of Motherhood hath made Him debtor to us. The mother may give her child suck of her milk, but our precious Mother, Jesus, He may feed us with himself, and doeth it, full courteously and full tenderly, with the Blessed Sacrament that is precious food of my life. ... The mother may lay the child tenderly to her breast, but our tender Mother, Jesus, He may homely lead us into [His sweet open side] ... where He saith: *Lo! How I loved thee.*[354]

Sacred Heart of Jesus, no sacrifice was too great for Your love of me: let me never limit my love for You!

December 18

St. John Cassian was an eremitic monk who here teaches that God's attributes cannot be circumscribed by human language. Being infinite, the most tender expressions fall short of capturing the great love of God.

> Finally, the blessed apostle, when considering the manifold bounty of God's providence … exclaims, "O the depth of the riches and wisdom and knowledge of God! How unsearchable are his judgments and how inscrutable his ways! For who has known the mind of the Lord?" [Rom 11:33–34] Whoever then imagines that he, by human reason, can fathom the depths of that inconceivable abyss, will be trying to explain away the astonishment at that knowledge, at which that great and mighty teacher of the Gentiles was amazed. … This providence and love of God — which the Lord in His unwearied goodness graciously shows us — He, therefore, compares to the tenderest heart of a kind mother, as He wishes to express it by a figure of human affection and finds no better comparison in His creatures. And He uses this example, because nothing dearer can be found in human nature, saying, "Can a woman forget her sucking child, that she should have no compassion on the son of her womb?" But not content with this comparison, He at once goes beyond it, and adds these words: "Even these may forget, yet I will not forget you" [Is 49:15].[355]

Sacred Heart of Jesus, let the full force of Your love be impressed upon our hearts, increasing our trust in You. St. John Cassian, pray for us!

December 19

Pope St. Leo the Great urged Christians to observe Christ's dual natures in the Nativity, participating in the grace and excellences of His divine-human heart through loving union.

> Consider, beloved, and ponder according to the light granted by the Holy Spirit, who it is that has drawn us into himself, and who it is that we have drawn to ourselves. For as the Lord Jesus was made our flesh by being born, so too have we been made His Body by being born again. Therefore, we are both members of Christ and the temple of the Holy Spirit.
>
> On this account, the apostle says, "Glorify God in your body." And while manifesting the pattern of His gentleness and lowliness, He infuses into us the same power with which He redeemed us, as He himself promises, "Come unto Me, all you who labor and are heavy laden, and I will refresh you. Take My yoke upon you, and learn of Me, for I am meek and lowly of heart, and you shall find rest unto your souls." Let us, then, take on [the yoke of Truth] which guides us, and be conformed to His lowliness whose glory we desire to be conformed, while He assists and leads us on to His promises. For He is able to efface our sins … according to His great mercy.[356]

Sacred Heart of Jesus, you invite all to gaze upon Your Nativity: May my eyes never depart from You! Pope Saint Leo, pray for us!

December 20

The *Didache* (c. 70–100), also known as *The Teaching of the Twelve Apostles*, recounts the apostolic instruction on Christian morality, theology, and sacraments. The tenth chapter contains post-Communion prayers similar to those recited in present-day liturgy. Here, refreshed by the Body and Blood of Christ, the Church prays to be made perfect in God's love.

> After you are filled, thus give thanks: We thank You, Holy Father, for Your holy Name, which You caused to tabernacle in our hearts, and for the knowledge, Faith, and immortality, which You made known to us through Jesus, Your servant; to You be the glory forever. You, Master Almighty, created all things for Your Name's sake. You gave food and drink to men for enjoyment, that they might give thanks to You; but to us, You freely gave spiritual food and drink and life eternal through Your servant. Before all things, we thank You that You are mighty; to You be the glory forever.
>
> Remember, Lord, Your Church, to deliver it from all evil and to make it perfect in Your love. Gather it from the four winds, sanctified for Your kingdom which You have prepared for it; for Yours is the power and the glory forever. Let grace come, and let this world pass away. Hosanna to the Son of David! If anyone is holy, let him come; if anyone is not so, let him repent. Maranatha. Amen.[357]

Sacred Heart of Jesus, deliver us from the exile of sin, reconciling all as one in You. Indeed, Your kingdom come!

December 21 | *St. Peter Canisius*

A Jesuit and Doctor of the Church, St. Peter Canisius (1521–1597) here renders thanks to the Sacred Heart of Jesus for protecting him throughout the night and surrenders his heart to the Lord, allowing his life's work to be divinized in and through the Sacred Heart.

> I praise, bless, glorify, and salute the most sweet and benevolent Heart of Jesus, most faithful of all lovers. And I thank You for the unfailing protection that You have rendered me this night: On my behalf, You unceasingly rendered praise, acts of thanksgiving, and all that I owe to God the Father. … I also offer my heart to You as a chalice that You might partake of, savoring Your very sweetness in those operations You condescend to work in me this day. Furthermore, I offer my heart to you as a most excellent pomegranate for Your banquet, that by consuming it, it may pass over into You, and there rejoice in You, and thus pray that every thought, word, deed, and act this day be directed according to Your good pleasure and most benevolent will. Upon every action, impress the sign of Your cross. This I pray in the name of the Father, and the Son, and the Holy Spirit. Amen. Holy Father, in union with the love of Your well-beloved Son, to You, I commend my spirit.[358]

Sacred Heart of Jesus, help me to give of myself without counting the cost, laying my life down for You! St. Peter Canisius, pray for us!

December 22

In the following series of spiritual counsels, St. Margaret Mary Alacoque proposes an examen centered upon the Sacred Heart of Jesus.

> If you are filled with pride and vain self-esteem, bury yourself in the humility of the Sacred Heart.
>
> … in an abyss of ignorance, go and plunge yourself into the loving Heart of Jesus. He will teach you how to love and please Him.
>
> … in an abyss of infidelities and inconstancy, go and hide yourself in the constancy and stability of the Heart of Jesus. Are you buried in poverty? Go to the Heart of Jesus, which is a treasure-house of all riches and of all good.
>
> … in an abyss of ingratitude for the great gifts you have received from God, go and hide yourself in the Heart of Jesus, the source of all gratitude. …
>
> … in an abyss of agitation, impatience, or anger, go and bury yourself in the sweetness of the loving Heart of Jesus so that He may render you meek and humble of heart.
>
> … in abyss of distractions and dissipation, go and rest in the tranquility of the Sacred Heart. …
>
> If you combat generously, you can lose yourself in the abyss of His purity and consolation. …
>
> If you are lost in darkness, He will clothe you with His light so that you can give yourself up blindly to His guidance.[359]

Sacred Heart of Jesus, have mercy on me, a sinner! St. Margaret Mary Alacoque, obtain for me true devotion to the Sacred Heart!

December 23

St. Peter Julian Eymard was profoundly devoted to the Blessed Sacrament and here instructs Eucharistic adorers to ever seek fresh appreciation for His mercies. As Our Lady meditated upon the birth of her Son, so ought Christians contemplate the Nativity of the Lord, wondering at the humble birth of Love Itself.

> "Adore incessantly our Eucharistic Jesus, but vary your adoration as the Blessed Virgin did. Recall and revive all the mysteries of religion in the Eucharist, else you will fall into routine. If the spirit of your love is not nourished by some form, some new thought, you will become dull in prayer." We should, then, celebrate all the mysteries in the Eucharist.
>
> It was thus that Mary acted in the Cenacle. When the anniversaries of the great mysteries, wrought under her own eyes came around, can we think that she did not recall their circumstances, the words, the graces connected with them? When, for instance, Christmas came around, can we imagine that Mary did not recall to her Son, then hidden under the Eucharistic veil, the love that greeted Him at His birth, His first smile, her own adoration, also that of Saint Joseph, the shepherds, and the Magi? She desired thereby to rejoice the Heart of Jesus by recalling to Him her love. And so it was with all the other mysteries.[360]

Sacred Heart of Jesus, You had nowhere to lay Your head on earth: recline upon my heart. St. Peter Julian Eymard, obtain for us reverence for the Blessed Sacrament!

December 24 | *Vigil of the Nativity of the Lord*

Today Christians gaze upon the Light of the World, born in a darkened cave in Bethlehem. Fr. Cajetan Maria da Bergamo (1672–1753) here marvels that Jesus condescended to be born in a stable and subject himself to the law, desiring only the Father's will.

> What humility, to be born in a stable — He who was the King of glory! What humility in Him, who was innocence itself, to appear as a sinner at the circumcision! What humility in the flight into Egypt to escape the persecution of Herod, as if He had been incapable of saving himself otherwise than by flight! What humility in His subjection to Mary and Joseph, He who was the King of the whole universe! What humility in living for thirty years in a hidden life of poverty, He who could have been surrounded by all the splendor of the whole world! With what humility He bore all the insults and calumnies He received in return for the Truths He preached and the miracles He worked, never complaining or lamenting those ills that were done to Him, nor the injustice that was shown to Him! Oh, if one could have looked into His Heart, one would have seen that His humility was not obligatory but voluntary, because "it was the will of the Lord" (Is 53:10).[361]

Sacred Heart of Jesus, Light of the World, born in the darkness of night, fill my soul with the radiance of Your love. Sacred Heart of Jesus, I adore you!

December 25 | *Solemnity of the Nativity of the Lord*

Christmas blessings! St. Robert Southwell's poem "The Burning Babe" describes a mystical vision of the Newborn Lord. The Divine Child speaks to the amazed narrator, explaining his tears and the flames upon His breast.

> As I in hoary winter's night stood shivering in the snow,
> Surprised I was with sudden heat which made my heart to glow;
> And lifting up a fearful eye to view what fire was near,
> A pretty babe all burning bright did in the air appear,
> Who scorchèd with exceeding heat such floods of tears did shed,
> As though His floods should quench His flames with what His tears were fed;
> Alas! quoth He, but newly born in fiery heats of fry,
> Yet none approach to warm their hearts or feel my fire but I!
> My faultless breast the furnace is, the fuel wounding thorns;
> Love is the fire and sighs the smoke, the ashes shame and scorns;
> The fuel justice layeth on, and mercy blows the coals;
> The metal in this furnace wrought are men's defiled souls;
> For which, as now on fire I am, to work them to their good,
> So will I melt into a bath, to wash them in my Blood:
> With this He vanish'd out of sight, and swiftly shrunk away,

And straight I callèd unto mind that it was Christmas day.[362]

Sacred Heart of Jesus may my soul ever exult in the Newborn Lord — my hope, my Savior, and my God! Sacred Heart of Jesus, burning with love, I adore You!

December 26

Peter Lombard (1096–1160) was one of the great Scholastic theologians; his *Sentences* served as a precursor to St. Thomas Aquinas's *Summa Theologiae.* In the following excerpt of this work, Peter explores several typological signs of baptism and the Eucharist. Because the signs present in the Mosaic covenant — the Red Sea and the manna — were themselves preceded by the bread and wine of Melchizedek, Peter Lombard concludes that the Christian sacraments were themselves prior to the Mosaic law. This argument follows that of Saint Paul in his Epistle to the Hebrews in which he argues the preeminence of Melchizedek's priesthood to that of the Levites (see Heb 7:1–28).

> Just as in the Red Sea we find baptism typified, so in the manna is the Lord's Body signified. These two sacraments were indicated when the Blood and water flowed from the side of Christ; because Christ came to redeem us from the devil and sin by the Blood of redemption and the water of cleansing, just as He freed the Israelites from the destroyer by the blood of the paschal lamb and from the Egyptians by the water of the sea. Melchizedek also prefigured the rite of this Sacrament when he offered bread and wine to Abraham. Wherefore, as Ambrose says, it is clear "that the sacraments of the Christians came before those of the Jews."[363]

Sacred Heart of Jesus, everlasting love, let all souls stream to the sanctuary of Your side. Satisfy us with Your life-giving drink, and renew us in Your Eucharistic Sacrifice!

December 27 | *St. John, Apostle and Evangelist*

In his *Sermons on the Song of Songs,* the eloquent St. Bernard of Clairvaux ponders verse 2:14: "O my dove, in the clefts of the rock." Taking the rocky cleft as the wounded Heart of Jesus, Saint Bernard urges deep contemplation, proposing St. John the Apostle as the foremost model of wisdom and adoration.

> Happy is the soul who has made it his study to frequently hollow out caves of refuge on this wall for itself, and still happier if its refuge be in the rock. For it is open to us to hew and hollow out our refuge even in the rock; but for this is required the sharper edge of purity, as it were. … And who can be thought qualified in these respects? Surely, he who said: "In the beginning was the Word, and the Word was with God, and the Word was God. He was in the beginning with God" (Jn 1:1–2).
>
> Does it not seem to you that this man is one who has plunged and whelmed himself, so to speak, in the abysses of the Word as in the depths of a sea, and who, from the recesses of the Heart of Jesus, has brought forth the very marrow of the deepest and most sacred wisdom?[364]

Sacred Heart of Jesus, grant me the heavenly gifts of purity, piety, and perseverance, that I may enter the inmost cell of Your Heart. St. John the Evangelist, pray for us!

December 28

Like the great Doctor of Prayer, St. Teresa of Àvila, Fr. Diego Álvarez de Paz (1560–1620), a Spanish Jesuit, here recommends contemplating the humanity of Christ in order to arrive at His divinity.

> Try to enter into the Heart of Jesus to contemplate it as it really is, that you may form your heart to the likeness of this Divine Heart. This Heart is the way by which we reach the place of our eternal rest, which is nothing other than the divinity of Jesus Christ. It is the gate by which we enter in to contemplate the divinity. If, then, you wish to attain to this contemplation, and to inflame yourself with the love of God, endeavor by earnest meditation to enter into the Heart of Jesus, the purest and holiest of all hearts, in order to conform your heart to it. …
>
> O Jesus, Savior of mankind, in the imitation of whom all our perfection consists, open to me, I beseech You, Your Sacred Heart, the gate of life and the fountain of the waters of grace, in order that, through this Divine Heart, I may enter into the knowledge of yourself, [drinking] the saving waters of true virtue, which quench all thirst for earthly things."[365]

Sacred Heart of Jesus, born in a stable-cave, cleanse my heart with the waters of meekness and humility, so I may perceive Your divine presence. Holy Mary and St. Joseph, pray for me!

December 29

In his encyclical *Deus Caritas Est,* Pope Benedict XVI (1927–2022) offers a summary description of Christian spirituality as it relates to the Sacred Heart of Jesus. Here he identifies those "rivers of living water" (Jn 7:38) that spring from the hearts of believers as the Holy Spirit, which conforms Christians' hearts to that of Christ.

> By dying on the cross — as Saint John tells us — Jesus "gave up his spirit" (Jn 19:30), anticipating the gift of the Holy Spirit that He would make after His Resurrection (see Jn 20:22). This was to fulfil the promise of "rivers of living water" that would flow out of the hearts of believers, through the outpouring of the Spirit (see Jn 7:38–39). The Spirit, in fact, is that interior power which harmonizes their hearts with Christ's heart and moves them to love their brethren as Christ loved them, when He bent down to wash the feet of the disciples (see Jn 13:1–13) and above all when He gave His life for us (see Jn 13:1: 15:13). …
>
> The entire activity of the Church is an expression of a love that seeks the integral good of man: It seeks his evangelization through word and sacrament, an undertaking that is often heroic in the way it is acted out in history; and it seeks to promote man in the various arenas of life and human activity.[366]

Sacred Heart of Jesus, renew us in Your grace, fulfilling in us Your redemption. Pope Benedict XVI, pray for us!

December 30

Pope Pius VI (1717–1799) led the Church through the tumultuous years of the French Revolution and was himself a victim of its cruel intolerance, having died in exile from the Papal States. He granted an indulgence to the following prayer — a benefit confirmed by his successor, Servant of God Pope Pius VII (1742–1823). This exclamatory prayer, here slightly modernized, praises the gift of the Eucharist and marvels at its exceeding benefits. Finding no explanation for so reverend a gift, the author concludes that the unrestricted love of the Sacred Heart must be its reason and source as love alone could account for such an offering.

> See where Your boundless love has reached, my loving Jesus! You, of Your Flesh and Precious Blood, have prepared for me a banquet whereby You would give yourself wholly to me. Who drove You to this excess of love for me? Your Heart, Your loving Heart. O adorable Heart of Jesus! Burning furnace of divine love! Within Your sacred wound, take my soul; that in that school of charity I may learn to love that God who has given me such wondrous proofs of His great love. Amen.[367]

Sacred Heart of Jesus, scorned by mankind, stir me to make reparation for the coldness of human hearts. Enclose me in the conflagration of Your love, consuming me as a living sacrifice. Sacred Heart of Jesus, with all my heart, I love You!

December 31

St. Claude de la Colombiére's "Offering to the Sacred Heart of Jesus" is a consummate expression of the Sacred Heart devotion, blending prayerful thanksgiving with solemn repentance. Burning with ardor, St. Claude encourages Christians to return love for such undeserved love.

> The principal virtues that we intend to honor in Him are: first, a most ardent love for God, His Father, joined to a most profound respect and the greatest possible humility. Second, infinite patience under trials, deep sorrow, and contrition for sins — the burden of which He had taken upon himself, the trust of a most affectionate Son, together with the shame of a grievous sinner. Third, tender compassion for our misery, immense love in spite of these miseries. …
>
> This Heart is still, as far as can be, in the same dispositions, and above all, ever burning with love for men, ever open to shower down every kind of grace and blessing, ever touched with our sorrows, ever animated with the desire to impart to us its treasures, and to give itself to us, ever ready to receive us and afford us shelter, home, and paradise, even in this life.
>
> Notwithstanding all this, He is met only with hardness, neglect, contempt, and ingratitude in men's hearts. He loves and is not loved in return; and men do not even recognize His love.[368]

Sacred Heart of Jesus, inspire us to still greater praise. Let all hearts give You thanks and every tongue sing of Your glory. I consecrate myself to You!

Consecration to the Sacred Heart of Jesus

By St. Margaret Mary Alacoque

I, *N.*, give and consecrate to the Sacred Heart of Our Lord Jesus Christ my person and my life, my actions, penances, and sufferings, not wishing to make use of any part of my being for the future except in honoring, loving, and glorifying that Sacred Heart. It is my irrevocable will to be entirely His, and to do everything for His love, renouncing with my whole heart whatever might displease Him.

I take You, then, O Most Sacred Heart, as the sole object of my love, as the protector of my life, as the pledge of my salvation, as the remedy of my frailty and inconstancy, as the repairer of all the defects of my life, and as my secure refuge in the hour of death. Be then, O Heart of goodness, my justification before God the Father, and remove far from me the thunderbolts of His just wrath. O Heart of love, I place my whole confidence in You. While I fear all things from my malice and frailty, I hope all things from Your goodness.

Consume then in me whatever can displease or be opposed to You, and may Your pure love be so deeply impressed upon my heart that it may be impossible that I should ever be separated from You, or forget You. I implore You, by all Your goodness, that my name may be written in You, for in You I wish to place all my happiness and all my glory, living and dying bound to You. Amen.[369]

Acknowledgments

Special thanks to the staff at OSV Books for their support and belief in this project. It would be impossible to name the cloud of witnesses who have inspired me along the way: the Benedictines of Cleveland, the friendship and guidance of Kenneth Howell, Molly Henley, and many others. Not being able to name everyone who has helped in some way, I will confine myself to thanking my mother.

Notes

1. Columba Marmion, *Le Christ dans Ses Mystéres* (Paris: St. Augustin, Desclée, de Brouwer et Cie., 1922), 444–445. Translated by Kronholz. Unless otherwise indicated, all works that have been translated into English for this book were translated by the author.

2. Basil the Great, "Letter to Maximus" in Philip Schaff and Henry Wace, *Nicene and Post-Nicene Fathers, Second Series, vol. 8* (New York: Christian Literature, 1895), 311. Works in the public domain cited in this book have been newly prepared, sometimes with slight changes to capitalization, punctuation, etc., and sometimes by updating and clarifying antiquated language.

3. *Summi Parentis Filio.*

4. Elizabeth Ann Seton, "Letter" in Sister Mary Agnes McCann, *Mother Seton: Foundress of the Sisters of Charity* (Mount St. Joseph-on-the-Ohio: Sisters of Charity, 1909), 18–19.

5. John Neumann, "Journal" in Johann Berger, *Life of John N. Neumann* (New York: Benziger, 1884), 67.

6. Carlo da Sezze, *Camino Interno dell'Anima* (Roma: Francesco Moneta, 1664), 170–171.

7. Angela of Foligno, *The Book of Divine Consolation of the Blessed Angela of Foligno,* trans. Mary Steegmann (London: Chatto and Windus, 1909), 56–58.

8. Laurent Justinien, *De L'incendie du divin amour* (Paris: Sagnier et Bray, 1849), 11–12.

9. Pauline Jaricot, *L'Amour infini dans la divine Eucharistie* (Paris: Les libraires associés, 1823), 64–66.

10. Gregory of Nyssa, "Against Eunomius" in Philip Schaff and Henry Wace, *Nicene and Post-Nicene Fathers, Second Series, vol. 5* (New York: Christian Literature, 1892), 81.

11. Paulinus of Aquileia, *Liber exhortationis ad Henricum Forojul,* ch. 52.

12. Aelred of Rievaulx, *Sermon 27.*

13. Hilary of Poitiers, "Commentary on the Psalms" in Philip Schaff and Henry Wace, *Nicene and Post-Nicene Fathers of the Christian Church, Second Series, vol. 9* (New York: Charles Scribner's Sons,1899), 243.

14. Methodius of Olympus, "Banquet of the Ten Virgins" in Alexander Roberts, James Donaldson, and A. Cleveland Coxe, *Ante-Nicene Fathers, vol. 6,* (New York: Christian Literature, 1886), 332.

15. Macarius of Egypt, "Homily 19" in A.J. Mason, *Fifty Spiritual Homilies of St. Macarius the Egyptian* (London: Society for Promoting Christian Knowledge, 1921), 157–158.

16. Mechtilde, *The Love of the Sacred Heart* (London: Burns, Oates, and Washbourne, 1922), 136–137.

17. This sentence highlights the Son of God's humility in becoming man, not that He dwelt in the human nature of another (the heresy of Adoptionism).

18. Hieronymus Palladius, *The Book of Paradise, vol. 1,* trans. E.A. Wallis Budge (London: W. Druglin, 1904), 433–434.

19. Margaret Mary Alacoque, "Letter" in Mary Philip, *Life of Blessed Margaret Mary Alacoque* (Edinburgh: Sands & Co., 1919), 213–214.

20. St. Bernard of Clairvaux, "Sermon 61 on the Song of Songs" in John Hodges, *Life and Works of Saint Bernard, vol. 4,* ed. Jean Mabillon, trans. Samuel J. Eales (Holland: Motley Press, 1896), 367–368.

21. Origen in Thomas Aquinas, *Catena Aurea, vol. I* (Oxford: John Henry Parker, 1862), 909. Here, a crucial distinction is tacitly made between Christ's *simple* and *chosen* will: Whereas Christ's human will, simply understood, would have naturally recoiled from suffering (e.g., "let this cup pass"), He ever chose the will of the Father (e.g., "not My will, but Yours be done").

22. Gertrude the Great, *The Exercises of Saint Gertrude,* trans. P. Guéranger (London: Burns and Lambert, 1863), 197–198.

23. Sister Athanasius Braegelmann, *The Life and Writings of Ildefonsus of Toledo,* The Catholic University of America Studies in Mediaeval History, New Series, Vol. IV (Washington D.C., The Catholic University of America Press, 1942), 95, 104.

24. Henry Suso, *A Little Book of Eternal Wisdom* (London: R. &. T. Washbourne, 1910), 105–107.

25. Francis de Sales, *Introduction to the Devout Life* (London: Longmans, Green, and Co., 1891), 258.

26. *Tinctam ergo Christi sanguine.*

27. Thomas á Kempis, *Meditations on the Life of Christ,* trans. H.P. Wright (New York: E.P. Dutton & Co., 1892), 210–211.

28. Angela Merici, "Last Testament" in Bernard O'Reilly, *St. Angela Merici and the Ursulines* (London: Burns and Oates, 1880), 233–234.

29. Thomas Aquinas, *Ninety-Nine Homilies of Thomas Aquinas upon the Epistles and Gospels for Forty-Nine Sundays of the Christian Year,* trans. John M. Ashley (London: Church Press, 1867), 16–17.

30. Mary of the Divine Heart in Louis Chasle, *Sister Mary of the Divine*

Heart (London: Burns & Oates, 1906), 181.

31. *The Ancren Riwle: A Treatise on the Rules and Duties of Monastic Life,* ed. and trans. James Morton (London: Camden Society, 1853), 293.

32. *Life of St. Joseph, Spouse of Mary, Foster Father of Jesus,* ed. John Bosco (Torino: Oratorio di Francesco di Sales, 1867), 73–75. Available online: http://www.donboscosanto.eu/oe/vita_di_s._giuseppe.php#_Toc228451742.

33. Pius XI, *Miserentissimus Redemptor* (Vatican City: Libreria Editrice Vaticana, May 8, 1928), par. 3.

34. Margaret Mary Alacoque, "Mémoire" in Monseigneur Bouguad, *Life of Blessed Margaret Mary Alacoque* (New York: Benziger Brothers, 1890), 165.

35. Maria Elisabetta C.G. Mora, *Life of the Venerable Elizabeth Canori Mora,* trans. Lady Herbert (London: R. Washbourne, 1878), 145, 162, 72.

36. Catherine de' Ricci, "Revelation" in F.M. Capes, *St. Catherine de'Ricci: Her Life, Her Letters, Her Community* (London: Burns & Oates, 1811).

37. Pius XII, Encyclical Letter *Haurietis Aquas* (Vatican City: Libreria Editrice Vaticana, May 15, 1956), par. 87.

38. Alphonsus Liguori, *Visits to the Most Holy Sacrament and The Blessed Virgin Mary,* trans. R.A. Coffin (London: Burns & Lambert, 1855), 218–219.

39. Pius IX, "Quanta cura" in Martin John Spalding, *Pastoral Letter: Promulgating the Jubilee* (Baltimore: Kelly and Piet, 1865), 31–32. [Encyclical: Pius IX, *Quanta Cura* (Vatican City: Libreria Editrice Vaticana, December 8, 1864), par 9.]

40. Francis Libermann, "Letter" in Prosper Goepfert, *The Life of the Venerable Francis Mary Paul Libermann* (Dublin: M.H. Gill & Son, 1880), 119.

41. Anne Catherine Emmerich, *The Dolorous Passion of Our Lord Jesus Christ* (London: Burns & Lambert, 1862), 71–72.

42. Johannes Tauler, "Sermon" in *The History and Life of the Reverend Doctor John Tauler,* trans. Susanna Winkworth (New York: Wiley & Halsted, 1858), 59–60.

43. Juan de Castañiza, *The Spiritual Conflict and Conquest* (London: Burns and Oates, 1874). 156.

44. Cornelius à Lapide, *The Great Commentary of Cornelius* à *Lapide: S. Matthew's Gospel, Chaps. X–XXI,* trans. Thomas W. Mossman (London: John Hodges, 1876), 76–77.

45. Fulton Sheen, *The Divine Romance* (Huntington, IN: Our Sunday Visitor, 1930), 60–61. [Seven addresses delivered in the Catholic Radio Hour, produced by the National Council of Catholic Men, in cooperation with the National Broadcasting Company, 1930.]

46. Mary of the Divine Heart in Louis Chasle, *Sister Mary of the Divine*

Heart (London: Burns & Oates, 1906), 56–57.

47. Claude de la Colombière, *The Sufferings of Our Lord Jesus Christ* (London: R. Washbourne, 1876), 51–52.

48. Jean Pierre de Caussade, *Abandonment: Or, Absolute Surrender to Divine Providence,* rev. H. Ramiére, trans. Ella McMahon (NY: Benziger Brothers, 1887), 65–66.

49. Walter Hilton, *The Scale (or Ladder) of Perfection* (London: Art and Book, 1901), 46–47.

50. Jean Vianney, "Catechism" in Alfred Monnin, *The Spirit of the Curé of Ars,* ed. John Edward Bowden (London: Burns, Lambert, and Oates, 1865), 72–73.

51. Bridget of Sweden, "Fifteen O Prayers" in *Revelations of St. Bridget on the Life and Passion of Our Lord and the Life of His Blessed Mother* (New York: D. & J. Sadlier & Co., 1862), 99–100.

52. Lúcia de Jesus Rosa dos Santos, *Fatima in Lucia's Own Words: Sister Lucia's Memoirs,* ed. Louis Kondor, trans. Dominican Nuns of Perpetual Rosary, (Fatima, Portugal: Secretariado dos Pastorinhos, 2007), 77–78.

53. Peter Damian, *De Gloria Paradisi.*

54. Giunta Revegnati, *Life and Revelations of Saint Margaret of Cortona,* trans. F. M'Donogh Mahony (London: Burns and Oates, 1883), 127–128.

55. Robert Southwell, "Saint Peter's Complaint" in *The Complete Poems of Robert Southwell,* ed. Alexander P. Grosart (London: Robson and Sons, 1872), 11, 16, 29, 42. .

56. Adam of Saint Victor, *S. Joannes Evangelista.*

57. Lorenzo Scupoli, *The Spiritual Combat* (n.p.: R.W. Dean & Company, 1801), 127–128.

58. John Chrysostom, "Homily 70 on the Gospel of John" in Philip Schaff, *Nicene and Post-Nicene Fathers of the Christian Church, vol. 14* (New York: Charles Scribner's Sons, 1906), 256–257.

59. Mary of Ágreda, *The Mystical City of God, vol. 3,* trans. Fiscar Marison (Mount Vernon, OH: Louis W. Bernicken, 1902), 430.

60. Saint Augustine, "Commentary on John, Tractate 61" in Philip Schaff, *Nicene and Post-Nicene Fathers of the Christian Church, vol. 7* (New York: Christian Literature, 1888), 419–420.

61. Julian of Norwich, *Revelations of Divine Love,* trans. Grace Warrack (London: Methuen & Co., 1901), 51–52.

62. *En ut superba criminum.*

63. Concepción Cabrera de Armida, *Holy Hours* (New York: Society of St. Paul, 2006), 39–40.

64. Margaret Mary Alacoque, "Instructions" in Mary Philip, *Life of Blessed Margaret Mary Alacoque* (Edinburgh: Sands & Co., 1919), 173.

65. Angela of Foligno, *The Book of Divine Consolation of the Blessed Angela of Foligno,* trans. Mary Steegmann (London: Chatto and Windus, 1909), 110–111.

66. Colette of Corbie, "Letter" in Louis Sellier, *Vie de Sainte Colette* (Amiens: Alfred Caron, 1853), 449–450.

67. Frédéric Pichon, *The Life of Monseigneur Berneux,* trans. Lady Herbert (London: Burns, Oates, and Company, 1872), 10, 144.

68. Ambrose, "On the Holy Spirit" in Philip Schaff and Henry Wace, *Nicene and Post-Nicene Fathers, Second Series, vol. 10* (New York: Christian Literature, 1896), 93.

69. Catherine of Bologna, *The Seven Spiritual Weapons,* trans. Hugh Feiss and Daniela Re (Eugene, OR: Wipf and Stock, 2011), 62–63. By permission of Peregrina Publishing.

70. Alfred Pampalon in Pierre Pampalon, *Une fleur Canadienne dans l'Institut de saint Alphonse, ou, Notice biographique du serviteur de Dieu, le R.P. Alfred Pampalon* (Ville Saint-Louis, Québec: École catholique des sourds-muets, 1907), 122, 113–114.

71. Francisco de Osuna, *Tercer parte del Abecedario espiritual* (Spain, Montserrat Abbey Library: I. del Reyno, 1638), 163–164, 172.

72. "An Epistle of Discretion" in Henry Pepwell, *The Cell of Self-Knowledge,* ed. Edmund G. Gardner (London: Chatto & Windus, 1910), 108–109.

73. Claude de la Colombiére in Louis de la Puente, *The Lights in Prayer* (London: Burns and Oates, 1893), 251–252.

74. Pius X, *E Supremi: On the Restoration of all Things in Christ* (Vatican City: Libreria Editrice Vaticana, 1903), par. 13.

75. Louise de Marillac in Alice Lady Lovat, *Life of the Venerable Louise de Marillac (Mademoiselle Le Gras)* (New York: Longmans, Green, and Co., 1917), 445, 385.

76. Mary of the Divine Heart in Louis Chasle, *Sister Mary of the Divine Heart* (London: Burns & Oates, 1906), 375, 385.

77. Patrick, "Confession" in Newport J.D. White, *St. Patrick: His Writings and Life* (London: Society for Promoting Christian Knowledge, 1920), 34–35.

78. Cyril of Jerusalem, *The Catechetical Lectures of S. Cyril: A Library of Fathers of the Holy Catholic Church, vol. 2* (Oxford: John Henry Parker, 1839), 152–153.

79. Alphonsus Liguori, *Visits to the Most Holy Sacrament and The Blessed Virgin Mary,* trans. R.A. Coffin (London: Burns & Lambert, 1855), 93–95.

80. Luis de Granada, *The Sinner's Guide* (New York: P. O'Shea, 1890), 73.

81. Columba Marmion, *Christ the Life of the Soul* (London and Edinburgh: Sands & Company, 1922), 39.

82. Mary Potter, *The Brides of Christ* (Chicago: Matre and Co., 1920), 5–6.

83. Guilelmus Parvus as quoted in Richard Frederick Littledale, *A Commentary on the Song of Songs* (London: Joseph Masters, 1869), 357.

84. Óscar Romero, *The Violence of Love,* compiled and trans. James Brockman (Farmington, PA: Bruderhof Foundation), 14–15. Reprinted from www.bruderhof.com. Copyright 2003 by the Bruderhof Foundation, Inc. Used with permission. Available online: http://www.romerotrust.org.uk/sites/default/files/violenceoflove.pdf.

85. John Paul II, *Ecclesia de Eucharistia* (Vatican City: Libreria Editrice Vaticana, April 17, 2003), par. 55, 56.

86. Mechtilde, *The Love of the Sacred Heart* (London: Burns, Oates, Washbourne, 1922), 120.

87. Augustine, "Tractate on the Gospel of John, 120" in *Nicene and Post-Nicene Fathers of the Christian Church, First Series, vol. 7,* ed. Philip Schaff (New York: Christian Literature, 1888), 434–435.

88. *O Esca viatorum.*

89. Thomas á Kempis, *Meditations on the Life of Christ,* trans. H.P. Wright (New York: E.P. Dutton & Co., 1892), 214–215.

90. Cornelius à Lapide, *The Great Commentary of Cornelius* à *Lapide: S. Matthew's Gospel, Chaps. X–XXI,* trans. Thomas W. Mossman (London: John Hodges, 1876), 76.

91. Note: Rolle's Middle English words and spellings have been modernized, and several now-obsolete terms have been updated.

92. Richard Rolle, *The Pricke of Conscience* (Berlin: A. Asher & Co., 1863), 143–144.

93. *Dignare me, O Jesu, rogo te.*

94. Henry Suso, *A Little Book of Eternal Wisdom,* trans. Richard Raby (London: Thomas Richardson & Son,, 1866), 43–44.

95. Margaret Mary Alacoque in Mother Mary Philip, *Life of Blessed Margaret Mary Alacoque* (Edinburgh: Sands and Co., 1919), 172–173.

96. Isidore of Seville in Oscar Daniel Watkins, *A History of Penance, Being a Study of the Authorities, vol. 2* (London: Longmans, Green, and Co., 1920), 572–573.

97. Mary Crescentia Höss in Ignatius Jeiler, *Life of the Ven. Mary Crescentia Höss of the Order of St. Francis,* trans. Clementius Deymann (New York: Benziger Brothers, 1886), 118, 130.

98. Urban IV in Darwell Stone, *A History of the Doctrine of the Holy Eucharist, vol. 1* (London: Longmans, Green, and Co., 1909), 345.

99. Jean-Baptiste de la Salle, *Méditations du Vénérable J.-B. de la Salle* (Versailles: L. Ronce, 1882), 86.

100. Julie Billiart, "Letters" in *Life of the Venerable Servant of God Julie Billiart*, ed. James Clare (London: Art and Book Company, 1898), 145, 117–118.

101. Henry Walpole, "Letter" in Richard Challoner, *Memoirs of Missionary Priests, vol. 1* (London: Thomas Richardson & Son, 1843), 343–345.

102. Gertrude the Great, *The Life and Revelations of Saint Gertrude* (London: Burns, Oates, & Washbourne, 1870), 114–115.

103. Gemma Galgani, "Letter" in *Lettres et Extases de Gemma Galgani* (Brunet: Arras (Pas-de-Calais), 1920), 106–107.

104. Mary of the Divine Heart in Louis Chasle, *Sister Mary of the Divine Heart* (London: Burns & Oates, 1906), 372–373.

105. Abbot Guéranger, *The Liturgical Year, vol. 1*, trans. Laurence Shepherd (London: Burns and Oates, 1908), 175–177.

106. Thomas á Kempis, *St. Lydwine of Schiedam, Virgin*, trans. Vincent Scully (London: Burns & Oates, 1912), 113–114.

107. Pauline Mallinckrodt, "Personal notes" in *The Life of Mother Pauline von Mallinckrodt* (New York: Benziger Brothers, 1917), 104–107

108. Bernadette Soubirous, "Private Notes, 1873" in Patricia McEachern, *A Holy Life: The Writings of Saint Bernadette of Lourdes* (San Francisco: Ignatius Press, 2005), 31–32.

109. John Henry Newman, *Meditations and Devotions of the Late Cardinal Newman* (London: Longmans, Green, and Co., 1894), 437–448.

110. Hugh of Saint Victor, *Explanation of the Rule of St. Augustine*, trans. Aloysius Smith (London: Sands and Co., 1911), 6–7.

111. Cornelia Connelly in *The Life of Cornelia Connelly* (London: Longmans, Green, and Co., 1924), 230–231, 29.

112. Origen, "Against Celsus" in Alexander Roberts, James Donaldson, and A. Cleveland Coxe, *Ante-Nicene and Nicene Fathers, vol. 4* (Buffalo, New York: Christian Literature, 1885), 432.

113. Anselm of Canterbury, *St. Anselm's Book of Meditations and Prayers*, trans. M.R. (London: Burns and Oates, 1872), 214–215.

114. Louis de Blois, "The Spiritual Mirror" in *Spiritual Works of Louis of Blois, Abbot of Liesse*, ed. John Edward Bowden (London: R. &. T. Washbourne, 1903), 154–155.

115. Louis de Blois in Joseph de Galliffet, *The Adorable Heart of Jesus*

(Philadelphia: Messenger of the Sacred Heart, 1890), 172.

116. Frederic Baraga, "Letter" in Chrysostom Verwyst, *Life and Labors of Rt. Rev. Frederic Baraga* (Milwaukee: M.H. Wiltzius & Co., 1900), 87, 89.

117. Mary Euphrasia Pelletier, "Discourse" in A.M. Clarke, *Life of Reverend Mother Mary of St. Euphrasia Pelletier* (London: Burns and Oates, 1895), 366–367, 369.

118. John Eudes in *The Love of the Sacred Heart* (London: Burns, Oates & Washbourne, 1920), 174–175.

119. *O filii et filiae.*

120. Marie of the Incarnation, *Lettres de la révérende mère Marie de l'Incarnation, vol. 1* (Paris: Librairie Internationale — Catholique, 1876), 381–382.

121. Louis-Marie Grignion de Montfort, *A Treatise on the True Devotion to the Blessed Virgin,* trans. Frederick William Faber (London: Burns and Lambert, 1863), 150–151.

122. Catherine of Siena, *The Dialogue of the Seraphic Virgin, Catherine of Siena,* trans. Algar Thorold (London: Kegan Paul, Trench, Trübner & Co., 1896), 154–156.

123. Pius V, *The Catechism of the Council of Trent,* trans. J. Donovan (Dublin: James Duffy and Co., 1908), 21–22.

124. Jean-Louis Bonnard, "Consecration to the Sacred Heart" in *Tong-King et Martyr ou Vie du Vénérable Jean-Louis Bonnard* (Lyon: Briday, 1876), 139–140.

125. Saint Athanasius, "Letter 2" in Philip Schaff and Henry Wace, *Nicene and Post-Nicene Fathers of the Christian Church, Second Series, vol. 4* (New York: Christian Literature, 1892), 511.

126. *Cor, arca legem continens.*

127. The One Hundred and Five Martyrs of Tyburn (London: Burns and Oates, 1917), 102–103.

128. Claude de la Colombiére in Louis de la Puente, *The Lights in Prayer* (London: Burns and Oates, 1893), 181–182.

129. John Bosco, *The Life of Dominic Savio* (London: Salesian Press, 1914).

130. *The Ancren Riwle: A Treatise on the Rules and Duties of Monastic Life,* ed. and trans. James Morton (London: Camden Society, 1853), 111.

131. John Croiset, *Devotion to the Sacred Heart of Jesus* (London: Burns & Lambert, 1863), 37–38.

132. Pachomius, "Sayings" in Hieronymus Palladius, *The Book of Paradise, vol. 1,* trans. E. A. Wallis Budge (London: W. Gruglin, 1904), 450.

133. John of Ávila, "Letter" in *The Letters of Blessed John of Ávila* (London: Burns & Oates, 1904), 46–47.

134. Damien de Veuster in May Quinlan, *Damien of Molokai* (London: MacDonald and Evans, 1909), 105–106.

135. Margaret Mary Alacoque, "Letter" in Mary Philip, *Life of Blessed Margaret Mary Alacoque* (Edinburgh: Sands & Co., 1919), 207–208.

136. "Vidi Aquam" in Abbot Guéranger, *The Liturgical Year, Paschal Time, vol. 1,* trans. Laurence Shepherd (London: Burns and Oates, 1908), 158.

137. Mary of the Divine Heart in Louis Chasle, *Sister Mary of the Divine Heart* (London: Burns & Oates, 1906), 354–355.

138. Vincent Strambi, "Sermon" in Kenneth Howell and Joseph Crownwood, *Mystery of the Altar: Daily Meditations on the Eucharist* (Steubenville, OH: Emmaus Road Publishing, 2020), 327.

139. Thérèse of Lisieux, *Soeur Thérèse of Lisieux: The Little Flower of Jesus* (London: Burns and Oates, 1912), 133, 312. Edited by Kronholz and revised in reference to the original French.

140. Peter Faber, *Memoriale* in Giuseppe Boero, *The Life of the Blessed Peter Favre, Quarterly Series, vol. 8,* trans. Henry James Coleridge (London: Burns and Oates, 1873), 283–284.

141. Jerome, "Letter to Abigaus" in *Nicene and Post-Nicene Fathers of the Christian Church, Second Series, vol. 6,* ed. Philip Schaff and Henry Wace (New York: Christian Literature, 1893), 157.

142. Raymond of Capua, *The Life of Catherine of Siena* (Philadelphia: Peter F. Cunningham, 1860), 124–125.

143. Bernardine of Siena in Paul Thureau-Dangin, *Saint Bernardine of Siena,* trans. G. von Hugel (London: J.M. Dent & Co., 1906), 195–196.

144. Eugène de Mazenod, "Letter" in Robert Cooke, *Sketches of the Life of Mgr. de Mazenod, vol. 2* (London: Burns & Oates, 1882), 48–49.

145. Madeleine Sophie Barat in *Life of the Venerable Madeleine Louise Sophie Barat* (Roehampton: Convent of the Sacred Heart, 1900), 584, 165. Edited by Kronholz.

146. John Baptist de Rossi in E. Mougeot, *The Life of St. John Baptist de Rossi,* trans. Lady Herbert (London: Thomas Richardson and Son, 1883), 170, 178–179.

147. *Summi regis cor, aveto* in Philip Schaff, *Christ in Song: Hymns of Immanuel,* trans. E.A. Washburn (London: Sampson Low, Son, and Marston, 1870), 322–323.

148. Mary Magdalene de' Pazzi in Placido Fabrini, *The Life and Works of St. Mary Magdalene de-Pazzi,* trans. Antonio Isoleri (Philadelphia: Antonio

Isoleri, 1900), 379, 423.

149. Philip Neri, "Maxims and Sayings" in *The Life of Saint Philip Neri, vol. 2* (London: Thomas Richardson and Son, 1847), 453, 456, 476.

150. Bede the Venerable, "Chronicle of the Six Ages of the World" in *The Historical Works of Venerable Bede, vol. ii,* trans. J.A. Giles, (London: James Bohn, 1843), 222.

151. Alphonsus Rodriguez, *The Practice of Christian and Religious Perfection, vol. 1,* trans. Regnier des Marais (Dublin: James Duffy, 1861), 111..

152. Paul VI, *Mysterium Fidei* (Vatican: Libreria Editrice Vaticana, September 3, 1965), par. 67–68.

153. Mary Aikenhead, "Letter" in *The Life and Work of Mary Aikenhead* (New York: Longmans, Green, and Co., 1924), 280, 399.

154. Camilla Battista da Varano in Filippo Maria Salvatori, *The Lives of S. Veronica Giuliani, Capuchin Nun and of the Blessed Battista Varani of the Order of S. Clare* (London: R. Washbourne, 1874), 327–328.

155. Justin Martyr, *Dialogue with Trypho the Jew,* trans. Henry Brown (Cambridge: Deightons; MacMillan, Barclay, and MacMillan, 1846), 224–225.

156. Leo XIII, "Consecration to the Sacred Heart" in Alexis M. Lepicier, *Jesus Christ the King of our Hearts* (London: Burns Oates & Washbourne, 1921), 254–255.

157. Margaret Mary Alacoque in Mother Mary Philip, *Life of Blessed Margaret Mary Alacoque* (Edinburgh: Sands and Co., 1919), 178–179.

158. Thomas á Kempis, *Meditations on the Life of Christ,* trans. H.P. Wright (New York: E.P. Dutton & Co., 1892), 212–213.

159. Pseudo-Dionysius the Areopagite in *The Works of Dionysius the Areopagite* (London: James Parker, 1897), 48–49.

160. Marcellin de Champagnat, "Prayer" in *Vie de Joseph-Benoit-Marcellin Champagnat* (Lyon: Perisse Frères, 1856), 19–20.

161. Anne of Saint Bartholomew, *Autobiography of the Blessed Mother Anne of Saint Bartholomew* (St. Louis: H.S. Collins Printing, 1916), 44..

162. Mary of the Divine Heart in Louis Chasle, *Sister Mary of the Divine Heart* (London: Burns & Oates, 1906), 179–180.

163. Ephrem the Syrian, *Select Works of Ephrem the Syrian,* trans. J.B. Morris (Oxford: John Henry Parker, F. and J. Rivington, 1847), 20, 34–35.

164. *Quicumque certum quæritis.*

165. Vittoria Colonna in Joseph de Galliffet, *The Adorable Heart of Jesus* (Philadelphia: Messenger of the Sacred Heart, 1890), 137–138.

166. Gertrude the Great, *The Life and Revelations of Saint Gertrude* (London: Burns, Oates, & Washbourne, 1870), 90–91.

167. Anthony of Padua, "Sermon" in C.M. Antony, *Antony of Padua: Miracle Worker* (London: Longmans, Green, and Co., 1911), 79–80.

168. Leo the Great, "Sermon 23" in *Select Sermons of S. Leo the Great on the Incarnation,* trans. William Bright (London: J. Masters and Co., 1886), 120-121.

169. Vincent de Paul in Abeé Maynard, *Virtues and Spiritual Doctrine of St. Vincent de Paul* (Suspension Bridge, NY: Niagara Index, 1877), 204.

170. Peter J. Arnoudt, *The Imitation of the Sacred Heart of Jesus* (New York: Benziger Brothers, 1904), 74–75.

171. Lutgarde, *The Heavenly Court of The Holy Cistercian Nun: Saint Lutgarde of Brabant,* trans. E.M. Walker (St. Benedict, Oregon: Benedictine Press, 1914), 36–37.

172. Elisabeth of Schönau in F.M. Steele, "St. Elizabeth von Schönau and her Vision," *The American Catholic Quarterly Review,* vol. XXXVI, no. 141 (January, 1911): 401–402; 403–404.

173. Joseph de Galliffet, *The Adorable Heart of Jesus* (Philadelphia: Messenger of the Sacred Heart, 1890), 104–105.

174. Methodius of Olympus, "The Banquet of the Ten Virgins" in Alexander Roberts, James Donaldson, and A. Cleveland Coxe, *Ante-Nicene Fathers, vol. 6* (New York: Christian Literature, 1886), 331.

175. Thomas More, *A Dialogue of Comfort Against Tribulation* (London: Charle Dolman, 1847), 313–314.

176. John Fisher, *The English Works of John Fisher* (London: N. Trübner & Co., 1876), 227–228.

177. Columba Marmion, *Christ in His Mysteries* (London: Sands & Co., 1924), 370–371.

178. Ray Palmer, *"Tibi dedo Jesu dulcissime"* in *The Poetical Works of Ray Palmer* (New York: A.S. Barnes and Company, 1876), 123–124.

179. Benedict XV, *Humani Generis Redemptionem* (Vatican City: Libreria Editrice Vaticana, June 15, 1917), par. 19–20.

180. Meister Eckhart in Odilia Funke, *Meister Eckhart,* Ph.D. dissertation (Washington, D.C.: Catholic University of America, 1916), 79.

181. John Paul II, *Dives in misericordia* (Vatican City: Libreria Editrice Vaticana, November 30, 1980), par. 13.

182. Irenaeus, "Against Heresies" in Alexander Roberts, James Donaldson, and A. Cleveland Coxe, *Ante-Nicene Fathers, vol. 1* (New York: C. Scribner's Sons, 1903), 458.

183. Claude de la Colombiére, "Prayer" in Eugene Seguin, *The Life of the Venerable Claude de la Colombiére* (London: Burns and Oats, 1905), 120.

184. Antonio Rosmini-Serbati, *Letters of Antonio Rosmini Serbati* (London: R. & T. Washbourne, 1901), 440–441.

185. Gaetano Bonanni, *Mois de juin consacré à honorer le précieux sang de Notre Seigneur Jésus-Christ* (Paris: Adrien le Clerc, 1842), 164–165.

186. John Eudes, *The Love of the Sacred Heart: Illustrated by St. Margaret Mary Alacoque & the Blessed John Eudes* (London: Burns, Oates & Washbourne, 1920), 181–182.

187. Cornelius à Lapide, *The Great Commentary of Cornelius à Lapide, S. John's Gospel, Chaps. XII–XXI,* Fourth Ed., trans. Thomas W. Mossman (Edinburgh: John Grant, 1908), 278–279.

188. Margaret Mary Alacoque, "Letter" in Mary Philip, *Life of Blessed Margaret Mary Alacoque* (Edinburgh: Sands & Co., 1919), 206–207.

189. Alexis M. Lepicier, *Jesus Christ the King of Our Hearts: Elevations on the Most Sacred Heart of Jesus* (London: Burns, Oates, & Washbourne, 1921), 30–31.

190. John of the Cross, "Dark Night of the Soul" in *The Complete Works of Saint John of the Cross,* trans. David Lewis (London: Longman, Green, Longman, Roberts, & Green, 1864), 393–394.

191. *Salvete Christi vulnera.*

192. Francis Libermann in Prosper Goepfert, *The Life of the Venerable Francis Mary Paul Libermann* (Dublin: M.H. Gill & Son, 1880), 104.

193. Veronica Giuliani in Filippo Maria Salvatori, *The Lives of S. Veronica Giuliani, Capuchin Nun and of the Blessed Battista Varani of the Order of S. Clare* (London: R. Washbourne, 1874), 135–136.

194. Pius XII, *Haurietis Aquas* (Vatican City: Libreria Editrice Vaticana, May 15, 1956), par. 53–57.

195. Secondo Franco, *Devotion to the Sacred Heart of Jesus* (Baltimore: John Murphy & Co., 1870), 133–134.

196. Mary Potter, *The Brides of Christ* (Chicago: Matre and Co., 1920), 43.

197. Columba Marmion, *Christ in His Mysteries* (London: Sands & Co., 1924), 366.

198. Alcuin in *Tracts Published Under the Superintendence of the Catholic Institute of Great Britain, vol. 1* (London: Catholic Institute of Great Britain, 1841), 9–10.

199. Bonaventure, *The Life of Christ,* trans. W.H. Hutchings (London: Rivingtons, 1888), 242.

200. Elizabeth of the Trinity, *The Praise of Glory: Reminiscences of Sister Elizabeth of the Trinity* (London: R. & T. Washbourne, 1913), 57.

201. Gregory XI, *Ave caput Christi gratum.*

202. Camillus of Lellis in Sanzio Cicatelli, *The Life of Camillus of Lellis, vol. 1* (London: Thomas Richardson and Son, 1850), 263, 223–224.

203. Robert Bellarmine, "Sermon 35" in *Sermons from the Latins,* trans. and adapted by James Joseph Baxter (New York: Benziger Brothers, 1902), 374–376.

204. Henry Suso, *Little Book of Eternal Wisdom* (London: R. & T. Washbourne, 1910), 96–98. .

205. Claude de la Colombiére, "Sermon" in Eugene Seguin, *The Life of the Venerable Claude de la Colombiere* (London: Burns and Oats, 1905), 113.

206. Robert Southwell, "Mary Magdalen's Funeral Tears" in *The Prose Works of Robert Southwell,* ed. W. Joseph Walter (London: Keating, Brown, and Co., 1828), 76–77.

207. Bridget of Sweden, *Revelations of St. Bridget on the Life and Passion of Our Lord and the Life of His Blessed Mother* (New York: D. & J. Sadlier & Co., 1862), 76–77.

208. John Cassian, "The Conferences" in *Nicene and Post-Nicene Fathers of the Christian Church, Second Series, vol. 9,* ed. Philip Schaff, Henry Wace, and The First Conference of Abbot Chaeremon (New York: Christian Literature, 1894), 419.

209. Mary of the Divine Heart in Louis Chasle, *Sister Mary of the Divine Heart* (London: Burns & Oates, 1906), 352–354.

210. William of St. Thierry, *Meditative Prayers,* 6. As cited in: Kenneth J. Howell and Joseph Crownwood, *Mystery of the Altar: Daily Meditations on the Eucharist* (Steubenville, OH: Emmaus Road Publishing, 2020), 30–31.

211. Teresa of Ávila, "The Dying Saint to Her Crucifix" in *Minor Works of St. Teresa,* trans. Benedictines of Stanbrook (London: Thomas Baker, 1913), 21–24.

212. Thomas á Kempis, *Meditations on the Life of Christ,* trans. H.P. Wright (New York: E.P. Dutton & Co., 1892), 315–316.

213. Mary Elizabeth Herbert, *Abyssinia and its Apostle* (London: Burns, Oates & Co., 1867), 122–123.

214. Peter Chrysologus, *Sermon 137,* pl. 25.

215. Ignatius of Loyola, *The Spiritual Exercises of St. Ignatius of Loyola,* trans. Elder Mullan (New York: P.J. Kenedy & Sons, 1914), 158–159.

216. Ignatius of Loyola, *Letters and Instructions of St. Ignatius of Loyola, vol. 1,* ed. A. Goodier, trans. D.F. O'Leary (St. Louis, MO: B. Herder Publishers, 1914), 101.

217. Alphonsus Liguori, *Visits to the Most Holy Sacrament and the Blessed Virgin Mary,* trans. R.A. Coffin (London: Burns & Lambert, 1855), 112–113.

218. Peter Eymard, "On Holy Communion" in Francis Xavier Lasance, *With God: A Book of Prayers and Reflections* (New York: Benziger Brothers, 1911), 415–416.

219. Peter Faber, "Memoriale" in Giuseppe Boero, *The Life of the Blessed Peter Favre,* Quarterly Series, vol. 8, trans. Henry James Coleridge (London: Burns and Oates, 1873), 275–276.

220. Jean Vianney, "Catechism" in Alfred Monnin, *The Spirit of the Curé of Ars,* ed. John Edward Bowden (London: Burns, Lambert, and Oates, 1865), 41–42.

221. Johannes Tauler, *De Vita Christi, c. 53* as cited in Richard Frederick Littledale, *A Commentary on the Song of Songs* (London: Joseph Masters, 1869), 169, 170.

222. Margaret Mary Alacoque in Mother Mary Philip, *Life of Blessed Margaret Mary Alacoque* (Edinburgh: Sands and Co., 1919), 180.

223. Cajetan in *The Life of Saint Cajetan*, trans. Lady Herbert (London: Thomas Richardson and Son, 1888), 229, 253.

224. Edith Stein (Teresa Benedicta of the Cross), *The Hidden Life: Hagiographic Essays, Meditations, Spiritual Texts* in *Collected Works of Edith Stein, Sister Teresa Benedicta of the Cross, Discalced Carmelite 1891–1942, vol. 4*, ed. L. Gelber and Michael Linssen, trans. Waltraut Stein (Washington, D.C.: ICS Publications, 2014), 114.

225. *"The Little Flowers" & the Life of St. Francis with the "Mirror of Perfection,"* trans. T. Okey (London: J.M. Dent & Sons, 1912), 90–91.

226. Columba Marmion, *Christ in His Mysteries* (London: Sands & Co., 1924), 375–376.

227. Francis Goldie, *The Life of the Blessed John Berchmans* (London: Burns and Oates, 1873), 160–161.

228. Jane Frances de Chantal, "Letter" in *The Spirit of Saint Jane Frances de Chantal as Shown by Her Letters,* trans. Sisters of the Visitation (London: Longmans, Green, and Co., 1922), 381–382.

229. Hippolytus, "Fragment from Homily, XI" in Alexander Roberts, James Donaldson, and A. Cleveland Coxe, *Ante-Nicene Fathers, vol. 5* (Buffalo: Christian Literature, 1886), 239.

230. Mechtilde, *The Love of the Sacred Heart* (London: Burns, Oates, and Washbourne, 1922), 165–166.

231. Mary of Ágreda, *Mystical City of God, vol. 4*, trans. Fiscar Marison (n.p.: Louis W. Bernicken, 1902), 511–513.

232. Anselm of Canterbury, *St. Anselm's Book of Meditations and Prayers,* trans. M.R. (London: Burns and Oates, 1872), 133–135.

233. Jeanne Delanoue, *Extraits ou Fragments des Discours ou Entretiens de la Soeur Jeanne Delanoue* (Angers: Imprimerie-Librarie Germain et G. Grassin, 1889), 142–143.

234. Ezequiél Moreno y Diaz, "Episcopal Letter" in Santiago Matute, *Los Padres Candelarios en Colombia: O Apuntes para la historia, vol. 2* (Bogata: Tipografia de los talleres Salesianos, 1897), 479–480.

235. John Eudes, "Salutations to the Sacred Heart" in *Life of Venerable Father Eudes,* trans. Henry Collins (London: Thomas Richardson & Son, 1880), 66–67.

236. Bernard of Clairvaux, *"Jesu dulcis amor meus,"* in John Wallace, *Early Christian Hymns* (New York: The Grafton Press, 1908), 246.

237. Pope Pius X, *Iucunda Sane: On Pope Gregory the Great* (Vatican City: Libreria Editrice Vaticana, March 12, 1904), par. 8.

238. Pope Benedict XIV, *Heroic Virtue: A Portion of the Treatise of Benedict XIV on the Beatification and Canonization of the Servants of God* (London: Thomas Richardson and Son, 1850), 196–197.

239. Mary of the Divine Heart in Louis Chasle, *Sister Mary of the Divine Heart* (London: Burns & Oates, 1906), 350–351.

240. Teresa of Ávila, *Minor Works of St. Teresa,* trans. Benedictines of Stanbrook (London: Thomas Baker, 1913), 17–18.

241. Dominic Barberi, *Lamentation of England* (Leicester: A. Cockshaw, 1831), 1, 22.

242. John Paul I, *Urbi et Orbi,* Radio Message of His Holiness, August 27, 1978 (Vatican City: Libreria Editrice Vaticana, 1978).

243. Augustine, "Commentary of the First Epistle of John" in Philip Schaff, *Nicene and Post-Nicene Fathers, vol. 7* (New York: Christian Literature, 1888), 340.

244. Augustine, "Commentary of the First Epistle of John" in Philip Schaff, *Nicene and Post-Nicene Fathers, vol. 7* (New York: Christian Literature, 1888), 503.

245. Gertrude the Great, *The Life and Revelations of Saint Gertrude* (London: Burns, Oates, & Washbourne, 1870), 79–80.

246. Giunta Revegnati, *Life and Revelations of Saint Margaret of Cortona,* trans. F.M. Mahony (London: Burns and Oates, 1883), 92, 94–95.

247. John Croiset, *Devotion to the Sacred Heart of Jesus* (London: Burns & Lambert, 1863), 38.

248. Gabriel of St. Mary Magdalene, *From the Sacred Heart to the Trinity: The Spiritual Itinerary of St. Teresa Margaret (Redi) of the Sacred Heart, O.C.D.,* trans. Sebastian V. Ramge (Washington D.C.: ICS Publications, 2006),

49–50.

249. Anonymous, *The Divine Cloud,* ed. Henry Collins (London: Thomas Richardson and Son, 1871), 15–17.

250. Gregory the Great, *Moralia in Job, vol. 1,* A Library of Fathers of the Holy Catholic Church, vol. 18 (Oxford: John Henry Parker, 1844), 232.

251. Mary Potter, *The Brides of Christ* (Chicago: Matre and Co., 1920), 8–9.

252. Teresa of Calcutta, *Where There Is Love, There Is God: A Path to Closer Union with God and Greater Love for Others,* ed. Brian Kolodiejchuk, (New York: Doubleday, 2010), 39.

253. Clement of Alexandria, "Stromata" in Alexander Roberts, James Donaldson, and A. Cleveland Coxe, *Ante-Nicene Fathers, vol. 2* (Buffalo: Christian Literature, 1885), 472.

254. Margaret Mary Alacoque in Mary Philip, *Life of Blessed Margaret Mary Alacoque* (Edinburgh: Sands & Co., 1919), 178, 176.

255. Columba Marmion, *Christ in His Mysteries* (London: Sands & Co., 1924), 378.

256. Theophylact in Cornelius à Lapide, *The Great Commentary of Cornelius* à *Lapide, S. John's Gospel, Chaps. XII–XXI,* trans. Thomas W. Mossman (London: John Hodges, 1892), 248.

257. Theodoret of Cyrus, "Letter" in Philip Schaff and Henry Wace, *Nicene and Post-Nicene Fathers of the Christian Church, Second Series, vol. 3* (New York: Christian Literature, 1892), 237.

258. Battista Vernazza in Friedrich von Hügel, *The Mystical Element of Religion as Studied in Saint Catherine of Genoa and Her Friends* (London: J.M. Dent & Sons, 1923), 359–360.

259. Catherine of Genoa, "Spiritual Dialogue" in *Life and Doctrine of Saint Catherine of Genoa* (New York: Christian Press, 1907), Part 3, ch. 1.

260. John Chrysostom, "Commentary on John" in Philip Schaff, *Nicene and Ante-Nicene Fathers, vol. 14* (Grand Rapids, MI: William B. Eerdmans, 1889), 117.

261. John of Ávila, "Letter" in *Letters of Blessed John of Avila* (London: Burns & Oates Ltd., 1904), 75–76.

262. Bridget of Sweden, *Revelations of St. Bridget on the Life and Passion of Our Lord and the Life of His Blessed Mother* (New York: D. & J. Sadlier & Co., 1862), 72–73.

263. Cyprian in Alexander, Roberts, in James Donaldson, and A. Cleveland Coxe, *Ante-Nicene Fathers, vol. 5* (Buffalo: Christian Literature, 1886), 360.

264. Hildegard von Bingen in Charles Singer, "Allegorical Representation of the Synagogue in a Twelfth Century Illuminated Ms. Of Hildegard of Bingen," *The Jewish Quarterly Review,* Vol 5, 1914–1915 (London: MacMillan & Company, 1915), 280–281.

265. Robert Bellarmine, *Steps of Ascension to God* (London: W. Freeman, 1705), 261–262.

266. Émilie de Rodat, *Lettres de la Vénérable Mére Émilie de Rodat,* ed. Henri Marty (Paris: Société Générale de Librairie Catholique, 1888), 62–63, 55–56.

267. *Auctor beate sæculi.*

268. Thomas á Kempis, *Meditations on the Life of Christ,* trans. H.P. Wright (New York: E.P. Dutton & Co., 1892), 209–210.

269. Thomas of Villanova, *Oeuvres de Saint Thomas de Villeneuve: religieux Augustin et archevêque de valence,* trans. from Latin by V. Ferrier (Paris: Lethielleux, 1886), 387.

270. Cornelius à Lapide, *The Great Commentary of Cornelius* à *Lapide, S. John's Gospel, Chaps. XII–XXI,* Fourth Ed., trans. Thomas W. Mossman (Edinburgh: John Grant, 1908), 281–282.

271. Mary of the Divine Heart in Louis Chasle, *Sister Mary of the Divine Heart* (London: Burns & Oates, 1906), 348–350.

272. Vincent Strambi, *Il Mese di Giugno Consecrato al Preziosissimo Sangue del Nostro Amabilissimo Redentore,* 5th ed. (Napoli: Tipografia della Stabilimento dell'Industriale, 1840), 40–41.

273. Juan Nieremberg, "Jesus Crucified, the Book of Life" in Joseph de Galliffet, *The Adorable Heart of Jesus* (Philadelphia: Messenger of the Sacred Heart, 1890), 181–182.

274. Vincent de Paul, "Exhortation" in Abeé Maynard, *Virtues and Spiritual Doctrine of St. Vincent de Paul* (Suspension Bridge, NY: Niagara Index, 1877), 127–128.

275. Francis Borgia, *Spiritual Works of St. Francis Borgia* (London: Thomas Richardson and Sons, 1875), 25–26.

276. Jerome, "Against Jovinianus" in *Nicene and Post-Nicene Fathers of the Christian Church, Second Series, vol. 6, ed. Philip Schaff and Henry Wace* (New York: Christian Literature, 1893), 369.

277. St. Thérèse of Lisieux, *The Story of a Soul: The Autobiography of St. Thérèse of Lisieux,* ed. T.N. Taylor (London: Burns, Oates, & Washbourne, 1912), Letter V to Missionaries.

278. Raymond of Capua, *The Life of St. Catherine of Siena* (Philadelphia: Peter F. Cunningham, 1860), 88–89.

279. Columba Marmion, *Christ the Life of the Soul* (London: Sands & Company, 1922), 259.

280. Francis of Assisi, "Prayers" in Paschal Robinson, *The Writings of St. Francis of Assisi* (Philadelphia: Dolphin Press, 1906), 145, 148–149.

281. Faustina Kowalska, *Diary of Saint Maria Faustina Kowalska: Divine Mercy in My Soul, 3rd ed.* (Stockbridge, MA: Marian Press, 2005), par. 1777.

282. Bruno of Cologne in Herbert Thurston, *The Life of Saint Hugh of Lincoln* (London: Burns and Oates, 1898), 30–31.

283. John Paul II, *Rosarium Virginis Mariae* (Vatican City: Libreria Editrice Vaticana, October 16, 2002), par 26.

284. Bartolo Longo, *The Fifteen Saturdays of the Most Holy Rosary,* trans. Luigi Caturelli (Valle di Pompei: Papal Typographical School for the Children of the Imprisoned, 1926), Sixth Saturday.

285. John Henry Newman, *Meditations and Devotions of the Late Cardinal Newman* (London: Longmans, Green, and Co., 1894), 572–574.

286. Francis Lucas Brugensis, "On John" in Joseph de Galliffet, *The Adorable Heart of Jesus* (Philadelphia: Messenger of the Sacred Heart, 1890), 177–178.

287. John XXIII, *Princeps Pastorum: On the Missions, Native Clergy, and Lay Participation* (Vatican City: Libreria Editrice Vaticana, November 28, 1959), par. 58–59.

288. Claude de la Colombiére, *The Sufferings of Our Lord Jesus Christ* (London: R. Washbourne, 1876), 54–55.

289. Henry Suso, *A Little Book of Eternal Wisdom* (London: R. & T. Washbourne, 1910), 159–160.

290. Gerard Majella, "Letters" and "Rule of Life" in Karl Dilgskron, *Life of Blessed Gerard Majella,* trans. Charles Dilgskron (New York: Redemptorist Fathers, 1886), 265, 315.

291. Teresa of Ávila, *The Letters of St. Teresa,* trans. John Dalton (London: Thomas Baker, 1893), 59.

292. Margaret Mary Alacoque in Mother Mary Philip, *Life of Blessed Margaret Mary Alacoque* (Edinburgh: Sands and Co., 1919), 94–95. Edited by Kronholz.

293. Ignatius of Antioch, "Letter to the Romans" in J.H. Srawley, *The Epistles of St. Ignatius, Bishop of Antioch, vol. 2* (London: Society for Promoting Christian Knowledge, 1910), 15–17.

294. St. Peter of Alcantara, *Pax Animæ* (London: Burns and Oates, 1876), 85, 26.

295. *The Jesuit Relations and Allied Documents, vol. 8,* ed. Reuben Gold

Thwaites, trans. James McFie Hunter (Cleveland: The Burrows Brothers Co., 1897), 182–283.

296. Paul of the Cross, "Letter" in George Spencer and Dominic Barberi, *The Life of the Blessed Paul of the Cross, vol. 2* (London: Thomas Richardson and Son, 1853), 87–88.

297. Camilla Battista da Varano in Filippo Maria Salvatori, *The Lives of S. Veronica Giuliani, Capuchin Nun and of the Blessed Battista Varani of the Order of S. Clare* (London: R. Washbourne, 1874), 381.

298. John Paul II, *Redemptor hominis* (Vatican City: Libreria Editrice Vaticana, March 4, 1979), par. 8.

299. Giovanni Agostino Gallicio in Joseph de Galliffet, *The Adorable Heart of Jesus* (Philadelphia: Messenger of the Sacred Heart, 1890), 104–105..

300. *Ancient Devotions to the Sacred Heart of Jesus by Carthusian Monks* (London: Burns, Oates, and Washbourne, 1953), 182.

301. Cyprian of Carthage, "Treatise 8: On Works and Alms" in Alexander Roberts, James Donaldson, and A. Cleveland Coxe, *Ante-Nicene Fathers, vol. 5* (Buffalo: Christian Literature, 1886), 483.

302. Mary of the Divine Heart in Louis Chasle, *Sister Mary of the Divine Heart* (London: Burns & Oates, 1906), 180–181.

303. Julian of Norwich, *Revelations of Divine Love,* trans. Grace Warrack (London: Methuen & Co., 1901), 181–182.

304. Catherine of Siena, *The Dialogue of the Seraphic Virgin, Catherine of Siena,* trans. Algar Thorold (London: Kegan Paul, Trench, Trübner & Co., 1907), 77–78.

305. *Liturgies: Eastern and Western, Vol. 1: Eastern Liturgies,* ed. F.E. Brightman (Oxford: Clarendon Press, 1896), 97.

306. John of the Cross, "Spiritual Canticle" in *The Complete Works of Saint John of the Cross,* trans. David Lewis (London: Longman, Green, Longman, Roberts, & Green, 1864), 395, 399–400.

307. Alphonsus Rodriguez, "Memoriale" in Francis Goldie, *The Life of St. Alonso Rodriguez* (London: Burns and Oates, 1889), 26–27.

308. Catherine of Genoa, "Spiritual Dialogue" in *Life and Doctrine of Saint Catherine of Genoa* (New York: Christian Press, 1907), Part 3, ch. 6.

309. Columba Marmion, *Christ the Life of the Soul* (London and Edinburgh: Sands and Company, 1922), 36–37.

310. "The Shepherd of Hermas" in *The Ante-Nicene Fathers, vol. 2,* ed. Alexander Roberts, James Donaldson, and A. Cleveland Coxe (Buffalo: Christian Literature, 1885), 31.

311. Charles Borromeo in C.A. Jones, *Life and Times of S. Charles Borro-*

meo (London: J.T. Hayes, 1877), 83–84.

312. *The Ancren Riwle: A Treatise on the Rules and Duties of Monastic Life,* ed. and trans. James Morton (London: Camden Society, 1853), 281, 283.

313. Eugène de Mazenod, "Personal Notes" in Robert Cooke, *Sketches of the Life of Mgr. de Mazenod, vol. 2* (London: Burns & Oates, 1882), 53–54.

314. Columba Marmion, *Christ in His Mysteries* (London: Sands & Co., 1924), 384.

315. Elizabeth of the Trinity, *The Praise of Glory: Reminiscences of Sister Elizabeth of the Trinity* (London: R. & T. Washbourne, 1913), 43–44.

316. Stephen the Sabaite, "Idiomela in the Week of the First Oblique Tone" in *The Hymns of the Eastern Church,* trans. J.M. Neale (London: J.T. Hayes, 1870), 88–89.

317. Leo the Great, "Letter (24) to Flavian" in George Anson Jackson, *The Post-Nicene Latin Fathers* (New York: D. Appleton and Company, 1884), 199–200.

318. Anne of Saint Bartholomew, *Autobiography of the Blessed Mother Anne of Saint Bartholomew* (St. Louis: H.S. Collins Printing, 1916), 73–74.

319. Adam of Perseigne, *The Book of Mutual Charity.*

320. Leo XIII, *Annum Sacrum* (Vatican City: Libreria Editrice Vaticana, May 25, 1899), par. 8–9.

321. John Eudes in *The Love of the Sacred Heart* (London: Burns, Oates, & Washbourne, 1920), 179.

322. Albert the Great, *On Union with God,* trans. Benedictine of Princethorpe Priory (London: R. & T. Washbourne, 1911), ch. xii, 77–79.

323. Gilbert Dolan, *St. Gertrude the Great* (London: Sands & Co., 1913), 24–24.

324. Mary of the Divine Heart in Louis Chasle, *Sister Mary of the Divine Heart* (London: Burns & Oates, 1906), 77–79.

325. Rose Philippine, "Letters" in Abbé Baunard, *The Life of Mother Duchesne,* trans. Georgiana Fullerton (Roehampton: James Stanley, 1879), 150, 215, 271.

326. Mechtilde, *The Love of the Sacred Heart* (London: Burns, Oates, and Washbourne, 1922), 70.

327. Tertullian, "Against Marcion" in *Ante-Nicene Fathers, vol. 3,* ed. Alexander Roberts and James Donaldson (New York: Christian Literature, 1885), 299–300.

328. Alphonsus Liguori, *Visits to the Most Holy Sacrament and The Blessed Virgin Mary,* trans. R.A. Coffin (London: Burns & Lambert, 1855), 105–106.

329. Lanspergius in John Croiset, *Devotion to the Sacred Heart of Jesus* (London: Burns & Lambert, 1863), 27–28.

330. Clement of Rome, "Epistle to the Corinthians" in Alexander Roberts, James Donaldson, and A. Cleveland Coxe, *Ante-Nicene Fathers, vol. 1* (New York: Charles Scribner's Sons, 1903), 10.

331. Catherine Burton in Thomas Hunter, *An English Carmelite: The Life of C. Burton* (London: Burns and Oates, 1876), 166.

332. John XXII, "Anima Christi" in *The Month, vol. 125* (London: Longmans, Green, and Co., 1915), 493.

333. John Fisher, *The English Works of John Fisher* (London: N. Trübner & Co., 1876), 229–230.

334. Leonard of Port Maurice, *The Hidden Treasure: Or the Immense Excellence of the Holy Sacrifice of the Mass* (Edinburgh: Marsh and Beattie, 1855), 151–152.

335. Thomas á Kempis, *Meditations on the Life of Christ,* trans. H.P. Wright (New York: E.P. Dutton & Co., 1892), 211–212.

336. Margaret Mary Alacoque in Mother Mary Philip, *Life of Blessed Margaret Mary Alacoque* (Edinburgh: Sands and Co., 1919), 42..

337. Edmund Campion, "Letter" in Bede Camm, *Lives of the English Martyrs, vol. 1* (London: Longmans, Green, and Co., 1914), 283, 287, 291.

338. Charles de Foucauld, "Letter" in René Bazin, *Charles de Foucauld: explorateur du Maroc ermite au Sahara* (Paris: Plon-Nourrit, 1921), 304.

339. Maurice Maeterlinck, *Ruysbroeck and the Mystics with Selections from Ruysbroeck,* trans. Jane T. Stoddart (London: Hodder and Stoughton, 1894), 146–147.

340. Francis Xavier, "Prayer" in Henry James Coleridge, *The Life and Letters of St. Francis Xavier, vol. 1* (London: Burns and Oates, 1872), 316.

341. John Damascene, "Ode IV" in *The Hymns of the Eastern Church,* trans. J.M. Neale (London: J.T. Hayes, 1866), 59–60.

342. Henry Suso, *A Little Book of Eternal Wisdom,* trans. Richard Raby (London: Thomas Richardson & Son, 1866), 193–194.

343. John Climacus in Cornelius à Lapide, *The Great Commentary of Cornelius à Lapide: S. Matthew's Gospel, Chaps. X–XXI,* trans. Thomas W. Mossman (London: John Hodges, 1876), 77–78.

344. Ambrose, "Exposition on the Christian Faith" in *Nicene and Post-Nicene Fathers, Second Series, vol. 10,* trans. H. de Romestin, E. de Romestin, and H.T.F. Duckworth (New York: Christian Literature, 1896), 227.

345. Marguerite Bourgeoys, "Reflection" in Etienne Montgolfier, *La vie de la venerable Marguerite Bourgeoys dite du Saint Sacrement* (Ville-Marie:

Montréal, 1818), 235.

346. Bonaventure, *The Life of Christ,* trans. W.H. Hutchings (London: Rivingtons, 1888), 62–63.

347. Columba Marmion, *Christ in His Mysteries* (London: Sands & Co., 1924), 377.

348. Margery Kempe, *The Book of Margery Kempe: A Modern Version,* The Life and Letters Series 103, ed. W. Butler-Bowdon (London: Jonathan Cape, 1940), 83.

349. Secondo Franco, *Devotion to the Sacred Heart of Jesus* (Baltimore: John Murphy & Co., 1870), 236–237.

350. Cornelius à Lapide, *The Great Commentary of Cornelius à Lapide, S. John's Gospel, Chaps. XII–XXI,* Fourth Ed., trans. Thomas W. Mossman (Edinburgh: John Grant, 1908), 246–247.

351. John of the Cross, "Dark Night of the Soul" in *The Complete Works of Saint John of the Cross,* trans. David Lewis (London: Longman, Green, Longman, Roberts, & Green, 1864), 444.

352. John Chrysostom, "Homilies on John" in Philip Schaff, *Nicene and Post-Nicene Fathers, vol. 14* (New York: Charles Scribner's Sons, 1906), 319.

353. Mary of the Divine Heart in Louis Chasle, *Sister Mary of the Divine Heart* (London: Burns & Oates, 1906), 68–69.

354. Julian of Norwich, *Revelations of Divine Love,* trans. Grace Warrack (London: Methuen & Co., 1901), 150–151.

355. John Cassian, "The Conferences" in *Nicene and Post-Nicene Fathers of the Christian Church, Second Series, vol. 9,* ed. Philip Schaff, Henry Wace, and The First Conference of Abbot Chaeremon (New York: Christian Literature, 1894), 434.

356. Leo the Great, "Sermon 23" in *Select Sermons of S. Leo the Great on the Incarnation,* trans. William Bright (London: J. Masters and Co., 1886), 10–11.

357. The *Didache* in Alexander Roberts and James Donaldson, *Ante-Nicene Fathers, vol. 7,* rev. A. Cleveland Coxe (New York: Christian Literature, 1896), 380.

358. Peter Canisius, "Morning Prayer of Salutation to the Sacred Heart" in Georgio Schlosser, *Beati Petri Canisii S.J. Exhortationes Domesticae* (Ruraemundae: J.J. Romen et Filiorum, 1876), 452–453.

359. Margaret Mary Alacoque in Mary Philip, *Life of Blessed Margaret Mary Alacoque* (Edinburgh: Sands & Co., 1919), 179–180.

360. Peter Julian Eymard, *Month of Our Lady of the Blessed Sacrament,* trans. by a Visitandine of Baltimore (New York: The Sentinel Press, 1903),

33–34.

361. Cajetan Mary da Bergamo, *Humility of Heart,* trans. Herbert Cardinal Vaughan (Westminster, MD: The Newman Bookshop, 1944), 129–130.

362. Robert Southwell, "The Burning Babe" in *The Poetical Works of the Rev. Robert Southwell,* ed. William B. Turnbull (London: John Russell Smith, 1856), 98–99.

363. Peter Lombard, "Sentences" in Elizabeth Frances Rogers, *Peter Lombard and the Sacramental System* (New York: Columbia University, 1917), 119–120.

364. St. Bernard of Clairvaux, "Sermon 61 on the Song of Songs" in John Hodges, *Life and Works of Saint Bernard, vol. 4,* ed. Jean Mabillon, trans. Samuel J. Eales (Holland: Motley Press, 1896), 373.

365. Álvarez de Paz in Joseph de Galliffet, *The Adorable Heart of Jesus* (Philadelphia: Messenger of the Sacred Heart, 1890), 203.

366. Benedict XVI, *Deus Caritas Est* (Vatican City: Libreria Editrice Vaticana, December 25, 2005), par. 19.

367. Telesphorus Galli, *The Raccolta,* trans. Ambrose St. John (London: Burns and Lambert, 1857), 132.

368. Claude de la Colombiére in Louis de la Puente, *The Lights in Prayer* (London: Burns and Oates, 1893), 249–250.

369. Margaret Mary Alacoque, "Consecration to the Sacred Heart" in Francis Xavier Lasance, *With God: A Book of Prayers and Reflections* (New York: Benziger Brothers, 1911), 543-544.

Index of Sources

A

B

C

D

E

F

G

H

I

J

K

L

M

N

O

P

Q

R

S

T

V

W

X

About the Author

Thomas J. Kronholz is a theologian, author, and classical pianist who holds advanced degrees in systematic theology and piano performance. In addition to lecturing at parishes and retreats, he teaches theology in the Diocese of Cleveland. In 2020, he coauthored *Mystery of the Altar: Daily Meditations on the Eucharist* with Kenneth Howell under the pen name Joseph Crownwood. He has dedicated his life to making Jesus known in the Holy Eucharist.